DIALOGUE

AND THE ART

OF THINKING

TOGETHER

A PIONEERING

APPROACH TO

COMMUNICATING

IN BUSINESS

AND IN LIFE

dialogue
and the art of
thinking together

William Isaacs

CURRENCY

New York   London   Toronto   Sydney   Auckland

A Currency Book
PUBLISHED BY DOUBLEDAY
a division of Random House, Inc.
1540 Broadway, New York, New York 10036

Currency and Doubleday are trademarks of Doubleday, a
division of Random House, Inc.

Book design by Richard Oriolo

LIBRARY OF CONGRESS CATALOGING-IN-PUBLICATION DATA

Isaacs, William.
 Dialogue and the art of thinking together: a pioneering
approach to communicating in business and in life /
William Isaacs.
      p.   cm.
Includes index.
 1. Communication in management. 2. Communication.
I. Title.
HD30.3.I8   1999
658.4'5—dc21   99-28182
                                                CIP

ISBN 0-385-47999-9
Copyright ©1999 by William Isaacs
All Rights Reserved
Printed in the United States of America
October 1999

9   10

For
Jody
and
Sam

Contents

Contents

PART V: WIDENING THE CIRCLE

Acknowledgments

No serious book simply arrives fully born. It is forged, some would say squeezed, out of the very marrow of one's psyche. This book has been no exception. I have been blessed to have had the assistance of many people over the years in this process, and in fact would have been unable to succeed without them. Acknowledging them is both a great pleasure and something of a risk, since one is inevitably unaware of all the contributions that have actually shaped one's life and work.

The most important statement I think I could make here is to acknowledge that there is a growing community of people around the world who have both a commitment to and real capacity for living the ideas represented in this book. Their contributions where they are will in the end be far more significant than any words in any book. As we cross the threshold to a new millennium, I am encouraged to know of many who are endeavoring both to reshape the institutions of the industrial age, and to bring new music into the world, and who have an increasingly conscious perspective on the changes required of all of us.

First, David Bohm's ideas, and perhaps even more important, his extraordinary and often breathtaking capacity for genuine inquiry, have shaped all aspects of this book. Sarah Bohm unwaveringly fostered the spirit of dialogue for me and many others. Martin Exeter set a standard of spiritual character that made undeniably visible the wholeness many only speak about. David Kantor has been a colleague, mentor, and friend for a decade. He has contributed in numerous ways to my thinking process and theory development. In my work I have tried to incorporate something of what remains most impressive in this man: his extraordinary capacity as an interventionist to help human beings to untie their own knots and liberate themselves. His compassionate ability on this score remains unparalleled, and is I believe an essential feature for enabling genuine dialogue.

Chris Argyris and Donald Schön taught me a great deal about the pervasive and self-defeating habits of action in human beings. Their work on conversation remains the gold standard of rigor in this domain. Peter Senge has been a friend and colleague for many years now too. He is a remarkable learner, and has a powerful ability to generate insights and communicate them in a way that allows many others to prosper. I want to thank him for his Foreword, and for his steady support and encouragement of both my work and this field. Ed Schein has also been a close friend and ally for many years now. Ed's comments and reading of the manuscript were of great value. In many ways my work stands on the shoulders of such giants as him, one whose clarity of thought and insight about what is valuable for human beings gave dialogue a needed boost at a critical moment.

Several colleagues have provided enormous help in the development of many of the ideas here. Peter Garrett has been a friend and colleague for some twenty years now. His partnership and originality of thought greatly helped David Bohm, and greatly helped me. He has made a significant contribution to the formulation of the principles of dialogue. And his inspired hand and lucid mind can be felt in virtually every other idea here.

Michael Jones brought a fierce and gentle determination to keep the awareness of beauty before us all. Mitch Saunders' friendship and creative wisdom provided an enormously potent field within which this work could form. Barbara Coffman facilitated some of the first dialogue sessions we held in the United States, and provides exemplary leadership in this field. Otto Scharmer has developed a fine theory of communication and field development that dovetails with my own work and greatly enriched it.

Diana Smith has been a steady inspiration to me, encouraging me to be true to my own voice. David Skaggs contributed much perspective for the section on dialogue and democracy. Mark Gerzon's reading of the manuscript pointed me in the right direction and greatly assisted in helping this book come to clarity. Jessica Lipnack and Jeffrey Stamps offered helpful and genuine encouragement. Bruce Allyn offered helpful advice and assistance in the section on the Hague Initiative, as well as being a friend and support for the overall journey. Chris Thorsen and Richard Moon have pioneered in the realm of physical analogues for dialogue, bringing aikido and dialogue together. They offered many helpful insights. Glennifer Gillespie and Beth Jandernoa have nurtured both me and this book. Danah Zohar inspired me to keep going, and provided genuine intellectual companionship. Diana and Jon Guilbert's dear friendship, vision, and straightforward feedback are a lifeline and source of real strength. Daniel Kim of Pegasus Communications has been a colleague and voice of encouragement for some years too, always encouraging me to take the next risk.

Cliff Barry and Mary Ellen Blandford have been immensely helpful to me over the years as both friends and advisors. Their thinking about intrapersonal structures and their skill in releasing the inner circuitry that keeps people stuck are both stunning and extraordinary; they have transformed my life and energized the thinking in this book.

Many people participated in The Dialogue Project at MIT, where this book got its start. I want to thank all of those who played their parts in this. Larraine Matusak championed the work at the Kellogg Foundation. Many people have been blessed by her vision, and I feel especially fortunate on this score. The Organizational Learning Center at MIT provided a safe haven for the project. Many people within the Center actively helped with the project, especially Jeff Clanon, Vicki Tweiten, Jean MacDonald, Angela Lipinski, Jane Punchard, and

George Roth. Their support and interest continue within the Society for Organizational Learning. Mary Fewel Tulin and Uli Dettling played important roles in shaping the dialogue research. Mary Ellen Hynes, Michelle Martin, and Nina Kruschwitz all ably administered the project and acted as the glue that held it all together.

The Dialogue Facilitator Group was the seedbed for many of these ideas. These people are exemplars of this work in the world, and include: Juanita Brown, Sarita Chawla, Barbara Coffman, Freeman Dhority, John Gray, Robert Hanig, Sue Miller Hurst, Ron and Susan Kertzner, Nomatemba Luhabe, Harold Massey, Ken Murphy, Marilyn Paul, Agota Rusza, and Mitch Saunders.

The team at DIA•*logos* has had enormous patience and been deeply committed to sustaining our business and keeping the spirit of it alive, even though I was often absent from it. Sabra Dalby's large heart and meticulous spirit nurtured and sustained us all. Joan Wickizer ran our office in ways that I still marvel at. B. C. Huselton was one of the early pioneers in the dialogue work while he was with Armco. He has been a constant and dear friend for many years, a determined strategist and an able representative of this work. I also want to thank Janet Gould, Carmen Barmakian, Eric DeLuca, Kate Pugh, Tiffany Roach, and Kristin Collins for their generosity and commitment.

The graduates of DIA•*logos*'s educational and leadership development programs have been enormously influential. They provided the living laboratory from which many others will benefit. Pam Paquin and Wendy MacPhedran both provided fine logistical support and authentic encompassment of the people who came through our doors.

Many more people than I can name, in many organizations around the world, have provided strong encouragement, access, resources, and time, enabling the dialogue work to proceed. Especially helpful have been Fred Simon and Nick Zeniuk, for-

merly of Ford Motor Company, David Marsing of Intel, Rob
Cushman of GS Industries, Linda Pierce, Tom Ryan, Bill
McQuillan, Jim Tebbe, and Beth Macy of Shell Oil Company,
Rick Canada of Motorola, Steven Olthof and all my friends at
KPMG Netherlands, Rolf Lindholm, Sven Atterhed, Emily Bliss,
Roger Martin, Mark Fuller of Monitor Company, and Lisa
Cheraskin and Bob Kelly from Eli Lilly.

John Cottrell, then president of the United Steelworkers of
America Local #13, is a true leader and good friend, who sustained genuine support and modeled authentic inquiry
throughout the process. I want also to thank the whole
Executive Board of Local #13, who provided such genuine, powerful, and committed participation to this work. Many people
have learned from and have been blessed by what they achieved.

Sister Lynn Casey and Barbara Sowada had the courage and
vision to bring dialogue to Grand Junction, inspired by the vision of a truly compassionate healthcare system. Barbara
Coffman, Mitch Saunders, and John Gray, with the assistance of
Elna Stockton and Uli Dettling, were the facilitators and researchers of the project, and provided able leadership for it.
Diane Weston wrote a wonderful reflection on the project which
proved quite helpful here. Many people in Grand Junction
worked hard to sustain and deepen this project, far more than I
can name here, including Denny Stahl, Roger Zumwalt, Mike
Weber, Paul Curly, Bruce Ward, Greg Omura, Denny Hartshorn,
Bernadette Prinster, Tish Wells, and Sally Schaefer.

All the participants in the Boston Urban Dialogue gave us
many insights into the nature of dialogue and the challenges of
bringing it into social contexts. Freeman Dhority and Ron and
Susan Kertzner provided powerful leadership for this process.

Harriet Rubin in many ways started this process by suggesting I write something about dialogue. She awakened my voice,
steered me away from the rocks, and continued to speak the

rude truth about my work, in a way which was enormously helpful. Roger Scholl at Doubleday took over from Harriet, and has brought an honesty and clarity to this work that has made it far stronger and more valuable. I am grateful for his tutelage. Stephanie Rosenfeld has capably managed many of the details of this project. Arthur Klebanoff, my agent, kept my perspective wide about the process and its potentials.

Tom Ehrenfeld provided valuable encouragement and help along the way. Cliff Penwell gave a careful reading of the manuscript, improving it at many points. Marietta Whittlesey read the manuscript and offered valuable input. Others who read drafts and offered vital support include Jim Cutter, Amy Edmondson, B. C. and Kaaren Huselton, Bill McQuillan.

Art Kleiner deserves very special mention. Art is a combination wizard, immensely talented writer, honest critic, brilliant editor, and genuine friend. He has helped me at every stage of this process, and been a remarkable support. One simply could not ask for or receive more.

My parents Jed and Susan Isaacs have been indefatigable fans and loving, ever present supporters, as have my brother John Isaacs and sister Jane Isaacs Schoenholtz and their families.

My wife, Jody Isaacs, has provided the kind of tender and insightful help and understanding that are truly rare commodities. She has endured much and offered a liveliness and joy into the field in which I have worked that the reader will surely feel. Without her this book, quite simply, would not exist. Finally I want to thank Sam, whose first three years of life coincided with the creation of this book. He has brought more perspective than anyone. His tender curiosity constantly inspired me to get down to cases, overcome the obscurity, and say what I meant. This book is for his generation and for the leadership that is so evidently emerging from it.

Cambridge, May 1999

F o r e w o r d

Several years ago, after a speech to a large group in Silicon Valley, I was asked to meet with a group of about twenty-five executives, mostly CEOs and executive VPs. Rather than present more, or have a question and answer session, I suggested that we put our chairs in a circle and do a "check-in." This is one of the simplest practices of dialogue, going around the circle and saying a few words about whatever thoughts and feelings are moving in me at the moment. The first several people made more or less perfunctory statements, expressing questions or commenting on the oddity of not sitting in the familiar "classroom" seating arrangement. Then one man said, "I think I know what this is about," and told a story.

He spoke of a camping trip he had taken the prior summer with his two teenage sons in the Sierra Nevada mountains. He said that, while they were there, he wasn't entirely sure how much his sons were enjoying the trip. It seemed like they complained a lot, about not being able to listen to their music, or use their computers, or call their friends. Then, several months after they returned, his sixteen-year old asked, "Dad, do you remember the camping trip we took last summer?" "Yes, I do," he responded. "You know the part I liked best," the son continued.

"What was that?" he asked. "Well," the son continued, "it was in the evenings—when we would sit and talk with one another."

From that point onward, the "check-in" among the group of executives became quite different. One after another told stories of heart and meaning. It seemed that everyone understood what was happening and what was expected. Some of the stories were simple, some more involved. Some people posed deep questions, questions which reflected core struggles in their lives. Others talked about issues that confronted them in their work and in their organizations—or in their families. It didn't really seem to matter what the specifics were. Everyone seemed to understand the opportunity present, the opportunity to reflect and to be heard, and to reflect further on what it meant to be heard. We spent the rest of the meeting simply going around the circle. Nothing else seemed quite so important.

It was only a few generations ago that, as people grew older, they did so with the idea that personal maturation had a lot to do with developing one's abilities in "the art of conversation." Although this was a fairly recent time, it seems very distant to us today. It was a time when the pace of life was different. It was a time when, with the day's work done, people sat and talked. It was a time when oral tradition was still alive, and the telling of old stories had not yet passed from day-to-day living. It was also a time when life and relationships still revolved around making meaningful and simple connections with one another.

Of course, these simple practices go back for a very long time. Few practices seem to lie more at the heart of human communities than talking and telling the old stories. As far as I know, no indigenous culture has yet been found that does not have the practice of sitting in a circle and talking. Whether it be council circles, or women's circles, or circles of elders, it seems to be one of the truly universal practices among humankind. As commonly expressed in Native American Indian cultures, "You talk and talk until *the talk* starts."

The very word *dialogue* and its etymology invites us to contemplate this ancient knowing. The ancient Greeks were perhaps the last western culture to have preserved this idea in the advent of the agricultural revolution, emergence of city states, and modern ways of organizing society. For the Greeks, *dia* • *logos,* flow of meaning, was seen as a cornerstone of civic practice, inseparable from self-governing. The *polis* or gathering place for governing, the root of our modern *politics,* was nothing but a physical space that designated and enabled the conversational space required for true self-governing. The capacity for talking together constituted the foundation for democracy, far more fundamental than voting. As one ancient Greek philosopher noted, "When voting started, democracy ended."

In a sense we are running an historic social experiment today. We are experimenting with whether or not a society can hold itself together without the core process that has always bound societies, the process of conversation.

Since 1990, when the community of organizations, consultants, and researchers that has become the Society for Organizational Learning (SoL) first formed, we have had ample opportunity to experiment with reestablishing dialogue as a core process in self-governing within large institutions. Bill Isaacs has directed this research, working with many colleagues to establish experiments within both businesses, nonprofit organizations, and diverse community groups. Some of these experiments have failed in the sense of establishing dialogue as an ongoing process. Some have succeeded, often beyond our highest expectations. And of course, it was exactly this variety of outcomes that forced Bill and his colleagues to ask, "What seems to differentiate among these situations?" "What do we not yet see that is at play when people attempt to truly talk together?"

Gradually, a body of knowledge began to take shape, the gist of which is contained within the following pages.

Bill invites us to think about dialogue on many levels, starting with observable behaviors, the basics of listening and respecting one another, of suspending one's views and voicing. But what makes these new behaviors possible is not simply trying to act differently. New behaviors that last come from new ways of seeing, from new awarenesses and sensibilities. Here something quite unexpected can happen, a deep movement within us that eventually opens up vistas of subtle dynamics to which most of us most of the time are blind.

For example, Bill introduces the "four-player model," a system for understanding the structures that lie behind group behavior, first developed by family systems therapist David Kantor. The dynamics of "movers, opposers, followers, and bystanders" not only characterizes a field of interdependent actions, they point to interdependent roles we tacitly assume—traditionally known as sovereign, warrior, lover, and magician. The interplay of these archetypal roles have inspired great stories, like the tales of King Arthur's Round Table, for a very long time. Viewed from the perspective of dialogue, an interesting finding emerged: a healthy "ecology of thought" is characterized by the presence of all four roles. In other words, there need to be followers—"I support this idea"—just as much as there need to be movers; but there also need to be opposers—"I do not agree, and let me explain why"—just as there need to be bystanders—"Here is how I am hearing where we seem to be going." Moreover, in a genuine dialogue, these are not static roles. Rather, people more or less naturally take on new roles as needed when they sense the need for a shift of energy in the conversation. By contrast most of our workplace conversations are characterized by rigid roles: by all movers, pushing past one another to champion their views; by disabled bystanders, paralyzed at not being able to bring their voice; or by cowed followers, fearful of offering anything but the meekest agreement to the voices of authority.

Gradually, Bill takes us still deeper, to consider the "architecture of the invisible," a subtle world of forces born of intention and awareness. Here, we begin to see conversation as a kind of "aperture" through which social realities unfold. The physicist David Bohm used to say that the tree does not grow from the seed. It is ludicrous to say the tiny seed produces the immense oak tree. Rather, Bohm suggested, the seed is a kind of aperture through which the tree gradually emerges. In a sense, it organizes the processes of growth which eventually create the tree. Just so, our conversations organize the processes and structures which shape our collective futures. The nature of the aperture rests in the spirit that shapes the undertaking.

These are unusual subjects for a "management book," but this is an unusual management book. For a very long time, our work within the SoL community has been guided by a simple premise that breakthroughs in human functioning will be required to build organizations that can thrive in the world of growing turbulence and interdependence the twenty-first century is bringing. Moreover, we have found again and again that these breakthroughs are both deeply personal and deeply systemic. I can think of no other book that lays bare this seeming paradox more elegantly and more usefully.

And I am no longer concerned, as I once was, that readers will find this material impractical. When the in-depth dialogue research began, I was a bit worried. The people with whom these projects were carried out were practical people, line managers, executives, and staff mostly coming from Fortune 100 companies. Dialogue seemed esoteric by contrast to the demands of their jobs. It was hard to imagine engineers sitting in tribal circles. Plus, there was so much to learn about how to develop dialogue and the individual and collective capabilities it demanded.

While I was right to anticipate the challenges, what I did not expect was the impact. In almost every setting where practices of dialogue have become embedded and part of everyday routines, the ensuing changes have become irreversible, as near as I can tell. People do not go back. They may practice "check-ins" or they may not. They may sit in circles without tables or they may not. They may use "talking stones" or other objects passed person to person in order to slow the pace of conversation or they may not. All these are artifacts, and the artifacts shift as circumstances shift. But once people rediscover the art of talking together, they do not go back. This rediscovery seems to awaken something deep within us, some recognition of what we have lost as our societies have drifted away from the core practices that can make them healthy. Once awakened, people do not go back to sleep. Teams change. People move from job to job, from company to company. But they continue to practice listening and suspending, and whenever they can they continue to get people together with the pure goal of simply talking, and thinking, together.

Goethe once called conversation "the most sublime of experiences." I have come to conclude that there is a deep hunger in the modern world for meaning and the core practices whereby human beings make meaning together. We may not go back to living in tribes. But we have an insatiable desire to live lives of dignity and meaning, and when we discover ways to do this, there is a quiet sigh of relief. We have found our way. Now we must move along it.

—*Peter M. Senge*
MIT and SoL, April 1999

Introduction: The Fire of Conversation

"Come now, let us reason together . . ."

—Isaiah 1:18

Following a summit meeting of world leaders, former Israeli Foreign Minister Abba Eban couldn't help expressing his disappointment. Together, he noted, the attending leaders brought "an extraordinary concentration of power, but their meetings don't seem to produce anything."

A child looking at such a gathering might expect great things—at the very least, a sense of direction and leadership. But what do we get instead? Usually only cautious steps, a scripted collection of position papers and talking points, policy speeches and press releases so polished that controversy slides right off them. Abba Eban's diagnosis of the central problem was succinct and right on the mark: These leaders "have not learned to think together."[1]

Most political and corporate leaders, academics, community builders, and families struggle with this same problem. It's not that they don't care. Most people care very deeply about the shape and quality of their lives and the institutions that foster them. Nor does this difficulty stem necessarily from a lack of money, power, intelligence, connections, vision, or anything else that people assume is necessary for success or greatness.

Something else is missing—something subtle, almost invisible, and yet powerful enough that it can prevent even the leaders of the seven largest industrialized nations of the world from providing truly great leadership, the kind of leadership that inspires and that brings out the best in people. Clearly, providing this kind of direction is every leader's dream: It is a dream so deeply held that it may often go unvoiced. Yet very few politicians—and not many of the rest of us—succeed in reaching this height.

What is lacking? Is it some innate quality of wisdom that only a few of us have? Or is it related, as Abba Eban suggested, to the fact that we don't know how to think or talk together in a way that summons up our own deeply held common sense, wisdom, and potential?

The underlying problem has to do both with our lack of personal capability and with the larger context in which we live. Most individuals can't seem to recognize the undercurrents beneath the surface of their conversations, undercurrents that can bring people together or tear them apart. At the same time, however, this is not merely an individual problem. It can't be "cured" merely by self-help programs or energetic corporate change initiatives. It is a symptom of a larger set of fragmenting forces not just resident in the body politic but in the culture of humanity as a whole.

THE PROMISE OF THINKING TOGETHER

If this is true—if the problem of thinking together is both personal and larger than personal—then what is needed is a powerful set of practical tools and practices that can help us deal with *both* dimensions. They must let us produce pragmatic, successful results out of difficult conversations. And at the same time they must call forth and help us address these fragmenting forces by helping us integrate the good, the true, and the beautiful within each of us and within the larger institutions in which we live. Presenting a way to address both dimensions is a central aim of this book.

Practical people may think that it isn't too important to make the world come alive in this way. But one of the most fundamental struggles for any leader—in business, in organizations, or in public life—stems directly from the separation that most of us feel between who we are as people and what we do as practical professionals.

As I shall emphasize again and again, these things cannot in the end be separated. What we do in private *does* impact how we perform in public. How we think *does* affect how we talk. And how we talk together definitively determines our effectiveness. Indeed, it could be said that all great failures in practical and professional life stem from parallel failures in this single domain of conversation. The problems that even the most practical organizations have—in improving their performance and obtaining the results they desire—can be traced directly to their inability to think and talk together, particularly at critical moments.

Here is an example: Two divisions within a very large corporation recently conducted a strategic thinking process, trying to address an important new market with unprecedented energy. The stakes were high. This new market could bring billions of dollars of new revenue to the company. The leaders of these divisions were polarized around two very different views about who should control the destiny of the new business and how they should invest in it. Each felt that this new business would strengthen his own division; each had already begun to "take it under his wing," when the CEO requested that they join together in a companywide approach.

Arguably, success in this new market depended on establishing new synergy, but neither the division heads nor their lieutenants were prepared to think openly and directly about the problem. Their positions were mutually contradictory: Each believed that to pursue the other division's approach would harm or at least limit their own growth. So they created task forces to study the problem, as if that in itself would be enough to overcome the contradictions. Privately, they acknowledged that they had a serious unresolved conflict. But as a group, they refused to admit the fact, much less discuss the fundamental underlying fears and issues—losing control, losing revenue, and ultimately losing face within the larger company. They dodged the issues and acted as if they were not. One of the task forces made some progress in loosening assumptions and making more possible an open conversation about the stakes, people's fears, and their beliefs about their bosses' proclivities. Yet even this team was unable to shift the well-defined and well-defended assumptions many people held, including the most senior ranks of the company.

The decision? To let each division pursue its own strategy for the new market without ever really exploring directly the new synergistic power they might have gained from working together. And they completely bypassed the inevitable contradictions and internal competition that would result when two divisions of the same company attacked the same market. Instead of creating a wholly new business that combined the best of both divisions, they fragmented themselves further and cannibalized each other's business. All the while they issued public statements of inevitability, stating that "present circumstances require us to go in this direction," and acting as if this were not just the only choice but the best choice.

This was failure of leadership, where the possibility of coming to a much more powerful, jointly committed course of action was abandoned in favor of one that did not require people to confront their assumptions, concerns, fears, animosities, and dreams.

And beneath it all lay that same inability to think together.

This is not an unusual situation. It is embedded in the very fabric of present-day human interaction. This kind of inability to think together has become so familiar that it might seem strange to talk about it as a deficiency. "That is just how human beings are," most people would suggest. It is actually counterproductive, the skeptics among us might argue, to get too close to one another's thoughts. To do so is to risk losing our objectivity, our distance, our cherished beliefs.

The idea of thinking together can sound like a dangerous illusion in which the quest for harmony leads people astray until they unwittingly sacrifice their individuality. But in assiduously avoiding false harmony, people can go to the other extreme—to an equally unwitting "argument" mode in which we stand in a stagnated pond of our own predispositions and certainties and blindly defend what we have as necessary and unalterable. In both cases—in false harmony and in polarized, argumentative stagnation—people stop thinking.

Another word for "not thinking" is "memory." Human beings live out of their memories, insulated from direct experience. Memory is like a tape recording; it plays back a once-experienced reality that may or may not apply well to the current situation. Like a tape, memory is limited. The parameters of its responses are already set. The emotions are already defined. Thus, when we face novel situations where the instincts of our memories don't

5

apply, we don't know how to respond. Instead, we fall back on the habits that most people learn from hard experience: to protect ourselves from one another's words, actions, and behaviors. Lacking any new way to operate that might let us move beyond the false "solutions" we remember, we cling to our views and defend them as if our lives depended on it.

In this book I suggest that we can do better than this. We can learn to kindle and sustain a new conversational spirit that has the power to penetrate and dissolve some of our most intractable and difficult problems. We can learn to do this in ourselves, in our closest relationships, in our organizations and communities.

The method and ideas about dialogue explored here are as old as the human race, and yet they are also being reinvented in our time. They represent an art of not just talking together but of thinking together that seems to have been all but lost in our modern culture. The simple premise of this book is that neither the enormous challenges human beings face today, nor the wonderful promise of the future on whose threshold we seem to be poised, can be reached unless human beings learn to think together in a very new way.

RIVERS OF FIRE

A few years ago a group of colleagues and I from MIT were invited to one of America's largest steel mills to introduce managers and steelworkers to a new way of talking together, to help them break through many years of intense division and strife.

Our first visit to the plant was like a visit to another world—on the surface, at least, it was an unlikely setting for dialogue. However, as I discovered, the place itself served as a perfect metaphor for deeper interaction.

Vast, loud, and oppressively hot, the steel mill lumbered

through its paces. As I stepped into the main hall of the plant, I saw a great expanse of machinery stretching almost two football fields in length. Above me 180,000 pounds of scrap steel were gradually being dissolved into a molten, white-hot brew by an intense arc of electric current. The steel seemed to roar as it melted.

Suddenly the clanging ceased, and an eerie silence pervaded the plant. The cycle of steel-making had shifted to another phase. Three thirty-foot-high by forty-foot-wide vats of molten steel, spaced out above me on a wide ledge, stood like jars on a giant's shelf. These were the "electric furnaces" that turned worn-out refrigerators, broken-down cars, and extinct buildings into raw new steel, which was later refashioned into bedsprings, steel wire, and steel balls. The steel grinding balls were used in the mining industry to pulverize raw metals like copper into a granular soil that could then be more easily processed.

I looked up to see a small vent opening at the bottom of the center vessel. Out poured a river of fire, bright red and white hot. The molten metal streamed like liquid light into a waiting railroad-car container below. Stepping back, I could see fireworks of red and white as other "hot" furnaces were tapped. Above me, catwalks stretched across fifty-foot-high ceilings. Brilliant bursts of yellow and red light lifted the darkness momentarily as sparks flew and molten fire fell into the giant waiting ladles.

Standing in a corner of this surreal drama, I felt I had stumbled on the inner workings of creation itself. Out of sight of the everyday world, I felt privileged to see these enormous forces being brought under control. This was creation on an almost mythical scale.[2] The men who ran this plant were like the forgers of the world. As I later told them, they were not steelworkers, they were "managers of fire."

Everyone worked purposefully. Everyone agreed it was safe.

In fact, there had been no major injuries in the mill for years. Most of the employees had worked there for more than twenty years, and some for as many as forty. Some had fathers who had worked in the same mill. Men who work near the molten steel have to wear thick violet glasses clipped to their hard hats to protect their eyes from the brilliant light of the white-hot steel. The look this gave them, otherworldly yet grounded, made it clear that the mill was not a foreign place but a kind of harsh home. One reason it all was safe here was that the molten steel was held inside these large vats. The process was contained by steel, fire enclosed by fire-forged steel.

Standing near these rivers of molten steel, I realized that these people already knew much about containing creative processes and managing the "fire of their thoughts." Here, after all, were some of the most intense forces known to man—3,000-degree molten metal, turned daily into usable steel—a power they handled with relative ease. Our work involved exploring how human beings could contain their intense emotional, intellectual, and even spiritual selves, especially those aspects that arise in conversation—and to find ways to turn them to creative uses. Containing this human fire often seems much more difficult than containing molten steel. Not surprisingly, the steelworkers understood this analogy instantly.

Over a period of two years our MIT research team worked with these steelworkers and with the senior managers of the company—two groups with a history of deep, bitter labor disputes between them—to find a way of conversing that would transform some of their deepest differences into a meaningful, useful dialogue. After some months, many of them experienced a radical change, one that—for a time at least—turned their swords into plowshares. We delved into the deep assumptions carried by both groups and as a result forged great mutual respect, coordination, and connection. Moreover, this mutual understanding was extended to action in the form of improved performance, fewer grievances, and, for the first time in generations, mutual action to solve chronic problems in the mill. The changed atmosphere helped to convince outside financial groups to invest over $100 million in the business. And despite the actions of people who sought to stop these explorations, many of the initiatives continue today. Understanding how processes like these work and why they unfold as they do, or fail to unfold in ways we intend, is one of the central focuses of this book.

A BOOK ON DIALOGUE

Writing a book about dialogue is in some respects a contradiction in terms. *Dialogue,* as I define it here, is about a shared inquiry, a way of thinking and reflecting together. It is not something you do *to* another person. It is something you do *with* people. Indeed, a large part of learning this has to do with learning to shift your attitudes about relationships with others, so that we gradually give up the effort to make them understand us, and come to a greater understanding of ourselves and each other.

But a book is supposed to be authoritative: As the author I am supposed to have answers for the reader. This presumption often leads the reader to question how quickly and easily he or she can extract that information from the pages. But dialogue does not work this way. Dialogue is a living experience of inquiry *within* and *between* people. A decade and a half of writing about and conducting dialogue around the world has led me to realize that the most important parts of any conversation are those that neither party could have imagined before starting.

So, without being overly prescriptive, this book will offer you a kind of road map to help you find your way. You'll discover what tends to encourage (or discourage) dialogue; what happens when you try to introduce it into difficult settings; and how to manage the internal changes that must take place in you in order to become effective at it.

DIALOGUE IN ALL WALKS OF LIFE

The dialogue process is a form of conversation that can be meaningful to people from a large number of backgrounds: from every walk of life, from every nationality, from many different professions and levels of responsibility within organizations and communities. People come to dialogue for many different reasons. Some want to resolve conflicts. Others wish to get along better with a particular person, a business partner, a boss, a spouse, a parent, a child. Still others wish to solve problems more effectively. The purpose that has brought you to this book may just be the beginning of what you may find useful in dialogue.

For instance, if you are an operational manager, then this book can help you enable people to work together in a highly coordinated and creative fashion, without the need for constant, heavy-handed, external controls. Many people seek breakthroughs in productivity and performance by developing measures and metrics, carrots and sticks. Dialogue achieves this by deepening the glue that links people together. This "glue" is the genuine shared meaning and common understanding already present in a group of people. From shared meaning, shared action arises. You will learn here how dialogue is generated out of all the interactions of the people, not a set of rules that they can apply from the outside.

If you are a corporate executive or senior leader in your organization, then you are likely faced with leadership challenges that are growing exponentially. If your organization is like many others, people will often withhold from you what they think you do not want to hear, for fear they may be punished. Thus you do not know what is going on around you. Dialogue can help you to uncover the undiscussed thinking of the people in your organization.

As a leader anywhere in your organization, you can learn to take dialogue one step further. The problems we face today are too complex to be managed by one person. We require more than one brain to solve them. Dialogue seeks to harness the "collective intelligence" (think of this as the collective intelligence quotient, or "CQ") of the people around you; together we are more aware and smarter than we are on our own. And together, we can perceive new directions and new opportunities more clearly than we can on our own. When many businesses are continuously reinventing themselves today, this capacity for collective improvisation and creativity is essential. And as a leadership method, the dialogue approach differs from other methods because you must develop it within yourself, and model it for others, before you seek to apply it to the teams you lead or the problems you face. In this sense dialogue invites you into greater balance as a leader.

If you are a diplomat or public official, all of these challenges may also apply to you. But you may be faced with a different set of issues—navigating the enormous cross-cultural problems that arise in our global and multicultural world. People from different cultures speak different languages, bring different underlying assumptions, carry different ways of thinking and acting. Dialogue can enable people to bring out these differences and begin to make sense of them, fostering communication and understanding among people. It does this by helping people create settings in which their differences can be safely and consciously reflected upon. Managers and executives will of course also face these difficulties as well, given the global nature of most firms today. Even within one team, people often come from startlingly different cultures—from different corporate divisions or different functions, which can be as diverse as ethnic cultures within a region can be.

If you are an educator, you may find this book confirms intuitions you already have about the conditions for learning—settings in which people listen well to one another, respect difference, and can loosen the grip of certainty they might carry to see things from new perspectives. Dialogue has promise in education because it challenges traditional, hierarchical models and proposes a method for sustaining "partnership"—between teachers and staff, teachers and students, and students with each other. Dialogue can empower people to learn with and from each other.

Finally, if you are a parent or family member, dialogue may help you bring a sense of healing, quietness and clarity to your interactions. For many of us, our families are the places where we first learned to listen and relate to people. But these experiences have not always been as fulfilling and satisfying as they might be. Some of the methods and ideas in this book may help you to transform your interactions at home. Once, a very senior investment banker came up to me after a talk I had given, looking a bit sheepish. He said, "Can I ask you something?" He continued, "I hope you don't take this the wrong way, but I was thinking about how what you said applied to my family. Do you ever work with families?" I asked him if he thought he might be insulting me because he was not asking about his business. He said, "Well, it seemed to go to something more important than my business."

Whatever reason you have for reading this book, dialogue offers a route for understanding and effectiveness that goes to the heart of human beings—the meanings we make, and the thinking and feeling that underlies what we do, individually and together.

THE THREE LANGUAGES OF THIS BOOK

For one thing, I have tried to write this book in a way that combines three distinct and different languages at once, languages that do not usually go well together.[3] The first is the voice and language of *meaning*, to give you a sense of the ideas behind this ancient practice, the concepts I have developed to make it more understandable, and the larger context in which it sits. The second is the language and voice of *feelings* and aesthetics. This is the sense of beauty, of rhythm, and of timing that we have in our conversations. How we *feel* deeply impacts what we *think*. The third is the language and voice of *power*—particularly the power of our actions. This voice speaks of the tools you need in order to act more effectively. Dialogue is not in the end merely about talking, it is about taking action. And at its best, dialogue includes all three of these voices: meaning, aesthetics, and power.

These three voices echo a more ancient set of ideas, one that opens before us not only today's practical challenges, but the underlying forces that impact how we live and work as human beings. To the ancient Greeks, human society was characterized by three value activities: the pursuit of objective understanding, the subjective experience of beauty, and the shared activity of coordinated and just action. They called these three the True, the Beautiful, and the Good. The True evolved into the pursuit of objective scientific truth, the Beautiful into aesthetics and art, and the Good into ethics and the challenges of collective action. As each developed, it produced its own language: The True focuses on objectivity, using "it" language, the Beautiful focuses on our subjective experience and uses "I" language, and the Good on intersubjective descriptions, and uses "we" language—speaking of what we express in taking action.[4]

As Ken Wilbur in his book *The Marriage of Sense and Soul* indicates, since the time of the Greeks, these three have evolved, but also separated, becoming fragmented and disassociated from one another. It is therefore unusual to combine, in any serious book on improving how we think and talk—that is, in part, learning to say the right next words to produce the right next action, an equally serious concern with the aesthetics, feelings, and timing of how to speak and think together. And while we may focus on effectiveness, or even how to remain human as we talk, we might leave out any reflection about whether our ideas are any good or just. Yet all three are essential. And it takes all three to have a genuine and balanced dialogue.

~

Dialogue is a very old idea. Yet it is not practiced all that frequently. One reason for this is that human beings have an inner ecology, a network of thoughts, ideas, and feelings that guide our actions. This ecology might be compared to a computer operating system—the set of instructions that inform a computer how to perform calculations. This human inner ecology is shared among human beings, and so when a problem arises in one part of the culture, it also tends to arise everywhere else as well.

Too many of us have lost touch with the fire of conversation. When we talk together, it is rarely with depth. For the most part, we see our conversations as either opportunities to trade information or arenas in which to win points. Difficulties that might otherwise be resolved or even dissolved persist. And often we find we simply do not have the wherewithal to genuinely consider new possibilities, new options. Such miscommunication or misunderstanding condemns us to look elsewhere for the creative intensity that lies dormant within and between us. Yet it is an intensity that could revitalize our institutions, our relationships, and ourselves. In the end, this book is about rekindling that fire.

PART I

WHAT IS DIALOGUE?

A Conversation

with a Center,

Not Sides

"I never saw an instance of one or two disputants

convincing the other by argument."

—Thomas Jefferson

When was the last time you were really listened to? If you are like most people, you will probably find it hard to recall. Think about a time when you saw others try to talk together about a tough issue. How did it go? Did they penetrate to the heart of the matter? Did they find a common understanding that they were able to sustain? Or were they wooden and mechanical, each one reacting, focusing only on their own fears and feelings, hearing only what fit their preconceptions?

Most of us, despite our best intentions, tend to spend our conversational time waiting for the first opportunity to offer our own comments or opinions. And when things heat up, the pace of our conversations resembles a gunfight on Main Street: "You're wrong!" "That's crazy!" The points go to the one who can draw the fastest or who can hold his ground the longest. As one person I know recently joked, "People do not listen, they reload." When televised sessions of the United States Congress or the British Parliament show the leaders of our society advocating, catcalling, booing, and shouting over one another in the name of reasoned discourse, we sense that something is deeply wrong.[1] They sense the same thing, but seem powerless to do anything about it.

All too often our talk fails us. Instead of creating something new, we polarize and fight. Particularly under conditions where the stakes are high and differences abound, we tend to harden into positions that we defend by advocacy. To advocate is to speak for your point of view. Usually, people do this unilaterally, without making room for others. The Israelis and the Palestinians could not agree over settlements on the West Bank. Sales managers fight with manufacturing managers over production schedules. Executives differ over the best use of capital. Friends argue about what constitutes morality. The headlines chronicle a multitude of times when people might have come together in a new way and yet somehow failed to do so.

There are, of course, many ways in which strong advocacy like this is reasonable. We have loyalties to our tribe, to our company, to our religion, or to our country. We do not live in a neutral world at all, but, rather, one in which the landscape is thickly settled with opinions, positions, and beliefs about the right and wrong way of perceiving and interacting with the world and each other. As a result, we have interests to protect, ideas and beliefs to defend, difficult or downright crazy colleagues to avoid, and our own way in the world to make. There are certainly times when we must defend our views.

But dialogue is an altogether very different way of talking

together. Generally, we think of dialogue as "better conversation." But there is much more to it. *Dialogue*, as I define it, is a *conversation with a center, not sides*. It is a way of taking the energy of our differences and channeling it toward something that has never been created before. It lifts us out of polarization and into a greater common sense, and is thereby a means for accessing the intelligence and coordinated power of groups of people.

Dialogue fulfills deeper, more widespread needs than simply "getting to yes." The aim of a negotiation is to reach agreement among parties who differ. The intention of dialogue is to reach new understanding and, in doing so, to form a totally new basis from which to think and act. In dialogue, one not only solves problems, one *dis*solves them. We do not merely try to reach agreement, we try to create a context from which many new agreements might come. And we seek to uncover a base of shared meaning that can greatly help coordinate and align our actions with our values.

The roots of the word *dialogue* come from the Greek words *dia* and *logos*.[2] *Dia* means "through"; *logos* translates to "word," or "meaning." In essence, a dialogue is a *flow of meaning*. But it is more than this too. In the most ancient meaning of the word, *logos* meant "to gather together," and suggested an intimate awareness of the relationships among things in the natural world. In that sense, *logos* may be best rendered in English as "relationship." The Book of John in the New Testament begins: "In the beginning was the Word *(logos)*." We could now hear this as "In the beginning was the Relationship."[3]

To take it one step further, dialogue is a conversation in which people think together in relationship. Thinking together implies that you no longer take your own position as final. You relax your grip on certainty and listen to the possibilities that result simply from being in a relationship with others—possibilities that might not otherwise have occurred.

Most of us believe at some level that we must fix things or change people in order to make them reachable. Dialogue does not call for such behavior. Rather, it asks us to listen for an already existing wholeness, and to create a new kind of association in which we listen deeply to all the views that people may express. It asks that we create a quality of listening and attention that can include—but is larger than—any single view.[4]

Dialogue addresses problems farther "upstream" than conventional approaches. It attempts to brings about change at the source of our thoughts and feelings, rather than at the level of results our ways of thinking produce. Like the Total Quality Movement, it seeks not to correct defects after they have occurred but to alter processes so that they do not occur in the first place. A similar analogy can be found in the environmental movement, which has moved in the past twenty years from trying to clean up waste after it spews out of the pipe to "source reduction"—eliminating toxins by redesigning core processes. Dialogue seeks to address the problem of fragmentation not by rearranging the physical components of a conversation but by uncovering and shifting the organic underlying structures that produce it.

The ideas I discuss in this book emerged out of work done first in association with physicist David Bohm beginning in the early 1980s and, later, at MIT's Center for Organizational Learning. Over this period of time, my colleagues and I have found increasing interest in dialogue and in efforts to apply it. Now many corporations like Ford, Hewlett-Packard, Shell, Amoco, Motorola, AT&T, and Lucent as well as communities, schools, and health-care systems have been experimenting with dialogue and producing powerful results.[5] At Ford, one manager initiated dialogues to begin many important meetings, reporting that people, at first skeptical, came to view these sessions as critical to their success. A colleague of mine, Peter Garrett, has held dialogues within maximum security prisons in England for four years now. He has found that offenders will attend these sessions when they will boycott everything else. The prison dialogues provide a setting where genuine healing can begin to occur and where the prisoners can begin to come to grips with their experiences, their emotions, and their situation, producing what some are now seeing as unprecedented change. Finally, there are groups of people in many countries now who meet informally for dialogue: friends in a home, a group of women from different countries who meet every year or so, citizen groups exploring the potential of dialogue to resolve difficult social issues, literally dozens of groups exploring the power of talking together. Here are some examples.

DIALOGUE IN ACTION

In South Africa, President de Klerk met privately with Nelson Mandela while he was still in prison in the late 1980s and early 1990s. They were not merely negotiating issues but engaged in dialogue about a totally new context for their country. These talks set the stage for the dramatic changes that subsequently took place.

John Hume, the Nobel Prize–winning Ulster politician, spent many years in behind-the-scenes conversation with Gerry Adams, leader of Sinn Fein, the political wing of the Irish Republican Army. The recent peaceful developments in that conflict resulted, according to Hume, from years of talking together privately, out from under the eye of public scrutiny and formal terms of engagement. Both had agreed that the most critical problem facing Ireland was learning to stop the violence, and they spoke in depth about this. Says Hume: "Twenty-five years we've been fighting violence. Five governments have failed to stop it. Twenty thousand troops and fifteen thousand policemen failed to stop it. So I thought it was time to try something else. Dialogue."[6]

The top leaders at Shell Oil in the United States have spent the past several years developing their capacity for dialogue. They see conversation as increasingly more critical as their leadership roles shift dramatically. Where once this group made the decisions about resource allocation, investment, and strategic direction, much of this is now left to the local operating businesses. In their new role they are coaches, advisers, and advance thinkers for new possibilities for the company. They look into the future, set the pace for the organization, and support one another as stewards of the new companies now formed within Shell.

With a less formal operating hierarchy, these leaders realized they needed a new way to think and work together. While at first it was hard for them to adjust to this new role and loosen their grip on discussions, now they ask for more agendaless space in their meetings to scan the future and reflect on the implications of the changes they have initiated. According to former CEO Phil Carroll: "Dialogue was at the heart of our work as leaders."

Dialogue not only raises the level of shared thinking, it impacts how people act, and, in particular, how they act all together. Several years ago we held a series of dialogues in Grand Junction, Colorado. We gathered thirty-five people from every major constituency in the health-care field for these sessions, which were held about once a month for over two years. Three CEOs from local hospitals, the CEO of the local HMO, the head of the physicians' organization, senior doctors, nurses, technicians, and the CEO of one of the major purchasers of health care in town—the largest local business—all participated.

Their objective was to create a "seamless system of health care." Many in the community were eyeing the changing national health-care picture and realized that some sort of shrinking financial pie was inevitable. The leaders of the different institutions were willing to try to create an alternative approach, and now that they had agreed to come together were very eager to move quickly to make change.

People were ready to roll up their sleeves and redesign the system. I asked them about their experience with collaboration. They replied that they had only created a hospice and that it hadn't represented a significant level of income. I asked them, "What is it about this effort that is likely to be different?" They were unable to say.

The pressure to collaborate, to find a way through these challenges, while occasionally expressed, had not been matched by action. People retained well-defended though polite institutional walls. Over the course of the year and a half during which regular dialogues were held, many issues previously undiscussed were explored, including the physicians' fears about loss of income in the new managed environment, and the pain of maintaining the image of the health-care practitioner as the last best defender of health in the community. At one point, somewhat to the surprise of many, it became clear that the local HMO might be purchased by a large out-of-state organization. This would have significantly reduced the degree of local control and autonomy that the community enjoyed. Already there had been significant changes in the ways people thought about collaboration. But with this possibility looming, they realized they had few choices. Their best option, they decided, instead of allowing the HMO to be purchased, was to band together to buy it themselves.

The collective voice of the community had shifted considerably—from one of polite competitors to willing collaborators. This was a move most agreed could not have been conceived of a year before. If someone was asked what had changed as a result of the dialogue, the answer was "everything"—a sea change in the ways people saw one another and worked together.

What distinguished the group of people who met to design a new organization and purchase the HMO was a remarkable level of candor. The voice that had emerged here was not one of overwrought anxiety or overconfident enthusiasm. The collective voice was, simply, honest about the hope they felt and the difficulty they faced. In the end, the takeover threats to the HMO were rescinded, and no collective action was required. But the community was assured of its expanded ability to think and act in alignment.

DIALOGUE'S TRADITION AND ITS LOSS

Dialogue presents a paradox. It is both something we already know how to do and something about which there is much to learn. On the one hand, the tradition of dialogue can be traced to the talking circles of the Native Americans, to the *agora*—or marketplace—of ancient Greece and beyond that to the tribal rituals of many indigenous peoples in Africa, New Zealand, and elsewhere. This indigenous heritage has led many people today to romanticize and oversimplify the practice. According to this view, dialogue is nothing mysterious or complex. We all know instinctively how to conduct our own circles for conversation. While this seems true, it doesn't explain the breakdowns and fragmentation of communication so often seen when people try to engage in dialogue. The genuinely difficult, systemic issues of our times seem singularly resistant to anything like a conversation without sides.

For instance, when one hundred nations finally gathered to create an agreement in Kyoto, Japan, about global warming, people held two very different conversations simultaneously: a public one about the agreement to be crafted, and a private one about what should *not* be discussed and who should not be confronted. This latter conversation was more about containing the conflicts and about protecting people's economic and political interests. Many of the most volatile and potentially high-leverage issues, like control of carbon dioxide emissions in third world countries, were left off the agenda. This meant that people did not explore the deep assumptions that drive this problem: the value of economic growth, the impact of global capitalism, the spreading tide of rapacious consumerism, and, most critically, our underlying mental models of the environment. Is it, for example, a resource to be managed? A web to be respected? A cost factor external to companies that must be borne by society? Political positioning, not an exploration of responsibility, was the focus of debate.

Few people imagined the Kyoto meeting to be a setting in which a reflective and searching inquiry could be achieved. To many "hardheaded realists" at meetings like Kyoto, the very proposal to use dialogue to solve such problems seems almost absurdly naive. To them it is a fantasy to think that people can talk together and work out their differences in the face of political influence, economic pressures, and cultural differences reaching back for centuries. But perhaps they feel that way because of a romanticized image of the simplicity of dialogue on the one hand, and because of defensiveness about their own positions, on the other.

Those who try to minimize the complexity of dialogue by reducing it to a few simple techniques about talking together will be sorely disappointed. Doing so fragments conversations in new ways by imposing oversimplified rules instead of stimulating an inquiry into what is preventing people from talking well. What is needed instead is a way of evoking what people already know about dialogue, while recognizing the ways we systematically undermine ourselves or fail to live up to the potential of our conversations.

We live in a singular time. After 150 years of industrialized life, people have a new appreciation for the value of older, traditional ways—but they have also learned that these ways cannot be taken up wholesale. Christopher Alexander, a professor of architecture at the University of California in Berkeley and one of the most widely regarded architectural theorists of this age, once offered a seminal story about this matter. For many centuries, peasants in Slovakia created beautiful shawls made of naturally dyed fabric. The tradition of shawl making was ancient. But when modern aniline dyes were introduced, the quality of these shawls rapidly deteriorated. The peasants, says Alexander, could recognize a flawed shawl by looking to their traditions and making adjustments in their craftsmanship accordingly. Their artistry was based in long-standing habits and familiar practices; they were unconscious agents of a tradition that had become embedded in them. Thus, when faced with a completely new set of technologies, they could not adapt. At the same time, however, the industrial techniques that replaced their craft lost the rootedness and quality of that old tradition. These peasants were agents of a tradition, although they were not conscious of it.[7]

Our relationship to conversation is similar. Most people living today do not recall how to create meaningful conversations. We do not easily recall traditions of speaking together—ones that might enable us to talk as naturally and authentically as the peasants of Slovakia dyed shawls. Instead, we have inherited a patchwork understanding. Sometimes we know things click when people talk, but more often we know only when they don't.

Sometimes we find ourselves in creative moments that evoke genuine dialogue. But, like Alexander's shawl makers, we have lost our unselfconscious ability in this domain. So many distractions and images, so much new information, have been introduced to us, we cannot draw upon a single tradition of conversation. Nor, living in our age, could we hope to simply fall back into an unselfconscious way of talking and thinking together. We require a very different way forward.

Yet we can learn to deliberately create the kind of conversations we want, especially at times when the stakes are high. Alexander's solution in architecture was to propose the creation of what he called a "pattern language." He identified creative features of the vernacular architectural tradition and made them accessible to creative people in industrial times. One of my hopes in this book is to articulate a pattern language for dialogue, one that will be continuously reinvented and developed by you and many others in thousands of conversations.

Thinking Alone and Thinking Together

In December 1997, around a crowded table in the Presidential Palace in Tatarstan, Russia, a group of senior Russian and Chechen officials and their guests were in the middle of dinner. Things had been tense earlier in the day. Chechnya had recently asserted its independence through guerrilla warfare and attacks on the Russians. They had shocked the world by forcing the Russian military to withdraw and accede to their demands for recognition as an independent state. The Chechens were deeply suspicious of the academics and western politicians who had gathered everyone into that room; the Chechens feared that they were Russian pawns intent on derailing Chechen independence. The Russians, for their part, were fearful of adding further legitimacy to what they considered a deeply troubling situation.

And yet, despite all this suspicion, after a few hours people began to relax. At the first toast of the evening the negotiator/facilitator of the session stood up and said: "Up until a few days ago, I had been with my mother in New Mexico in the States. She is dying of cancer. I debated whether to come here at all to participate in this gathering. But when I told her that I was coming to help facilitate a dialogue among all of you, in this important place on the earth, she ordered me to come. There was no debate. So here I am. I raise my glass to mothers." There followed a long moment of silence in the room.

It is in courageous moments like these that the promise of dialogue shows itself. Displays of such profound directness can lift us out of ourselves. They show us a broader horizon and put things in perspective. Such moments also remind us of our resilience and invite us to look harder for a way through whatever difficulties we are facing.[8]

Yet these moments are usually rather fleeting. It is easy to fall back into old ways of interacting. In this session in Tatarstan, participants managed to avoid any further unraveling of existing agreements between Russia and Chechnya. This was considered a genuine accomplishment, and even evidence of forward movement. But everyone remained firmly within their original positions, and within a month the guerrilla leaders and hard-liners in the Chechen government had forced the new Chechen president out of office. The new group made it clear that they would never have agreed to speak with the Russians, as the former president risked doing. They were unwilling to begin thinking together.

Of course thinking together is not as easy as it sounds. In my experience, most people do not even consider the possibility. Most of the time they are *thinking alone*. When Russians and Chechens, Northern Irish and British, management and union, husband and wife, differ, they are usually defending their positions, looking for evidence that they are right and that others are wrong. They assume they have to make their points without making themselves too vulnerable to the opinions of their opponent. They withhold information, feel hurt or betrayed, and lose respect for the other person or party. They want to fight or flee. In such conversations someone has to win and someone has to lose. Our meetings and our institutions can be very lonely places.[9]

When I learned physics in high school I was taught to think of atoms as a set of microscopic billiard balls zooming past one another and sometimes colliding at high speeds. That image seems to fit the way most people interact when they're talking about difficult issues. They zoom past each other. Or they collide abruptly and then veer away. These collisions create friction—which we describe as things "heating up." We don't like the way that "heat" feels, so we respond to it by trying to cool things down, to at least get to "maybe," to compromise.[10] We never learn to live over time in close contact with the heat, to understand why it emerges, or to explore our mutual understanding of the conditions that produced it in first place. We do not discover our resilience or our ability to completely alter the experience.

Thinking alone is so taken for granted, so deeply embedded in our modern ways of living that to suggest anything else is possible or needful often comes across as Pollyannaish. Yet it may be our headstrong belief that this is the only way to go that is getting us in trouble.

THREE LEVELS OF ACTION IN A DIALOGUE

How can we learn, as individuals, to take actions that might be conducive to evoking dialogue? How can we create dialogue in settings where people may not have initially been willing to engage in it? How can we broaden the dialogue process to include more people? How can we prevent reentrenchment? These are some of the central questions this book seeks to answer.

The key to answering them requires we address three fundamental levels of human interaction. Together these three create a foundation by which we can think together, and are the focus of the remainder of this book. We must learn to:

1. Produce coherent actions. One of the more puzzling things about our species is that we sometimes live in folly: We do things we do not intend. You may have noticed this about yourself. A dialogic approach requires that we learn to be aware of the contradictions between what we say and what we do. Dialogue requires that we learn four new behaviors to overcome these limits. Developing *capacity for new behavior* puts us in position to resolve incoherence and produce effects we intend.

2. Create fluid structures of interaction. Human beings do not always see the forces that are operating below the surface of their conversations. As individuals, this leads people to misread both what others are doing and the impact that they themselves are likely to have on others. In groups and organizations, it leads people continuously to find that efforts to make change are neutralized by other, well-intentioned individuals who have very different goals and ways of seeing the world. It is possible to develop an intuitive understanding of the nature of these forces, and to develop ways of anticipating and managing them. We can develop *"predictive intuition."* Predictive intuition is the ability to see these forces more clearly, enabling us to liberate stuck structures of interaction, free energy, and promote a more fluid means of thinking and working together.

3. Provide wholesome space for dialogue. What is often missed when people try to create dialogue is that our conversations take place in an envelope or atmosphere that greatly influences how we think and act. The space from which people come greatly influences their quality of insight, clarity of thought, and depth of feeling. This space is composed of the habits of thought and quality of attention that people bring to any interaction. By becoming more conscious of the *architecture of the invisible* atmosphere in our conversations, we may have profound effect on our worlds.

To understand how each of these levels works, consider this example. A colleague recently told me about a major capital project in a factory of his that was supposed to cost one hundred million dol-

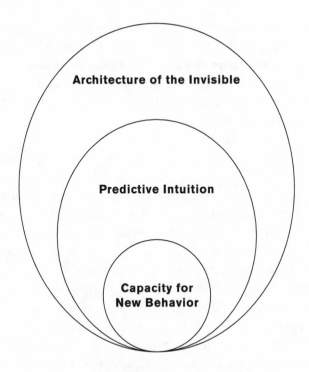

Architecture of the Invisible

Predictive Intuition

Capacity for New Behavior

lars in new investment. Very early on, the people planning the project realized that its true cost would likely be much higher than anyone had anticipated—perhaps as much as twice the initial estimates. They also quickly came to the conclusion that their senior managers and outside investors would reject any proposal that went over the number they had already publicly stated they were intending to spend. So the planners created a proposal that looked like it would work for the cost that had been stated. Do some things now and other things later, they told themselves. Within two years these same people were spending hundreds of millions of *additional* dollars to correct the problems that arose by using parts and materials that cost less but were not really designed for the purposes intended.

There is something familiar, obvious, and a little sad about a story like this.

They should have "done it right" the first time or not done it at all, right? Perhaps, except that this is far easier said than done! How often have you done something you knew was not quite right only because there did not seem to be any alternatives? Or you didn't realize until much later that the situation was awry in some crucial way?

How can we understand this situation?

First, their actions lacked coherence. These people *acted in ways that were problematic:* They judged and did not admit to it. They covered up and acted like they were not. They pushed for their point of view but resisted others who pushed for theirs. They attributed that others would not be interested or open to tackling the "real" difficulties and so did not raise them. In so acting, they remained unaware that they were doing to others what they attributed others would do to them. Despite all the questions about how to pull off a project of this size, no one really looked into how they were systematically undermining their own efforts.

Second, everyone in this story was caught in a web of traps: the senior managers who went public with their original numbers and were closed to hearing alternatives; the engineers who rearranged the project to fit the original figures out of a belief that this was what their managers wanted; the banks who were trying to get their money out of the situation; the investors who were focused only on short-range financial returns rather than on the long-range thinking and acting behind them; and the managers who felt compelled to hedge, to cover up this fact, and to jury-rig a solution for their cover-up. Clearly this problem is not unique. Everywhere we look, myopic vision, petty misunderstandings, and small deceits escalate into gross, wasteful calamities that seem like they could be avoided if people would only talk to each other with a different kind of conversational presence and "fire."

Most of the time, people do not intentionally set out to undermine their own projects. Yet this is certainly what happened in this case: Most of the managers who created the initial plan were eventually fired, costs were vastly underestimated, and a planned initial public offering (IPO) to the stock market was delayed by years. It would be easy to lay blame on a few seemingly incompetent or shortsighted managers rather than acknowledge there was a whole system of forces conspiring to limit effectiveness. What lay at the foot of this system? Blaming others for their political intrigue and failure to speak openly, while doing the same themselves.

These people were caught in certain roles and underlying *structures of interaction* that made them feel they *had* to relate together in the ways they did, but of which they were unconscious. Such structures guide people as to what counts as acceptable behavior. For instance in this case, some of the management team wanted to invite wide and open participation in the planning and decision making—including shop floor personnel who might have important roles in a new facility. But other managers and the investors wanted only the "experts" on the project to have a say, and to regulate quite carefully what got said to whom. They were concerned about the "qualifications" of the people. In the end, their approach won.

The beliefs of each of these groups are also part of the structure and led people to respond in certain ways. So, for instance, the investors believed they *had* to think first about the numbers. The engineers believed they *had* to do only what managers required of them. The managers believed they *had* to produce positive results as judged by others. These are all very real rules, ones that people feel they have to follow in this and in every situation, typically without reflection. And there can be very serious ramifications if they fail to follow them.

Third, and most important, these people had fallen into widely shared and widely taken-for-granted *habits of thinking and feeling* about their problems, what I refer to as the invisible architecture of human beings. To try to isolate one element and lay blame on it is to repeat exactly the problem that caused this disaster in the first place. It is this very *way of thinking and acting* that is at the root of the problem. It is a way of thinking that fragments, or divides, problems and fails to see the underlying interconnections and coherence of the situation. Dividing things up is not the problem. Forgetting the connections is.

For instance, several managers came to believe that the perspectives of the union people about the viability of the new technology were simply not worthy of serious consideration. In so doing, they were denying a fundamental reality: that all the perspectives were part of an underlying whole, however seemingly challenging, unacceptable, or unsavory. It seemed sensible to reject such things. People feared there would be too many cooks, believed union people were not experts, and were convinced they would try to impose conditions management would not like. It could all be a potentially huge waste of time to engage them, they told themselves. But this meant that critical information got buried and corrections that might have been made were not.

People also became convinced, not surprisingly, that their own perspective on the problem was essentially right, and that others had it wrong. But thinking in this way also prevented them from gaining a wider perspective—one that would enable them all to say "Wait a minute, what are we doing here? What are *we* missing?" People were not interested in what they were missing, just what *others* had already missed.

These two habits, among many others—losing respect for and so rejecting what is uncomfortable and unfamiliar, and becoming fixated on one's own certainties—pervade human consciousness. In this case they produced a detached and defensive atmosphere, hindering serious reflection and honest inquiry. This underlying atmosphere turns out to be a critical determining factor in whether we can talk successfully or not, because it leads us either to see one another as inextricably related aspects of a larger fabric or as separate and disconnected parts, bringing up troublesome but largely disconnected problems that must be managed and eventually overcome. When we find ourselves in the latter mode, we tend not to talk together well.

This atmosphere within our own consciousness is generated, very simply, by the ways we think and feel—the levels of internal freedom we allow ourselves, the inclusiveness we are able to sustain, the authenticity we are able to muster, the flexibility of perspective we are able to take, and the stability and spaciousness we have in our hearts.

Of course our atmosphere is not separate from others. Our feelings and habits of thinking are part of a complex web that links us all together; it is our "ecology of thought." This ecology is the living network of memory and awareness, one that is not limited to any single person but is in fact held collectively. It is the matrix that informs us the world is a certain way and that problems can be solved in only a certain way. Out of this ecology comes the collective atmosphere in which we all live and work.

The capital project disaster at the factory came down to a failure at all three of these levels: the self-defeating actions people took, the competing underlying structures or rules of interaction that guided people, and the fragmented quality of atmosphere in which it all took place. This prevented the right people from talking and thinking together about the problem in a way that all the concerns could safely and intelligently come out in advance. Everyone knew something about the issues. Everyone had a part of the problem. But they all were unable or unwilling to raise them. Everyone was in a hurry to justify the project. No amount of market analysis, technical engineering calculations, financial projections, or hand wringing could have dealt with this situation. Failing to talk together effectively, these people sowed the seeds of their own disaster.

What is needed to bring about dialogue? Coherent new

actions and behavior, fluid structures and an ability to predict problematic ones, and a wholesome atmosphere and understanding of the space out of which our conversations arise.

THE DESIGN OF THIS BOOK

I have organized this book into five parts to seek to address these matters:

The first part, entitled *What Is Dialogue?*, invites you to consider the overall territory covered in this book—the meaning of the word *dialogue*, some of the reasons why dialogue fails, and what we might do about it. As I discuss in this section, human beings already *do* think together, but in a way that blocks creativity. The second part, *Building Capacity for New Behavior*, explores the four essential behaviors required to bring about dialogue for both individuals and groups: listening, respecting, suspending, and speaking our voice (voicing). These chapters also explore four principles for dialogue that underscore these behaviors and that inform us about how to apply them.

The third part, entitled *Predictive Intuition*, proposes a way of anticipating and naming the forces that can undermine any conversation. These include a way of understanding the different languages people speak, a framework for anticipating how people manage power, and an approach for detecting self-defeating patterns of action. This part also explores how we might understand the traps that arise at key interfaces between people in organizations, and outlines several ways to shift the structures of a group's conversation.

In the fourth part, *Architecture of the Invisible*, I show that conversation takes different forms depending on the quality of the setting, or climate, in which it occurs. This section explores the different "fields" in which conversation takes place. This part shows that as we focus on the quality of the setting in which our interactions occur, we are prompted to adopt a new model of leadership. I also discuss the different contexts for conversation and the qualities that distinguish them.

Finally, in the fifth part, *Widening the Circle*, I explore the ways dialogue is being applied in large organizations, in communities, and in society. I offer examples of dialogic approaches in a number of very interesting and promising arenas. I close with some reflections on the new language of wholeness that many are seeking to articulate today. Dialogue seems to be one of the ways in which it is possible to welcome the diversity of voices that people bring to the table—and move to a new level of collective insight.

THE EVOLUTION OF CONVERSATION—
A MAP OF CONVERSATION TYPES

As you actively begin to work on all these levels of dialogue, you will find that the path to dialogue goes through several distinct steps or phases. When you begin to talk with someone, you often begin with a *conversation*. The roots of this word mean to turn together *(con verser):* You take turns speaking. As you listen and participate, some things will strike you as relevant and others as irrelevant. You may like some parts of what is being said and dislike others. You select and process information; in other words, you *deliberate*. The word *deliberate* means to "weigh out." You weigh out what you like and do not like; you pay attention to some things and not to others. It is at this point that you face a choice: to *suspend* what you think, relaxing your grip and remaining open, or to *defend* it with the assumption that you are right. Typically, this is not a choice you make consciously. And more often you find yourself reacting, generally defending your position or point of view.

The Route to Dialogue

If you can make this choice deliberately, two possible routes open before you. One takes you in the direction of reflective dialogue, where you become willing to think about the rules underlying what you do—the reasons for your thoughts and actions. You learn to see more clearly what you have taken for granted. A Gary Larson "Far Side" cartoon illustrates this well. In it, several cows are happily grazing in a field. One of the cows suddenly looks up, startled, and says, "Grass! We've been eating grass!" In dialogue, we begin to reflect on what we have been doing but not noticing. This can be both startling and powerful.

Reflective dialogue can then give rise to generative dialogue, in which we begin to create entirely new possibilities and create new levels of interaction. A jazz musician improvising and inventing new music is engaged in generative dialogue with the music and his band. But generative dialogue in words is more rare. I first experienced generative dialogue in 1984 where physicist David Bohm, at the inspiration of Peter Garrett and Donald Factor, had gathered a small group of people to reflect on Bohm's work. The attendees were unusual; many had the experience of living in intentional communities, where the aim was to develop contemplative awareness and a sense of shared responsibility within group settings. There were also scientists, academics, psychologists, educators, even graduate students like myself.

At first Bohm read several of his academic papers, giving people opportunity to comment on it. It soon became clear that Bohm's own inquiry was not merely about physics but about the insights physics might provide for a wide range of human experience. Bohm, unlike most physicists, was attempting to look beyond the exterior surfaces of the material world to the implications for the interiors of human beings.

At the time, he was developing an approach he called "the implicate order."

The implicate order is the idea that underlying the physical universe is a sea of energy that "unfolds" into the visible, explicate world that we see around us. In this picture, reality unfolds from this invisible sea and then folds back up again. Bohm began to speculate that these ideas might serve as a metaphor for understanding other levels of experience, including thought and consciousness itself. He had begun to identify the implicate order in the external world, but now he was positing that there was a direct correlation to it in thought that could also emerge or be evoked within us.

Listening to a controversial but well-regarded physicist speak about his ideas was interesting, though not in itself a breakthrough. Yet one evening this began to change. David spoke about what he thought of as the pain, or fear of imagined pain, of living in the present moment. Most people, he noted, avoid the present, tending instead to live in their memories or imagination about the future. We spoke about the possibility that if we could come into the present all together, and somehow break through this barrier of attention, we might release an enormous amount of untapped or repressed energy. I recall thinking at the time that we ought not to simply talk about this, but do it. So I said just that—could we not allow ourselves the opportunity here and now to be together, to think together, in a way that goes beyond the pain and fog that we traditionally carry around? As I said this, something shifted in that room; others said similar things; we began to experience a change of atmosphere and clarity of insight. I think of these moments as the beginnings of a dialogue among us, and a more particular initiation for me into this territory.

Bohm arrived the next morning, saying he had planned to read one of his papers, but that he felt it would now be better simply to talk together. As we reflected on the possibilities of the implicate order, and the sensitivity required to understand it, our conversation itself became a living example of the kind of new experience that Bohm was suggesting. It surprised everyone in the room, including Bohm—this theoretical idea in which a conversation could in itself somehow lead people past their natural defenses into genuine contact with one another and a more invisible, implicate reality was not just a theoretical possibility. We were watching it happen. And we could feel the result. Bohm later reflected on the experience:

> In the beginning, people were expressing fixed positions, which they were tending to defend, but later it became clear that to maintain the feeling of friendship in the group was much more important than to hold any position. Such friendship has an impersonal quality in the sense that its establishment does not depend on close personal relationship between participants. A new kind of mind thus begins to come into being which is based on the development of a common meaning that is constantly transforming in the process of the dialogue. People are no longer primarily in opposition, nor can they be said to be interacting; rather, they are participating in this pool of common meaning which is capable of constant development and change. . . . Thus far we have only begun to explore the possibilities of dialogue in the sense indicated here, but going further along these lines would open up the possibility of transforming not only the relationship between people, but even more, the very nature of the consciousness in which these relationships arise.[11]

Generative dialogue emerged as people let go of their positions and views. They found themselves attending simply to the flow of conversation, a flow that enveloped us and lifted us to a new level of shared understanding about dialogue.

This progression, from defending to suspending, and on to dialogue, has remained a common thread in my exploration of this field ever since. The diagram below shows this core choice, and the two roads that emerge from it:

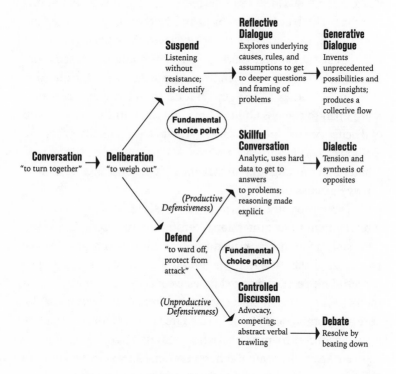

Discussion

The other direction on the diagram is toward *discussion*. As indicated before, while people may aspire to have dialogue, much of the time their conversation reflects the tendency to think alone: People choose to defend their views and sustain their positions. The word *defend* comes from roots that mean "to ward off an attack." This is the billiard-ball model of conversation. In a discussion, people see themselves as separate from one another. They take positions to put forth arguments and defend their stakes. And they try to resolve differences definitively—if *x* is correct, then *y* must be wrong. The roots of the word *discussion* are the same as *concussion* and *percussion,* and mean "to shake apart." David Bohm referred to discussions as Ping-Pong matches. The ball bounces back and forth at a quick pace, and the point of the game seems to be to win the exchange.

As shown above, there are two basic kinds of discussion. In one, we "defend well" and produce what I call "skillful discussion." We stick to our guns but do so in a way where we remain open to the possibility of being wrong. In the second kind of discussion, we "defend badly"—that is, unilaterally, where all we hope to do is win and not lose. We are not open to the possibility that we might be mistaken. This is controlled or unproductive discussion.

Discussion in one form or other is the dominant mode of interaction in most professional settings, in part because the billiard-ball model has prevailed in organizations and professional society as the best way to obtain valid results. Discussion is a powerful mode of exchange but, as we shall see, a limited one. It tends to force people into either/or thinking. It focuses on closure and completion. But it does so from the standpoint that the way to gain control over a situation is to try to contain and guide separate "particles" into a coherent order. It does not presume an existing or underlying wholeness; in fact, it presumes the absence of one. So when someone says, "We have to *make* a clear decision here," they are saying that they do not perceive an underlying coherence that would naturally indicate what direction to take. Lacking this, we believe we must impose a decision.

Unproductive or controlled discussion devolves frequently into *debate,* whose roots mean to "beat down." People do not simply raise different views, they try to overcome others with their views. One way they do this is through what I have called "abstraction wars" in meetings.

Abstraction Wars

Many conversations, for example, consist of one party lobbing an abstract description of a problem at the other and acting as if what they said was clear, obvious, and unambiguous. In a meeting of doctors and administrators seeking to reform health care I heard an administrator from a thriving hospital say: "Doctors are getting paid way too much, and it is not right." Someone swiftly countered with "What do you mean? I do not think they see it that way, and would see you as being slightly hypocritical." What were these two people talking about? How much is "way too much?" According to what criteria? Who is the "they" that would not agree? None of this is clear from these people's words, though each thought he was being perfectly clear. What is more, each added additional charged layers of meaning beneath the surface of his words. What the first man was saying under the surface was "I know what is right and you do not, and I am not open to discussing it." The second one insinuated that the administrator was also very well paid, though he was acting like he was not, and that compensation was not the issue. His response might be restated as "I see your abstraction, and I raise you one."

Finding the Right Problem

Other problems with discussion arise because people use it for *every* form of knowledge generation. In the beginning stages of defining a problem, for example, a mode that seeks to force closure and completion is limiting. MIT Professor Donald Schön spoke of the need for "problem finding." We must discover *what* problem we want to address before we try to solve it. Discussion, because of its tendency to decompose issues, leads us to look for those parts of problems that are already known. Dialogue, in contrast, asks us to consider the context or field in which the problem arises, to open ourselves to new options and the thinking underlying our assumptions, not simply to go for closure.

I was in another meeting with a group of senior doctors and nurses from around the United States where this came clear. The doctors were speaking about their success at virtually eliminating the problem of infants being born with low birth weights in their hospitals. One doctor, looking at a set of statistics, declared, "There is no problem here." To him the issue had simply gone away. A senior nurse, listening to this, nearly exploded. "This is typical of you doctors," she snapped. "Where you see nothing, I see *everything*. We have worked for months, in the communities all over, to educate mothers about prenatal care. This problem did not just go away. We have worked very hard on it."

The doctor was looking at the statistics and how to measure their change. The nurse was looking at the context out of which the changes had appeared.

Many of us believe that truth emerges after we take two conflicting ideas and somehow smash them together. The resulting spark is supposed to shed light on the situation. But more often than not, what actually happens is that one party simply beats the other down. A discussion attempts to get people to choose one of two alternatives. A dialogue helps to surface the alternatives and lay them side by side, so that they can all be seen in context.

Discussion is not always without merit though. Done well, it provides the benefit of breaking things into parts in order to understand them more clearly. A "skillful discussion" seeks to find some order among the particles while they are still "hot." It involves the art of putting oneself in another's shoes, of seeing the world the way she sees it. In skillful discussion, we inquire into the reasons behind someone's position and the thinking and the evidence that support it. As this kind of discussion progresses, it can lead to a dialectic, the *productive* antagonism of two points of view. A dialectic pits different ideas against one another and then makes space for new views to emerge out of both.

COMPARING DISCUSSION AND DIALOGUE

We need both discussion and dialogue. There are times when it is fruitful to think alone, or use discussion, and there are times when it is essential that we think together, or engage in dialogue:

Discussion is about making a decision. Unlike dialogue, which seeks to open possibilities and see new options, discussion seeks closure and completion. The word *decide* means "to resolve difficulties by cutting through them." Its roots literally mean to "murder the alternative."

Dialogue is about exploring the nature of choice. To choose is to select among alternatives. Dialogue is about evoking insight, which is a way of reordering our knowledge—particularly the taken-for-granted assumptions that people bring to the table.

Some Ford managers with whom I was working several years ago used dialogue to generate an insight that ended up transforming the product development process they were managing. They were building the new Lincoln Continental. They found that the engineers, in the early phases of the project, were struggling to develop designs that met both the cost criteria set out by the finance department and the creative vision set out by the marketing people. The engineers kept floundering. They were in a dilemma. When they moved in one direction, one of the departments would resist; when they went the other way, the other would raise hell.

During the dialogue we conducted with the project's top

teams, it became clear that they were trying to build a "Lexus at a Cadillac price." (A Lexus was known at the time to be at the top of its class in luxury and quality. The Cadillac was priced at the level these managers wished to meet, yet without a concurrent loss of quality.) Each team felt this dilemma—electrical, noise and vibration, body and engineering. And no one had questioned the implicit premise so far. Now, talking together about it, they realized that this unstated (and nearly undiscussable) goal was compromising the efforts of the whole group. Once named, it began to lose its hold on the teams. People could see that as stated, a "Lexus-Cadillac" was not possible, but that other options *were*. They began generating alternatives, making more explicit the tradeoffs they were facing.

This was an example of an insight: It reordered people's existing knowledge. It did not tell them something they did not, in a way, already know. But it helped them to see what they already knew in a very new light. They had been holding discussions about which horn of the dilemma was the "right" one—tedious battles that had frustrated everyone over some months. Now they saw that this was the wrong question altogether.

Discussion produces important and valuable results. It is necessary for many of the situations we face. But it is too limited for many of the most intractable problems before us, especially those where people bring fundamentally different assumptions to the table, have reasonable differences of view, and deep investments in getting what they want. While we need both, we must broaden our repertoire.

Finding the Freedom of Conversation

The problems with our talking together do not stem from an absence of words. We have an inflationary glut of words: more words, less and less meaning. Five-hundred-channel television services, millions of Web sites, and an endless stream of opinion from every media source about the latest political or social scandal race their way to you in a frenzied contest for your attention. Given so many different perspectives, we lose sight of any "common sense" we might make of it all. As a result, whatever "gold standard" of commonly held and deeply shared meaning that might have lain beneath our words is scattered and lost. Our world is filled with piles of words, many of which are full of sound and fury, signifying nothing. Perhaps more critically, we find it very hard to say what the gold standard of meaning is, or how we might restore it.

Dialogue can give us a way to regain that gold standard. It does this by helping to create an atmosphere in which we can perceive what really matters to most to us, and to one another. Doing so gives us access to a much finer and subtler kind of intelligence than we might ordinarily encounter.

To listen respectfully to others, to cultivate and speak your own voice, to suspend your opinions about others—these bring out the intelligence that lives at the very center of ourselves—the intelligence that exists when we are alert to possibilities around us and thinking freshly. My colleague, musician Michael Jones, calls this the "intelligence of the heart."

Through dialogue we learn how to engage our hearts. This does not mean wallowing in sentimentality. It refers, instead, to cultivating a mature range of perception and sensibility that is largely discounted or simply missing from most professional contexts. Daniel Goleman, in his book *Emotional Intelligence,* has documented extensively the dysfunction that emerges due to emotional immaturities and stunted emotional development. People easily regress into reactive states, and intelligence gets thrown out of the window. Dialogue provides a means by which we can learn to maintain our equilibrium. It lets us reconnect and revitalize our emotional capacity because it compels us to suspend our habitual reactions and frozen thoughts. It requires that we learn to include and take into account opinions different from our own. Dialogue requires that we take responsibility for thinking, not merely reacting, lifting us into a more conscious state. Ralph Waldo Emerson once wrote of this as "the high freedom of great conversation."

EVOKING THE DREAM

Learning to inquire together about what matters most is some of the most significant work I can imagine. Our isolation, our investment in positions and roles, our defense of our own limits, fuel the condition of thinking alone. Dialogue represents a new frontier for human beings—perhaps the true final frontier. In it we can come to know ourselves and our relatedness to the whole of Life.

Almost everyone dreams about the power that could be harnessed by groups of people thinking together. This dream seems present every time people come together: This time, they wonder, might something be different? We hear in this a promise, however difficult it is to realize, that somehow this work might activate the collective power of human beings—something that goes vastly beyond what any one of us can do on our own. This potential is not only a dream, I believe, but a deep memory, one still smoldering in embers of ancient fires. But to access that dream and make it a practical reality today requires that we relight these passions and recall the memory of a unique but deeply familiar kind of speaking and listening.

Why We Think

Alone and What We

Can Do About It

You enter a conference room to find people sitting around, waiting for the meeting to begin. They are talking together informally, in twos or threes, over coffee, standing by the window, or sitting together. The atmosphere is relaxed and casual. Soon several others arrive, looking hurried and distracted. Someone sets out an agenda and a timetable and asks if there is anything missing from the list.

Now the atmosphere changes. People are no longer so relaxed. They withdraw and assume a "professional" demeanor—they become more authoritative and more formal. The change is tangible. You know these people. You already have a good sense of what they think about the subjects you are discussing—where this one will agree, where that one will be made *uncomfortable, when the boss will cut off conversation. In fact, you have known these things for some time: different words, same music.*

As you listen, you do not always hear what the others are saying—you realize that sometimes you miss key pieces of their statements while you are making notes and thinking about all the telephone calls you still need to return before the end of the day. You are on a kind of automatic pilot, able to jump in when needed. One part of you considers this efficient, since you can both listen and keep track of the rest of your other responsibilities—back and forth between worlds.

Then the conversation starts moving faster. People begin to make their points more aggressively, pushing for their views. You jump in, ready to push for yours. You and two others are doing most of the talking now. Others withdraw and sit by, quiet. You wonder why they say little, but mostly you are focused on what you have to say and the forward motion you want this group to achieve. The conversation begins to heat up. People disagree. It is an old, familiar fight. You know who is likely to win. It is uncomfortable, and several people are looking down at their hands or at their notes. Finally the boss speaks and tells everyone that "we should move on now." The battle is over for the moment.

Conversations like these go on in corporations and institutions all over the world, all the time. Sometimes the people concerned make decisions, sometimes not. Often after they make a decision, they find out that people had very different understandings of what was meant, very different levels of commitment, and not always a real willingness to admit this. As a result, these so-called agreements unravel. People often are simply unaware of how differently others interpret what has happened. They remain quite unaware of the impact what they said and did has had on others.

The theory of dialogue suggests that these situations reflect a series of problems in how we think, for we have learned to think alone. And what I mean here by "thinking" involves the whole of us—our emotions, our ways of feeling in the body, our ideas, and our qualities of character and being.

TOWARD A THEORY OF THOUGHT

If I were to ask you how you ride a bicycle, you will find it hard to say. You do not rehearse the laws of gyroscopic motion before each ride. You simply get on and pedal. Just as we know how to ride a bicycle, so it is with our thinking process: We just know how to do it. We don't think about it. Both of these are examples of "tacit" knowledge.[1]

Tacit knowledge is the understanding that enables us to produce behavior without thinking about it. In fact, it is a kind of knowledge for which we *do not have words*. We can make up stories about how our thinking works, but we cannot describe the mechanisms, only the result. We know how to use language, for instance, but *how* we do it remains largely implicit. How you come to understand these words, for example, and how you make sense of them is simply not something that we can easily describe.

The idea of tacit knowledge is coming into common use today, particularly in connection with the field of "knowledge management." In the corporate arena, many people have tacit—unwritten and unexamined—know-how about how to bake bread, make steel, write software, and many want to capture this knowledge and share it, turn it into explicit knowledge. While it is indeed possible to write down the recipe or algorithm by which tacit know-how works, there is a fundamental misunderstanding in this approach. Tacit knowledge *cannot* be turned into explicit knowledge. It is a different thing altogether. Tacit knowledge is defined precisely by the fact that *we have no words* for it. Yet we can't ignore it because it affects the way we act.

The problems people have with thinking have their roots at

the tacit level. Because of this, the problems—the kinds of false starts and misconnections described in Chapter 1—are not easily changed or grasped. The tacit processes governing thinking are like the soil out of which our ideas and actions grow. While we do not particularly notice this soil, it becomes increasingly clear that, particularly under high-stakes circumstances, human beings do not come together well to solve their problems. The soil, in a sense, has become polluted, and whatever emerges from it will be affected accordingly. We tend to polarize, limit our group intelligence, hold on to our positions, and withhold information that is needed to solve the critical problems that we all face. To change the soil, we must become conscious of how this process works.

The dialogue process can help us to address four habits of thought that tend to sustain "thinking alone," and prevent dialogue. To change these habits and shift the way we approach and solve problems, we must develop entirely new capabilities. In the pages that follow, I will outline each of these limiting habits, as well as offer a principle for dialogue that can enable us to transform them. Each of these four principles is at the heart of the truly alive and dialogic individual and organization.

ABSTRACTION, FRAGMENTATION, AND PARTICIPATION

If I raise my hand and ask "How many fingers am I holding up?" most people will answer four or five (depending on whether they think a thumb is a finger!). But the "idea of fingers" is an *abstraction*—we have separated out, or abstracted, a part of our body and given it a name.[2] To abstract is to "extract" or pull out meaning—according to the roots of the word. We do this effortlessly and automatically. It is, after all, a useful division. We do not think for a moment that our fingers are separate from our hand or our body.

Similarly, when we hold up our organization to examination, we see different teams, divisions, functions. But when we do so in these cases, however, we seem to readily forget that they are still connected, still part of a larger whole. We make these distinctions but then come to believe that these divisions are real.

A striking example: When the first astronauts went into space and looked back on the earth, they realized that there were no lines on the planet. Listen to this Syrian astronaut, part of a Russian space mission, speaking of his first journey into orbit: "From space I saw Earth—indescribably beautiful—with the scars of national boundaries gone.[3] The dividing lines disappear when you get enough perspective. The lines were made in the minds of human beings, in many cases drawn in the boardrooms of Europe and applied in places like Africa or South Asia. Yet now these lines have significant reality to them: Institutions have formed around them, identities are invested in them. The fragmentation on earth remains pervasive: We see divisions among and within people everywhere we look.

We make divisions like these all the time, and then forget that we have done so. The results of this is "fragmentation"—a word whose roots mean to "smash." We fragment the world, and in the process the parts lose their connection to the whole. As pointed out by quantum physicist David Bohm, to fragment is to divide things up that are at a more fundamental level actually connected. So we find different divisions of the same company competing with one another, acting as if they were parts of different companies. Republicans battle with Democrats about the principles of moral leadership while they try to share the responsibilities for governance. Ethnic groups in central Europe divide their land and families in the struggle for autonomy. Unions and management within a company fight about wages and work rules. And husband and wife often quarrel about whether or not to ask for directions or how much to discipline their children.

The Fragmentation of the Good, the True, and the Beautiful

But perhaps one of the most devastating divisions, as writer Ken Wilbur has shown, lies among the three main value spheres of human activity: ethics, science, and art. In our modern world these three have been quite completely divided. The scientific and technological culture—and its awesome and powerful pursuit of truth—has taken a position of dominance. But science has gone way beyond dominance to the point of denying that anything but its own canons of evidence and standards of meaning constitute fundamental reality. Science is now "new science," increasingly illuminating the complexity and systemic interdependencies in the world with a holism once thought only the domain of religion. But in its sophistication it has taken over, forcing all other dimensions to respond to its arguments and discoveries.

Science has assumed the position of supreme authority, leaving the other domains as second class, background voices. Believe all you want, what is *real* is what "objective" science says is real. From within science itself there is little truck with anything but observable phenomena that can in some measure be empirically tested and externally validated. Now, there are, of course, many challenges to this claim, from many directions, both scholarly and religious. Many of them make sense. But none have swayed the overriding momentum of the remarkable successes achieved by the modern scientific mind-set.

This stance has been a great blessing to the world, bringing far deeper clarity about the physical universe, the human body, and nature's system of evolution than has ever been known. Yet it has done so, arguably, at the expense of the other spheres of human activity. When everything is seen through the lens of the canons of modern science, it "flattens," as Wilbur argues, the depth dimensions of our world. Nothing is real unless it has a specific and measurable external location, whether consciousness, the artistic impulse, or altruism. You can make colorful scans of the electrochemical activity of your brain as you think, letting you locate an idea in your skull just behind your nose. This may well tell you something fascinating about *where* you think. But it cannot tell you *why* you think or what difference your thought will make to others, or, indeed, whether you should think what you do at all. Art and aesthetics and ethics have all been relegated to the margins, to make way for science.

In one modest effort to begin to reintegrate these domains, we have brought the arts into the educational seminars we run for business leaders. For instance, Michael Jones sometimes plays improvisational piano in our sessions. He does this to activate people's imagination and give them a feeling for the improvisational "music of conversation." People have had two very different sorts of reactions to these experiments. Some embraced the music as evidence of the restoration of sanity, quietly hoping that those hard-nosed pragmatists would finally begin now to "understand." Others found it quite a stretch to understand why we would ever want to do such a thing: Wasn't the program about dialogue, about solving problems, about business? What does music have to do with that, other than perhaps as nice background entertainment?

Both the overenthusiatic embrace and the underenthusiastic incredulity showed me how far away from genuine integration we really were. Art and (management) science were still armed camps, with people guarding the doors, defensive when others threatened their domain, thrilled when the other's resistances appeared to be weakening. Divisions also reign between science and ethics. On matters for which human beings must find agreement about the right thing to do, science is silent. Science develops techniques for cloning human cells, for example, possibly enabling us to regenerate damaged or diseased tissues in the body. But it has nothing at all to say about the ethical ramifications of these abilities. It is "value free." It tells us the what and how, but not the why or whether.

The ancient Greeks called the three spheres of ethics, science, and art the Good, the True, and the Beautiful. Today each has been refined, differentiated, and ultimately fragmented to an extraordinary degree. But once all three were considered necessary for a genuine education and balanced leadership. To the Greeks, the soul itself was a reflection of the purpose, science, and the music of the spheres of the universe. The cost of the divergence of these three is that now we have only guarded walls between them, and very little sense that they might in fact be intimately and inextricably linked.

As a result, our social fabric is deeply fragmented. This fragmentation pervades the way human beings think and talk, in families, between friends, in businesses, in communities. It is a reflection of divisive forces that we have inherited and usually take for granted, and about which there often seems little we can do. The process of abstraction is a great gift but also one that, gone unmonitored, leads to fragmentation and so produces relationships based in the fiction of isolation. As Bohm once put it; "Thought creates the world, and then says, I didn't do it." Whatever image our minds make up is not the thing imagined. It is always both more and less.

Principle of Participation

To heal the problems of abstraction in thought we might apply the *principle of participation,* of recalling the ways in which we are an intimate part of the world around us. This means learning to pay attention to the details of our experience. One way to discover this principle is to practice the art of looking at something without needing to have a name in our heads for what we are looking at.

Try looking at a tree. You may find that immediately associations occur to you—the wish to be outdoors, the name "tree," the kind of tree, thoughts about the health of the tree. Can you gradually release these thoughts, one at a time, and simply be present to perceive the tree? As each thought about the tree arises, just notice it and let it go. If you do, you may find that the tree almost seems more alive, more "there," perhaps more distinctive than you had once thought. It may even become unfamiliar in a way. You are starting to participate more directly in your experience of the tree.

The principle of participation takes us back into a more direct experience of the world and of ourselves. When we label the world we lose track of the difference between our labels and our experience. Zen Buddhists call this "beginner's mind": "In the beginner's mind there are many possibilities, but in the expert's mind there are few."[4] At the center of the principle of participation is the intelligence of our hearts, the freshness of our perceptions, and ultimately the deep feeling of connection that we may have with others and our world.

But the principle of participation takes us beyond merely feeling connected, to a realization that the world is not simply "out there," but is in fact in each of us as well.

We generally experience ourselves as simply being in the world. We say, "I am here, the world is there." We experience things, we walk around in the world, occasionally we can influence it. We tend to see it as "objectively" there. We are in the world. If we become empathic, we may develop a sense of how others feel. But all this still comes from a paradigm of fragmentation—where the particles are separate from one another, though they may generate "webs of connection."

"I am in the world, and the world is in me"

The principles that lie behind dialogue flow from another source, in particular David Bohm's unique insights about quantum physics. Bohm's work led to the suggestion that what appears in an explicit sense as separate particles, as an external, independent world, is also intimately linked. Though we may say we are in the world, we may also in this sense come to see that the world is also in *us*. Everything that happens to us happens in our consciousness. As you read these words, they will become part of you—part of what you are aware of. They will influence you, whether you choose to discard them or accept them, depending on the degree of emotional connection you have with them.

Think of people that matter to you. Their influence does not leave you simply because they are not physically present. They continue to live in you, active forces that guide your life.

Initially it is somewhat challenging to think this way, but I have found that there is some real power and potential in it. As we begin to do this, we see that "I am in the world, and the world is in me."

Bohm called this way of seeing things the "holographic paradigm"—suggesting that the whole of the world is enfolded within our awareness, in fact within every aspect of the world. To get a sense of this, consider this simple example: If you walk around a room, you are aware of the whole of the room from whatever corner of it in which you stand. Despite the fact that you look from different perspectives, you still have a sense of the total room. This suggests that your eye and mind somehow enfold the total room in each and every aspect of it. The problem with our thought is that we do not generally even consider this way of seeing the world. This kind of holographic participation happens subconsciously. But in considering it and becoming conscious of it, we can begin to entertain many new possibilities.[5]

We may think, then, of participation in an entirely new way, not simply as connection but as a mutual enfolding.

IDOLATRY, MEMORY, AND UNFOLDING

A second characteristic in how we think relates to the fact that we often confuse our memory with *thinking*. What is true thinking? To think truly is to say things that may surprise us—things we have not said before—that are not in our memory. Such words change us. To think is to sense the emerging potential of a situation, to perceive what is not yet visible, and to give it voice.

To think is also to listen to our own automatic reactions and gain perspective on them. It is to ask, Now, why did I do that? Visiting my parents as an adult, I find it remarkable that I return to ways that seem to bear little resemblance to the person I believe I am today. I seem to regress. I get defensive or competitive, at times aggressive—and I see others as the source of this behavior! (*They* made me do it). Later (if I and those close to me are lucky) I notice this and reflect on it, taking responsibility. Whatever "they" did, I was the one who behaved as I did. "They" may have gotten under my skin, but it was my skin that had something under it! The behavior that plays itself through me in those awkward circumstances is like a tape-recorded program. It is not thinking.

What we usually call thinking is often merely the reporting or acting out of patterns already in our memory. Like a prerecorded tape, these thoughts (and feelings) are instantly ready for playback. And they do so quickly in our professional as well as personal lives. In the meeting described at the beginning of this chapter, people came with predictable views and ways of working. In this case, their words were largely repeated from memory, through already established positions, assumptions, and beliefs, and by means of preestablished but not-always-spoken rules about what is "legal" to say. All of this is usually more dense, heavier, than the process I described above. Though such encounters are often fast-paced and highly charged, they are strangely lacking in self-awareness.

True thinking moves more slowly, more gently than this. Usually we do not imagine we have time for it. Thinking has a freshness to it, like a flow of water softly moving through the mind, and requires space. The fruit of thinking is sometimes a seemingly simple, quiet idea that stands out among a crowd of passing thoughts. It arrives unannounced. Truth, a mentor of mine once said, is like a deer that comes to stand at the edge of the woods to drink. If you make too much noise, it runs away. How quiet are you?

Bohm differentiated between these processes by calling the fresh responses we have "thinking" and the habitual reactions of memory "thoughts." "Thought" is not only the past of thinking, it is the product of thinking. The problem, however, is that thoughts re-present themselves in consciousness as if they were "real" and active now.

Consider this example: The first time you learned to drive a car, you had to think about it. You did not know where the brakes were, how to judge the distance to the curb on the passenger side, how to turn into traffic. Eventually, you learned. Your ability to drive became part of your memory. Now, have you ever had the experience of getting into your car, driving to work, arriving, and then realizing that you had absolutely no idea how you got there—what route you took, what scenes you passed? In that instance, what drove the car? I suggest it was *thought*—memory acting to guide your instincts and reactions without your needing to be aware of them. Clearly, this is a very useful ability. Your thought is essential. It would be unfortunate if we had to relearn to drive every time we got in a car!

As my colleague Peter Garrett has suggested, feelings work in the same way; "feelings" form in the present moment, "felts" are memories of feelings from the past. When we hear patriotic marching music, many of us experience "felts" of patriotism.

The presence of "thoughts" and "felts" becomes a problem when we simply live out of our memories without realizing it. Then our memory controls us—tells us how to respond, what to feel, how to interpret what is happening. But an unfamiliar situation may require a totally fresh response. It may require that we innovate, that we *think* anew. And even though this is easy advice to exhort ourselves and others to follow, it is hard to do because the grip of emotion on us convinces us that we do see clearly, often leaving us with the options only of fleeing or fighting.

Imagine yourself walking down a dark street. You see a shadow and imagine it to belong to an assailant. Your heart starts to race; you look for the nearest streetlight, the nearest escape. Then you look again and realize that what you saw was indeed only a shadow, perhaps your own. You relax. The thoughts and feelings triggered came from your memory. It took monitoring your reaction and reviewing your circumstance to realize that this in fact was not a dangerous situation, but one that you had manufactured within yourself. Clearly it is useful to be on the alert when walking at night! But I suspect we see and react to shadows as if they were real more often than we might think.[6]

I refer to these problems of memory as *idolatry*. An idol is a collective representation or image that is not perceived as such but instead comes across as "real."[7] A rainbow is perhaps the best illustration of an idol. A rainbow is not simply "there." It is a product of our eye, the angle of the sun, and water droplets in the air. These three combine to produce the vision of a rainbow. A rainbow is a construction even though it appears as physical reality. And, rainbows are not the only instance of these representations.

When we think of idols—false gods that people fell down to worship—we may think of people only in ages past. But I believe that our own age is actually rife with idols—the false gods or images that we have unquestioningly accepted to guide us in the way we operate, which in turn blind or limit us to other possibilities. We hold to these without even realizing that we are doing so. The idols of this day are the conjured perceptions that advertisers produce of happy people and material success. An acquaintance of mine, a man who works for one of the largest accounting firms in the world, recently told me that he understood easily the notion of idols. "It's a 'partner' in our firm," he said. Partners in his firm ostensibly are owners, but when a company reaches seven hundred partners, then it begins to become clear that partners are really high-level employees; a yet-smaller group actually controls the fortune and direction of the firm. Idols are the perception of an assailant on the street that we fear, or the view that we are a "partner" when others still control our destiny.

When people hear the word *dialogue* (as in, "the former opponents held a successful dialogue") they often assume it means achieving a level of understanding and experience that is missed in ordinary conversations. Among beginning dialogue groups that have touched the potential of the art, this experience is often translated as "feeling better together," or perhaps "gaining insight not before known." Dialogue, when successful, may become a projection screen onto which people place their highest hopes or fantasies about the potential of human exchange and conversation. And inevitably, when a group does this, it is disappointed. For instance, people may have a "peak experience" with groups or on a team, and then spend much of their time using that experience as a reference point, trying to re-create it. The experience becomes an *idol,* and gradually loses its value because it is based in a memory, not a present-moment experience.

When you think about your competitors or colleagues, or the next project you will embark on, to what extent are you thinking and to what extent are you basing your views on what others have told you, what you have stored in memory, what you believe but do not really know for sure? What percentage of your views are assumptions, or already received wisdom? And most important, how do you know the difference? What is locked in reactions stored in your memory, and what is fresh, original thinking? What might you do to unleash a totally new way of seeing?

We can remedy these problems of memory by learning to apply the principle of unfolding. *This principle for dialogue is based on a premise of David Bohm's. The idea is that there is an invisible patterned reality waiting to unfold into present visible form. At one level, you can know it as growing confidence in yourself that life continues to move forward despite what you or I do. This notion differs quite fully from our conventional ideas about how we understand and experience the world.*

At a conference I attended in 1983, Bohm gave a particularly striking image of this in nature. Typically, when you plant a seed, he said, you assume it will cause a tree to grow in its place. The seed causes the tree to grow, we say. But the total environment could be also seen as unfolding into a tree—the air, the soil, the water—all emerging from a common, "enfolded," or invisible, source, and then appearing in the world. In this sense the seed is the aperture through which the tree unfolds. When the tree dies, it folds back up. It only looks like a linear progression to our eyes, Bohm said. Nature itself could be constantly unfolding and folding back up again.

Our thoughts and feelings are also constantly unfolding and folding back again, much the same way. Authenticity is the art of perceiving potential, and of being willing—daring, even—to bring this out. This principle implies the gradual process of learning to tell the truth about what we feel and know. It is the art of finding our own voice, whether through others or on our own. To find and speak our own voice is to sense the potential that is present and waiting to unfold through us.

In this sense we are the seed through which a new reality unfolds, emerging from the "implicate order." But it is not only the physicists who have explored this principle. Ralph Waldo Emerson in an essay called "Self-Reliance," calls every person to come to the point of listening to himself, to the unfolding potential within him:

"The power which resides in him is new in nature, and none but he knows what that is which he can do, nor does he know, until he has tried."

As we do this, we no longer confuse who we are with any image of what we believe ourselves to be or what we were told we should be. We unfold our genuines selves.

CERTAINTY, FLOW, AND AWARENESS

Not only do we unwittingly operate from memory, we often develop partial understandings and see them as complete. Or we may rigidly hold on to our views. A colleague of mine calls these "noble certainties."[8] Our nobly certain interpretations blind us and limit our freedom to think.

A woman I met recently found herself deeply bound to an issue about animal rights. She found it intolerable that some people felt it acceptable to hunt and kill bears in New England, especially when hunters had all but eradicated them from that part of the world earlier in this century. She saw those who disagreed with her as "Neanderthals" and others who shared her views as "sensible." At the same time, she was quite concerned about how she was interacting with people with whom she did not agree, and wanted to understand how to change—mostly, at first, so that she could be more influential.

While it was quite painful to her to think about animals suffering and dying, it eventually became equally disturbing to hold on to a belief that caused so much polarization between her and others. She realized that she was, in fact, fixated on this belief, and that it was blinding her to other possibilities. But then came a much more startling realization: "If I do not hold on to this belief," she asked, "what else is there? I may be left with nothing."

Beneath the reluctance to let go of our beliefs is the fear that there will be nothing underneath—a kind of anxiety about existence itself. Perhaps we cling to our certainties because we believe this is all we may have. The habit of certainty relieves us, at least momentarily, from having to confront this possibility.

As I noted above, we form images and then act as if they were the reality. Though these images are incomplete, this does not stop us from holding on to them quite firmly. A particularly striking example of this occurs in organizations that form "visions" that are subsequently used in ways very different from what anyone intended. Many organizations today are oriented around some set of visions and values—it has become fashionable and even necessary to be "value led." Yet the application of visions in practice shows how the grip of certainty can prevent reflection and perception of other possibilities. It can even produce paradoxical results.

Take Herman Miller, a furniture company that became famous for its elegant designs and the creation of the "action office" concept—the now infamous cubicles and open-space designs. Herman Miller was employee-owned and placed a deep value on participation by all workers in key decisions. Yet what started out as a core value ended up as handcuffs. "Participation" came to mean that people expected to have a say all the time. Participation became paralysis, where no decisions were made without extensive consultation with everyone. Critical decisions were held up for months—in some cases, years. There was no way the company could revise the concept of participation to mean "appropriate" participation without seeming to violate the original value. A fixed and partial interpretation of "participation" prevailed, one which people neither saw nor questioned. After much work, a cultural transformation has begun more recently to take place there, but not without a high cost—erosion of market share, high turnover at the top, low morale.

The inability to reflect—to see that a single way of understanding can limit us—restricts both individuals and organizations. This, too, is a function of the overall problem of fragmentation in thought. We take the fragment as a whole and then fix our grip on it. How firmly do you hold on to your views? Do you have room for other points of view?

Underpinning the problem of certainty is another limiting feature of thought that tends to see the world as essentially unchanging, static. To our eyes, things are not changing all that much. We look around and, at the physical level, most of the time things seem quite stable. There are some gradual shifts, perhaps, in the landscape, which we usually notice more after having been away for a while. It is especially striking to discover, in many cases, that some part of the external landscape that we had once accepted as fixed is suddenly changed. I remember, for example, the transformation of an old, decrepit building around the corner from our street. One day after a trip I came back to realize that it was gone! I had to look again—at first I did not see the gaping hole where the house had stood. I had expected something else to be there. The building had been demolished in an afternoon, and a construction site had taken its place.

The impairment of our senses is a function of our brain's continuous attempt to give us a coherent and stable view of things. We fill in missing details in order to have this coherence. But then we miss the gaps!

While it is comforting to believe we live in a fixed and certain world, the only thing that turns out to be certain is change itself. As Buckminster Fuller once put it, "Life is a verb." Everything is in motion, in process. Some of these processes are too slow for us to see, or too fast; but everything is moving.[9]

The problems that arise from too much certainty might be remedied with an awareness of this sense of motion, of process. Staying conscious of this can lead us to relax our grip on certainty, to expand our view, and to see the world from a new and higher perspective. The principle *I pro-pose here is that of* awareness. *This is another key principle for dia-logue. It entails developing the capacity to see the living processes that underlie all things, and to begin to become aware of ourselves and the impacts we have—right in the moment of their occurrence. It is also the ability to let go, to "suspend" our certainty, the rigid opinion we may have formed about something, to see things from another point of view. With awareness, we can entertain multiple points of view at once, even if they are dramatically opposed or in contradiction with one another. This awareness that everything is in motion, in process, can relieve us of the pressure to have everything fixed and worked out, since the only reliable thing we can know is that this situation, too, shall change.*

VIOLENCE, INCLUSION, AND COHERENCE

A final characteristic of thought relates to the fact that we impose our views on others and the world. We judge. We decide things are this way or that. We then defend our interpretation, looking for evidence that we are right, ignoring or discounting evidence that we are wrong. Our defensive judgments are ways we impose ourselves on others, implying or saying that they should not be the way they are.

To defend ourselves against another's idea is to deny that we have any connection to that idea, or to what is behind it. In these situations we often fail to see the underlying coherence or sense in others' views. We reject them, see them as partially or downright wrong. But to do so is to miss the fact that others' thinking and experience emerged out of a legitimate source, one that becomes understandable as one inquires into it. To fail to inquire is to insist, in this sense, on fragmentation. When the steelworkers of Armco told their managers that they did not trust them, and that they would listen very carefully to what any manager said for evidence that he did not mean what he said, it became clear that a very high wall was erected in the room. Two groups of people were defending themselves against the saber-toothed idea that something new might harm them, with the same flight-or-fight reaction you might expect in a situation of real physical danger.

Maintaining defensiveness of this sort leads to kind of violence that is perhaps one of the deepest problems of thought. The word *violence* comes from roots that mean "the undue use of force." Thought that imposes or defends is violent. It applies force to try to make someone be different. It imposes from the outside a false logic that creates the violence we see in the world. And it all begins between our ears.

To remedy the problem of defensiveness and violence in thought, then, we might apply the principle of coherence. *Dialogue, as considered in this book, builds from the premise that the world is an undivided whole, and that the central problem we face is that we do not see this. The world is already whole. The challenge lies in coming to understand the ways in which this is true. Maya Angelou, the poet and writer, once quoted a black Roman author, Terence Afar, who had a precise read on this point. He said: "I am a human being; therefore nothing human is alien to me." All the nobility and all the ugliness is in some fashion included, he meant, in himself.*

Our problem is that generally we do not see the coherence, only the fragments. Our training and experience makes it very hard to understand what we might even mean by the word whole. *We are much more aware of the parts, of the differences between us. So we focus on finding quantitative measures for our world without always remembering to ask what the underlying meaning of these measures really is. In physics scientists often become overly focused on the formal equations that explain quantum theory and not the meanings behind them. In business we focus on the performance "numbers" without always remembering to ask, Are these in fact relevant to the quality and creativity of my people? We get involved in the technical details because it is easier to do this.*

We also make the mistake of thinking that if we can somehow get the parts in connection, that will produce a sense of wholeness. This is, of course, the premise of the digital age, and the apparent promise of the Internet. But this produces what I later will call "connection without contact." *It is the story of Humpty Dumpty. Once we have broken the world into parts, we cannot put the pieces together again. Electronic connections do not of themselves make for an appreciation or curiosity about the underlying coherence of the world.*

We need something more. That is the understanding of coherence—the eye that looks for coherence first, that notices the tendency to break the world into unrelated parts or put unrelated parts together and call them the same. This is the eye of the artist in us, which appreciates the whole, though certainly does not discount or miss the details. With the principle of coherence in mind, we learn to inquire into what is, not constantly to try to produce what we imagine should be. We learn that things fit together in ways we could not have understood or imagined. We may not always like what we discover, but we learn to see how it all fits. Practically speaking, you learn that, for example, even the most odious actions by people in your world may be the result of a set of forces that have some validity. The next time you have a fight with your partner or spouse, remember to take seriously the possibility that they, too, are a part of your world, and that the way they see things makes sense too—not only for them, but potentially for you too. The next time something difficult or ugly arises in you, you might ask the same question: "Where does this come from? How does it work?" Ultimately, we perceive the coherence of the world as we extend forgiveness—to ourselves and to others.

These four pathologies of thought—abstraction, idolatry, certainty, and violence—underlie most of the difficulties we face—in ourselves, in our families, our organizations, our society. Together they reinforce our experience of fragmentation. At the same time, the four principles for dialogue—participation, unfolding, awareness, and coherence—make up the outlines of a way of being human that might help us to overcome these difficulties and provide a basis for bringing about a very different way of working and living.

The Timeless Way

of Conversation

Almost everyone can recall times when they had a particularly great conversation. Perhaps it was late at night with people at school, on a long walk with a friend, at a family gathering, or perhaps even through correspondence. Dialogue, as we have seen, is a practice for deliberately and consciously evoking powerful conversations like these. But while it is a practice, and even an art form, it cannot be described solely in terms of technique. There is no recipe for "getting started with dialogue."

A key reason for this lies in the difference between conducting a dialogue and other forms of facilitation. In dialogue, you yourself are part of the method. You cannot be separated from it. To engage in dialogue is to engage with yourself in a profoundly new way. There are no steps that you can use on others, independent of how you yourself function. There are, however, definite and reliable practices to follow—if not steps to take—that determine whether the conditions for dialogue are present or not.

For instance, you have to learn a stance, a way of looking at the world, from which you build your own conversations from scratch to meet the particular needs, and the particular conversational field, of each situation. That's why you need to understand the theory and principles of dialogue—the interlocking forces that determine "how and why" dialogue works. Without an underlying theory about why things work—in this case, why and where dialogue is effective—we can go only a short distance toward proficiency.

And without a theory we will never be able to sustain the practice of dialogue beyond a small group of intuitive "masters" because we will always have slightly different, shifting standards about what success is and what should or should not be included. And we will always get relatively unpredictable results. In this chapter I want to explore briefly why we must go beyond this. I build on a basic theory of dialogue, and outline why such theory making can no longer remain the provenance of academics.

Admittedly, many people have a kind of allergic reaction to studying theory—it seems too academic to them: "Just tell me what to do!" But I will suggest this: To open yourself to begin to understand the theory behind dialogue is to open yourself up to the forces that make human endeavors effective or not. Once you are aware of these forces, you can no longer simply blame people for situations that don't work out. And you can begin to set up conversations that will engender better results.

WHY LUCK ISN'T ENOUGH

One senior consultant recently came to my office and started to tell me about a dialogue he had helped to arrange among a rather extraordinary group of CEOs, entrepreneurs, and educators to explore how the workplace could be transformed in the twenty-first century. With a slight grin on his face, he began: "Well, we had no idea what we were doing! I had read a little. We wondered what would happen, but it seemed to be the right thing to do, so we tried it. And it really worked! We kept looking at each other and asking, is this supposed to be happening? But everyone was delighted: People who had never met before came together and created something new. We all learned. And everyone expressed a keen desire to continue."

Fortune sometimes favors the unprepared mind when it comes to dialogue! Not knowing "what we are doing," we make room for possibilities that we cannot anticipate or control. Ironically, having a clear sense in advance of what is possible often squelches the unexpected and unpredicted.

At the same time, as my colleague Diana Smith likes to put it, without conscious consideration, the mastery remains beyond mystery. Luck is not enough to reliably produce the dialogic experience over time. The problem here is not with the feelings of elation that arise from an initially successful experience with dialogue; there is an important difference between having an experience and being conscious of what led to that experience. It means developing practical and articulable knowledge that can be conveyed to others.

Without practical knowledge, people inevitably become dependent on others to re-create an experience for them, since they themselves have no understanding of how it happened. Put differently, they may dance to the music but they may not understand how to play it. In my view, the promise of dialogue is that everyone can come to an understanding of how to play the music of dialogue.

This is especially necessary because my own, and other people's, experiments with dialogue have not always turned out positively. Sometimes disaster strikes.

Another manager told me about a very senior group that had come together within Ford to launch a new production process. They decided to use dialogue as the way to help everyone explore their perspectives and bring out new insights. But in the meeting the managers—all of whom had well-developed points of view, and all of whom knew each other well—could not quite grasp what dialogue was, why they were using it, and what they were supposed to say. They said things like "What is the objective here? What are we trying to do?" They suppressed their genuine differences and uncertainties, believing that dialogue required this of them. The conversation became very abstract. People resorted to their familiar positions and ways of interacting. In the end they said, "This dialogue stuff doesn't seem to work! Maybe we don't have what it takes. Or maybe it isn't what people claim."

IF YOU MEET A METHOD ON THE ROAD, KILL IT!

When we undertake any task, like run a meeting, negotiate an agreement, discipline a child—even meditate—we operate from a set of taken-for-granted rules or ideas of how to be effective. Understanding these tacit rules is what I mean by *theory*. The word *theory* comes from the same roots as the word *theater*, which means simply "to see." A theory is a way of seeing. The problem comes when we decide that a particular way of seeing is the "right" way. Without a theory, however—some way to assess what is happening—we shall be forever doomed to operate blindly, subject to chance.

We need to become conscious of what we are doing so that we can refine it and share it. This does not mean that we must make a theory of dialogue formal and explicit, but that we in some fashion make it understandable and usable to others. So I am not referring exclusively to theory of the sort we have come to understand from the physical or social sciences. Instead, by "theory" I mean a way of seeing the world based on a clear principle that is predictive of certain results: "Under X conditions if you do Y, you will get Z." There was a book published a few years ago with the title *If You Meet the Buddha on the Road, Kill Him!* The idea, which comes from the paradoxical teachings of Zen Buddhism, was that our minds seek to grasp and hold on to things and so claim to know them, but that for certain kinds of experiences—especially those of self-knowledge and self-awareness—this kind of knowing actually gets in the way. Strange though it is to say, this is as much a theory as any formal law of physics.

Kurt Lewin, a fascinating renegade of an academic, challenged convention by proposing many new ideas within social science, all of which were designed not only to promote new ideas but also to promote new action. He said that there is *nothing so practical as a good theory*. With a theory you could not only explain the existing facts, said Lewin, you could point to what you do not yet know. Theory opens the way for deeper inquiry. Edwards Deming, the father of the Total Quality Movement, put it even more succinctly: "No theory, no learning." He meant by this that without an underlying theory of how things worked, you would never know if you were tinkering with a system, making it worse, or improving it.

Michael Jones, a colleague and friend of mine, is a very accomplished improvisational pianist. He has spent many years cultivating in himself a particular feel for the piano—not an intellectual set of steps, but more a sense of *touch*. His approach to the piano has more to do with emptying himself of distractions than filling himself with ideas. He literally seeks to feel the entire instrument, the room in which he is playing, himself—the totality—and to let the music come from this space. While it is difficult to name what he is doing, it is also quite precise. It is based on a very particular way of seeing—and feeling—that says that authentic music must come directly from the soul, not from one's images about it. It makes a very clear distinction between music that is an imitation of this quality and music that is not. This is a distinction that you can *hear*. And it demonstrates a method that has as much to do with emotional maturity of the pianist as piano technique—to enable the artist to bring out his or her genuine voice. Michael does not often speak in quite these terms, but they are familiar to him as a description of what he is doing.

The method for dialogue that I describe in this book has this quality to it. It turns out to be the kind that points you to certain experiences and abilities that, once understood, must be let go of completely in order to experience things for yourself. The paradox here is that in the end dialogue is a quality of being, not a method at all. It is the difference between reading the menu and eating the meal. You do not in the end want a theory about yourself, but a direct experience of you. Maps and theories can be quite useful, but they are not the same as the real thing.

THE TIMELESS WAY OF CONVERSATION

Christopher Alexander has developed a way of tackling this problem of knowing and "not knowing" that holds particular promise for dialogue. In his seminal book *The Timeless Way of Building,* he proposes that there is a way of building that is thousands of years old, and that underlies the great buildings of the world, which are "as ancient in their form, as the trees and hills, and as our faces are." Alexander proposes that we must discover a way of building that works like nature. He says that human beings *already have within them* this timeless way, but it has been covered over for ages by our illusions, methods, and rules. Alexander argues that at the core of all successful acts of building and all successful processes of growth, even though there are a million different versions of these acts and processes, there is one fundamental invariant feature, which is responsible for their success.[1]

At its core, this single invariant process is *alive*. Alexander shows us that this single process is not an external method, but an internal one, indeed one that lies deep within us. The challenge, he argues, is that we must rid ourselves of all the images and methods that have led us to try to control the act of building from the outside in order to discover it. Liberating ourselves in this way, we discover that beneath the chaos in and around us is what Alexander calls "a rich, rolling, swelling, dying, lilting, singing, laughing, shouting, crying, sleeping *order*."[2] As we become more and more in touch with this order, we find we can create from it, build from it, and speak from it.

Alexander proposes that there is a secret to discovering this order and bringing it forth in building. He bases this in the assertion that human beings can tell the difference between things that are true to their inner nature and things that are not, whether in people or in buildings. We can recognize this quality within people and within buildings because they have a certain aliveness and freedom and depth to them. I know, for instance, someone who is both wise and charismatic. He seems to have an inner consistency to him. Alexander uses words like *comfortable* to give a sense of this quality. Such people are comfortable in their own skin, and they show this by the ways they interact with others; they have an ease, a gentleness, a no-need-to-force-things kind of genuineness.

We can find these same qualities in conversation. Conversations where people are generally being true to themselves, speaking their own voice and listening in a way that sustains listening from others feels *good*—if not always entirely comfortable. One gets the sense that something important is happening. Alexander points out that no one single word can capture this quality. It is very precise, he says, but confounds people because *it cannot be named*. It can, however, be recognized, and its absence felt.

Alexander says that to use the method he advocates we must first develop a discipline that enables us to discover a true and liberating relationship between ourselves and our surroundings, and—once we have found it—to abandon trying to apply it, and act as nature does.[3] This is a self-erasing methodology of architecture. At its core is the conscious rediscovery of a different way of being.

What Alexander proposes for architecture is also true for dialogue. What follows here is a description of a path that I believe can bring out this same inner aliveness, not merely in buildings but in conversation itself. Just as human beings have developed innumerable ways to block creativity in architecture and many other domains, so, too, have we blocked the creative possibilities that lie in every conversation. My intent in the next few chapters is to uncover an approach that can change this.

This ability for unselfconscious and highly creative exchange seems to have once been present for all human beings but now is largely a distant memory. Wherever one looks throughout history, one can see evidence of tribal gatherings, community events, and councils, where the central glue of human organizing was conversation—often around a fire—usually carried on for days at a time. These rituals of conversation typically included everyone in a tribe. In South Africa, for example, indigenous people still hold gatherings where the eldest and the youngest are all treated with the same respect, where everyone is seen and recognized.

Dana Meadows, a professor of environmental studies at Dartmouth and a newspaper columnist, told me a story many years ago of a time when she visited Georgia in the former Soviet Union. A dinner was to be held for the special American guests. Neighbors suddenly appeared with food, offering it simply because they had heard of the event and wished to contribute. At the dinner, Dana recounted, each person from oldest to youngest was given a chance to speak, to say what was happening in their lives, to share their accomplishments. All were fully *seen* by the attending crowd, drawn out of themselves. I will never forget her conclusion: *"This* is the secret to health!" In a setting like this, every person can be fully received, realize they belong, has a chance to voice what he or she is doing. This is the same part of the world featured in a popular yogurt commercial on television that implied people here live to a very ripe old age because of the yogurt in their diet. I have since wondered whether it was rituals of this sort, rather than the yogurt, that made the difference!

This unselfconscious capacity for conversation cannot be achieved simply by declaring it so or seeking to reinvent a lost society. For we have largely lost the ability to simply talk and think. Today we often see talking together as a "waste of time" if we do not have a specific objective. Under pressure, our conversation fails us. So while this ability to converse may be interesting to hear about, most of the time we simply cannot re-create it, especially in professional settings, where the norms all seem designed to prevent any kind of genuine contact.

Using dialogic practices, we need to see how conversation can evolve with groups of people, and finally extend to much larger, more complex settings like organizations and communities. The principles that underlie all these levels are the same. It is a method, or theory, that, once learned and incorporated into our conversations, must be dropped completely so that we can live and speak naturally again.

B U I L D I N G   C A P A C I T Y

F O R   N E W   B E H A V I O R

When you hear a word like *dialogue,* you probably think of conversations with others. But strange as it may sound, dialogue begins with yourself. In fact, all great practices always begin with the individual, no matter how many people one eventually touches. The saying "Physician, heal thyself" stems from long tradition that saw the deep connection between the individual and the wider world with which the healer interacts. This same tradition applies to dialogue. To be effective, we must first ask ourselves, How successful am I at listening to and speaking with *myself?*

The four practices named in Chapter 1, listening, respecting, suspending, and voicing, are the key building blocks to accomplishing this task. This part explores each of these, providing you with ways you might both understand and develop them within yourself.

DEFINING A PRACTICE

A "practice" is an activity that you do repeatedly to help you to bring about a particular experience. Yoga, playing the scales in music, the particular sequence for asking questions when taking a medical history, all have deliberate design and intention that, when used well, produce a defined result: expansion of awareness, musical accuracy, or vital information to aid in a diagnosis. You cannot tell a medical student how to sense the story behind a person's presenting medical difficulties, so that he can swiftly perceive the underlying causes. But you can give him the scaffolding that leads him to discover this deeper understanding for himself.

A practice is usually theory based, meaning it derives from deep principles that have been developed over time. In this sense it is not a recipe so much as a meditation: It requires constant repetition, over years, with the understanding that one will always be learning. A practice, finally, usually arises in the context of a community: groups of people establishing a tradition for accessing this knowledge. The community reinforces the necessity of the practice, supporting continuous reflection and improvement. Often the most senior members of the community guide the newer members in developing their understanding.

The practices I recommend for dialogue are not fully developed in the same way that some of the others mentioned here are. After all, yoga and the healing arts have been under conscious development for several thousand years. I believe dialogue, to be effective in groups and in larger social settings, requires a similar kind of development, a set of practices that can help us to understand it and let it blossom.

Taken together, the dialogue practices I propose here create a sense of wholeness in conversation. When you express them together, you experience balance, resilience, strength, life. When one or more are absent, conversations are less whole, less effective—they feel dead. The idea here is that wholeness is reflected in a certain set of *capacities for action* and that these can be articulated and brought forth by individuals, groups, organizations, and larger social communities. The practices provide a way to anchor these in yourself.

As you will see, they also work together and underscore the principles of participation, coherence, awareness, and unfolding. The practices described in the following chapters are each underscored by a principle that flows from the invisible architecture for dialogue. These deeper principles inform the way you can use each of the practices described here. So beneath the practice of listening is the principle of participation; behind respecting is the principle of coherence, behind suspending, the principle of awareness, and behind voicing, the principle of unfoldment. In this part I will discuss these practices and show you how to develop them within yourself.

But we cannot stop there. If we are conscious only of ourselves, we will be ineffective in groups. Dialogue requires that we learn to think together with others. The four individual practices can also be applied in groups of all sizes. Group level practices draw directly on the individual practices but expand to take into account a wider frame and broader sense of the dynamics of interactions among people.

Listening

The heart of dialogue is a simple but profound capacity to listen. Listening requires we not only hear the words, but also embrace, accept, and gradually let go of our own inner clamoring. As we explore it, we discover that listening is an expansive activity. It gives us a way to perceive more directly the ways we participate in the world around us.

This means listening not only to others but also to ourselves and our own reactions. Recently a manager in a program I was leading told me, "You know, I have always prepared myself to speak. But I have never prepared myself to listen." This is, I have found, a common condition. For listening, a subject we often take for granted, is actually very hard to do, and we are rarely prepared for it. Krishnamurti, the Indian philosopher, put the challenge this way:

> I do not know if you have ever examined how you listen, it doesn't matter to what, whether to a bird, to the wind in the leaves, to the rushing waters, or how you listen in a dialogue with yourself, to your conversation in various relationships with your intimate friends, your wife or husband. If we try to listen we find it extraordinarily difficult, because we are always projecting our opinions and ideas, our prejudices, our background, our inclinations, our impulses; when they dominate, we hardly listen at all to what is being said. In that state there is no value at all. One listens and therefore learns, only in a state of attention, a state of silence, in which this whole background is in abeyance, is quiet; then, it seems to me, it is possible to communicate.[1]

To listen is to develop an inner silence. This is not a familiar habit for most of us. Emerson once joked that ninety-five percent of what goes on in our minds is none of our business! We often pay great attention to what goes on in us, when what is actually required is a kind of disciplined self-forgetting. This does not have to be difficult. It is within the reach of each of us.

To do this you do not have to retreat to a monastery or to be converted to some new belief. You do, though, have to do some deliberate work to cultivate settings inside yourself and with others—where it is *possible* to listen. In other words, you must create a space in which listening can occur.

The ways we have learned to listen, to impose or apply meaning to the world, are very much a function of our mental models, of what we hold in our minds as truths. But the physical functioning of our ears, and how they differ from other senses, can shed light on how we can learn to "make sense" in new ways.

THE SENSE OF HEARING

The sense of hearing is ever present. You cannot turn it off; there is no switch. You can close your eyes. You can become less sensitive to or even limit your sense of touch, or taste, or smell. But unless you are deaf (or becoming deaf), you cannot stop yourself from hearing without external aid.

In her book *A Natural History of the Senses,* Diane Ackerman says that hearing's job is:

> partly spatial. A gently swishing field of grain that seems to surround one in an earthly whisper doesn't have the urgency of a panther growling behind and to the right. Sounds have to be located in space, identified by type, intensity, and other features. There is a geographical quality to listening.[2]

Our hearing puts us on the map. It balances us. Our sense of balance is intimately tied to our hearing; both come from the same source within our bodies. We listen in a way that tells us about the dimensionality of our world. Hearing is *auditory,* of course, relating to sound. The word *auditory* and *oral* have the same roots as the word *audience* and *auditorium.* Their most ancient root means "to place perception." When we listen, we place our perceptions.

Our culture, though, is dominated by sight. We see thousands of images flashed across our minds in an hour of television or the Internet. The result of this external bombardment of visual impressions is that we tend now to think in these ways. In the Western world we have begun to be habituated to this quick pace, and are impatient with other rhythms. But seeing and listening are very different.

The substance of seeing is light. Light moves at a far more rapid pace than sound: 186,000 miles per second as opposed to 1,100 feet per second. To listen, in other words, you must *slow down* and operate at the speed of sound rather than at the speed of light.

The eye seems to perceive at a superficial level, at the level of reflected light.[3] While the eye sees at the surface, the ear tends to penetrate below the surface. In his book *Nada Brohmn: The World Is Sound: Music and the Landscape of Consciousness,* Joachim-Ernst Berendt points out that the ear is the only sense that fuses an ability to measure with an ability to judge. We can discern different colors, but we can give a precise *number* to different sounds. Our eyes do not let us perceive with this kind of precision. An unmusical person can recognize an octave and, perhaps once instructed, a quality of tone, that is a C or an F-sharp. Berendt points out that there are few "acoustical illusions"—something sounding like something that in fact it is not—while there are many optical illusions. The ears do not lie. The sense of hearing gives us a remarkable connection with the invisible, underlying order of things. Through our ears we gain access to vibration, which underlies everything around us. The sense of tone and music in another's voice gives us an enormous amount of information about that person, about their stance toward life, about their intentions.

To listen well, we must attend both to the words and the silence between the words. I once held a dialogue retreat in Amsterdam with a group of consultants, managers, and civic leaders. On the first day, people were quite frustrated and contentious: Some found the conversation going too slowly, others felt there seemed to be no coherent theme. People developed many different opinions about what was happening and what ought to happen. The afternoon of the second day I opened the proceedings by simply asking people to reflect on the day's events. To people's surprise, there was a profound silence. The silence filled the room like a rest between the notes. The silence seemed to take us in, bring us alive, evoking a profound state of listening. In that state all one's words feel inadequate, almost an imposition. Slowly people began to put their thoughts into words. Many later reported that like a jazz ensemble playing together, they felt they had to improvise, that all of their previous ideas seemed out of place. They tried to speak in a way that matched the intensity of the silence.

LISTENING AND THE PRINCIPLE
OF PARTICIPATION

Our capacity to listen puts us in contact with the wider dimensions of the world in which we live. It lets us connect to it. Listening can open in us a door, a greater sense of participation in the world. I see listening, properly understood and developed, as an immediate gateway that can connect us with the much-touted but much-misunderstood notion that we live in a "participative universe," one of the four key principles that underlie the approach to dialogue proposed in this book.

The principle of participation builds upon the realization that individuals are active participants in the living world, a part of nature as well as observers of it. At the heart of the matter here is the idea that human beings participate intimately in their worlds and are not separate from them.

Ideas like these fly directly in the face of what science has told us about the world over the last three hundred years. We have had the belief that man was separate from nature and needed to control it. Descartes, in many ways the founder of modern rationalism, declared in the seventeenth century that there was an absolute split between thinking man and the world he observes. Today, what we

call "real" are the things we can quantify and measure objectively—
views stemming directly from Descartes and the canon of modern
science that grew from it—"specific location." This idea is simply
that if you cannot find a precise measurement and location for
something, it does not really exist.

There is clearly validity to this perspective at the physical
level of things. But it gets more problematic as we move into
thoughts and feelings. Science now has attempted to help us
"locate" our thoughts by conducting brain scans; but as I indicated earlier, this tells us only about the external surface, not
the interior contours of our thought.

The principle of participation that lies behind the practice
of listening is well demonstrated by a hologram. A hologram is
a three-dimensional image created by the interference pattern
of two interacting laser beams. This interference pattern is captured on photographic film or a holographic plate. When a laser
is directed at this special plate, it produces a three-dimensional
reproduction of the image that was recorded.

All the information contained on the plate is enfolded into
every part of the plate. For instance, if you were to break this
plate up into smaller pieces and shine the laser through it, you
would still see the whole image. As the pieces of the plate get
smaller, the image becomes dimmer and more diffuse as well;
there is less information on it. The density of information on
the original plate made the image bright and clear. But every
piece of the holographic plate contains the whole image.
Similarly, as David Bohm argued, information about the whole
of the universe is "enfolded," or contained, in each part.

To get a sense of how this might work, consider the experience of listening to music.[4] Music acts in a slightly different
way. Music, too, is experienced as a living whole. Though any
one note may be discerned individually, it is held in the context
of reverberations of the notes that came before and the antici-

pation of those that will follow. Each part of the music contains information about the whole piece. If we heard one note at a time, we would not tend to think of this as music. Bohm suggests that the universe itself is like this: Each part is enfolded into every other part. There is a surface-level order that has only a relative independence, like the individual notes of a piece of music. Everything is interconnected.

We are part of a much larger universe in ways that may continue to surprise us. Henri Bortoft tells us in his book *The Wholeness of Nature* that the night sky is also enfolded in each aspect of it:

> We see this nighttime world by means of the light "carrying" the stars to us, which means that this vast expanse of sky must all be present in the light which passes through the small hole of the pupil into the eye. Furthermore, other observers in different locations can see the same expanse of night sky. Hence we can say that the stars seen in the heavens are all present in the light which is at any eye-point. The totality is contained in each small region of space, and when we use optical instruments like a telescope, we simply reclaim more of that light.[5]

A telescope focuses the light, making the holographic image brighter and stronger.

Language Is Holographic

Our language is also holographic. Each word contains not only the wider context of paragraph and sentence but the deeper context of our lives. When you first interact with someone, their initial words carry the entire hologram of their consciousness to you. The full meaning might not be completely clear to you initially, since the information may not be focused enough—like seeing without a telescope, not enough light has been captured to let you see what is actually there. But when you know someone for a long time, or have a close relationship, the richness of the information changes. I can remember hearing my mother say my name at different times while I was growing up and knowing that just that one word could mean anything from "I want you to do something for me" to "You are in big trouble." Most of the time I knew precisely which it was. These meanings, and many others, were enfolded in me and her and influenced how we both interacted.

Every part of ourselves is enfolded in every part of our conversations whether we realize it or not. But we cannot always tell the extent of our participation. There is not enough information to produce a clear and coherent understanding. We lack a focusing process—a way of containing the enormity in a small space. Dialogue is the focusing mechanism for the hologram of conversation. Through it we can expand our awareness to include ever-greater wholeness. Dialogue is a process that can allow us to become aware of our participation in a much wider whole. Like the telescope, it focuses the available light more completely so that we can see more.

The Earth Listens to Us

The mechanistic view of life that we have inherited tells us that the world is an objectively existing, separate place. We hear the sounds of the world. But this view of things is quite insular. In preparing ourselves for dialogue, it is helpful to recall that there was a time when human beings were much more intimately involved in the landscape, where our very language mimicked and was developed from the music of the earth itself. We not only listen to the earth; it listens to us.

Writer David Abram, in his book *The Spell of the Sensuous,* outlines the ways in which human language was deeply rooted in the physical sounds of the earth—the birds, the forces of weather, the rivers. To the indigenous peoples, the earth itself spoke. Oral cultures had a deep attunement with the nuances of their physical surroundings. It was the arrival of written language, according to Abram, that gradually marked a shift away from human beings feeling that they are participants with the earth, toward a more objective stance.

When someone claims that his indigenous ancestors had a more intimate connection with the earth than he does, this may seem quaint to modern, sophisticated ears. The idea that the earth "spoke" to the indigenous peoples may fit into one's picture of an earlier animistic culture—one in which all of nature was endowed with conscious life. But most would not see it as anything more than that—a belief—that science has long since disproved.

But notice: When you read these words, it is very likely that you are hearing them inside your head as you go along. The words of our written language *speak to us.* We endow them with voices. They come alive. We enter into a strange, almost dreamlike state with the words. Says Abram,

> Our senses are now coupled, synaesthetically, to these printed shapes as profoundly as they were once wedded to cedar trees, ravens, and the moon. As the hills and the bending grasses once spoke to our tribal ancestors, so these written letters and words now speak to us.[6]

Animism is not dead; *it has just changed form.* It is in fact a fundamental human capacity—our ability to let our senses fuse with the world around us and so enable us to participate directly in it.

Through a detailed process that Abram traces in his book, this capacity has gradually been redirected toward written language.

LEARNING TO LISTEN

Learning to listen begins with recognizing how you are listening now. Generally, we are not all that conscious of how we listen. You can begin to listen by listening first to yourself and to your own reactions. Ask yourself, What do I feel here? or How does this feel? Try to identify what you feel more carefully and directly. Beginning with the perception of your own feelings connects you to your heart and to the heart of your experience. To learn to be present, we must learn to notice what we are feeling now.

Be Aware of Thought

As you begin to listen, you can also begin to notice what you are thinking. Focus your thoughts on someone you care about for a moment. Almost immediately, you may find that you are flooded with thoughts and images of that person. You may also experience a range of feelings. Your memory plays a very powerful force in how you perceive those around you.

To listen is to realize that much of our reaction to others comes from memory; it is stored reaction, not fresh response at all. Listening from my predispositions in this way is *listening from the "net" of thought* that I cast on a particular situation.[7]

Let me give you an analogy. England has been inhabited continuously for many centuries. A large number of people occupy a relatively small geographic space. As a result, almost every corner, every piece of land, is settled, cultivated, occupied. There is a certain density to people's memories about this place, and you can feel this as you travel in the country. It is not a land of wide-open spaces that have yet to be explored fully. Here you get the sense that everything has been explored very fully for a very long time. It is rich as a result. Every stone in every building has many stories it could tell compared to, say, a stone in rural Nevada.

The landscape of our listening works in similar ways. We know well and have explored fully certain parts of our inner lives. Listening in this mode, from the net of our thought, from this rich background, may make us feel quite clever. After all, we seem to know a lot about what is being said, have things to say, reactions to express, opinions to voice. But just as a densely populated area like England can feel claustrophobic, this kind of listening is not always very expansive. This net of our thought, however finely woven, is still based on memory. It is limited, even unintelligent, in the sense that it cannot respond in a new way to what is happening. The word *intelligence* is quite revealing on this score. It comes from two Latin roots, *inter* and *legere,* which mean "to gather between." Intelligence, then, is the active, fresh capacity to think, to gather between already existing categories. In other words, we can learn to listen either from the net we already have, or to the spaces between.

"Be aware of thought" was a piece of advice Krishnamurti often offered. He would ask someone, "Why do you walk that way?" And they might respond, "Because I do." He would retort, "Well, that's your thought." To be aware of thought is to learn to watch how our thoughts dictate to us much of our personal and collective experience. Much of what human beings do happens simply by virtue of our agreements that it should. By agreement alone—not because there is any particular reason, some countries drive on the left and others on the right, for instance. What do you do that is simply your thought?

Stick to the Facts

A common joke about someone who has an overinflated sense of himself is "He is a legend in his own mind." We need to learn to listen with a great deal more humility. This typically means literally coming down to earth and connecting what we think with the experiences that lead us to think it. While this may seem obvious and easy, in practice people continually jump to conclusions, speak abstractly, and fail to notice they are doing so. A new discipline of listening to what is said can make a real change.

This is not always so easy to do. We are often unaware of the extent to which we assume what we see is what is there. A colleague of mine tells the story of a man who went one day to pick up his high-school-age daughter and another girl. As he drove up to the place he was to meet her, he saw her leaning on a black BMW sedan. Standing nearby were two young men, both with pagers and cell phones. One had a ponytail. This man's immediate thought: drug dealers! But he noticed how he had begun to judge them, and stopped himself. He went up and started to talk to them, and found that they were volunteer firemen, that the BMW was used and much older than he had realized, and that the young men were very gentle, very bright, and capable.

As they were driving away, his daughter's friend burst into tears. When asked what was wrong, she said, "I wish my parents would talk to me the way you just talked to them."[8]

The Ladder of Inference

We need to distinguish between the inferences we make about experience and the experience itself. One powerful tool for helping to do this is called the Ladder of Inference. This tool, developed by Chris Argyris, a professor at Harvard, is a simple model of how we think.[9] It suggests that what we experience we process and create inferences about our experience, typically at lightning speed, without noticing that we are doing so. What we do not notice principally is the difference between a direct experience and our assessment of it.

For instance, if I called a meeting for two and someone

showed up at two-thirty, several people might think to themselves, "She's late." Someone else might further think that she did not care about the meeting. A third person might say, "She is always late on Thursdays." All of this happens in milliseconds: The assessments are made, the reactions are in, it all seems obvious and true. But is it? In what ways?

We draw conclusions like these all the time. Our conclusions have the simple reasoning that "this is the way it is." But I have found that these sorts of conclusions are never fully accurate.

For instance, in the story above, what is the directly observable data? Many people would say it is the fact that she was late. But is late really directly observable data?

Can you see, touch, smell, hear, or feel "late"? "Well, yes," a student once replied to this question. "The clock says two-thirty, the meeting started at two, she's late! What's the discussion about?" he exploded. Gradually, we explored the idea that "late" is an inference drawn from the fact of the clock striking two-thirty, a foot crossing the threshold, a prior statement about the meeting time, and an agreement to meet. People sometimes hear this as doubting whether this person is late. I am sure she was, *by the standards of our community*. But that is a long way from saying that is an observable fact. It may be a valid judgment.

Why is this important? One of the ways we sustain the culture of thinking alone is that we form conclusions and then do not test them, treating our initial inferences as facts. We wall ourselves off, in other words, from the roots of our own thinking. And when we are invested in an opinion, we tend to seek evidence that we are right and avoid evidence that we are wrong.

Errors of this sort can have devastating consequences. Some thirty years after the Cuban Missile Crisis, several academics brought together the Russian, Cuban, and American leaders in charge at the time of the crisis to reflect on the causes of this near-devastating conflict. A series of three meetings were held in

Boston, Moscow, and Havana. Included on the Russian side were Ambassador Dobrynin, Soviet Foreign Minister Gromyko, the son of Nikita Khrushchev, and the Soviet generals responsible for installing the missiles in Cuba. American participants included Robert McNamara, Ted Sorenson and other members of Kennedy's inner circle, and for the Cubans, Fidel Castro himself. Simply getting these leaders together was an important step toward greater dialogue about international conflict. Their meetings revealed some important facts not previously understood or well known, and shed light on the disastrous consequences of drawing conclusions.

One important component of this crisis was the fact that the Cubans installed missiles without notice ninety miles off the coast of the United States. A U-2 spy plane caught sight of these and noted one striking fact: There was no camouflage on them. It seemed to some in Kennedy's inner circle that the Soviets were aggressively moving forward, not even bothering to camouflage their missile installations.

Thirty years later another side to the story emerged. As it turns out, the Russian army, which installed the missiles, was accustomed to installing missiles in Russia, where there was no need for camouflage. Like any good military bureaucracy, when ordered to install missiles in Cuba, they did it the way they normally did: without camouflage. Some three decades later in conversation, the Russian general in charge of the installation made it quite clear that there was no ulterior intent in leaving the camouflage off. What was taken by some as clear evidence of aggressive intent was essentially based on an erroneous presumption.[10]

We jump to conclusions all the time. Many of us assume that this is a normal way of conducting business: to set things up in oppositional fashion, draw sharp conclusions, and let the chips fall where they may. What we miss in this is the systemic way in which we may err. We do not remain in touch with our experience but draw abstract inferences from it. And then we assume our inferences *are* the reality, just as Kennedy's advisers did. But we can learn to listen in a way that challenges this process, that distinguishes all the stories people make up about a set of facts from the facts themselves.

We can notice how we progress from our conclusions about subjects to assumptions we construct about them and finally to beliefs that we adopt—views that, once they take hold, tend to remain relatively stable and hard to change. These beliefs then reinforce what we select out to see. We can easily become locked into a way of thinking that is hard to change.

Listening this way can help us resolve differences. We can become more attentive to the "data" that leads us to make our conclusions, and so open a much different quality of inquiry.

For example, a company with which I am familiar was in the process of making the transition from an entrepreneurial firm to a more mature, managed firm. Previously, things had been quite informal. Now, by contrast, the corporate setup included a human resource manager, more policies, and structure. One event triggered a crisis. The human resource manager sent out a memo asking that everyone make deliberate requests for vacation time. (Previously people had just informed one or two of their coworkers and left.) One manager took a look at this memo and thought the spirit of the place was being destroyed. "Oh, no, we're becoming more like IBM," he thought to himself. Another manager saw the memo and thought, "Finally, structure!" People saw two very different meanings in the same event, or data.

The managers locked horns over this, and the memo became a symbol of the very problem that the company now faced. As we looked more closely, however, we discovered something interesting: The first person had reacted not to the memo but to the way the memo arrived on his desk—unannounced, as if it were a done deal. The second person saw the memo—a copy of which had also been sent to his mailbox—and was delighted. These differences show that people extract different meanings out of the same data, or they can see entirely different data. In this case the same memo evoked very different responses.

What happens when people bring controversial things to your attention? Do you have reactions that seem utterly justified to you but may not in fact be based on experience that you can point to directly? When we make claims about the inevitability of our choice of interpretations, we run the risk of closing off others and limiting ourselves. The ladder of inference invites us to see the difference between what we think and what leads us to think it.

Follow the Disturbance

Slowing down our thinking and listening in this way is not so easy, in part because the landscape is not neutral. Some of the memories we have are painful. They move very swiftly and grab us by the scruff of the neck. By the time we realize their influence, we are caught.

Often when we listen to others we may discover that we are *listening from disturbance;* in other words, we are listening from an emotional memory rather than from the present moment. If I say something to you that you do not like, you may be triggered by what I say, perhaps intensely so. Your future listening will be colored for a while by this. If I call you an idiot, it will be very hard for you not to react to this, to defend yourself against it. The simple word *idiot* conjures up for many a host of reactive memories—most of them probably quite painful, perhaps even to the point where one cannot hear anything but disturbed feelings and thoughts.

Both the steelworkers and the managers I worked with were deeply skeptical, for instance, that they could have a conversation together that would make any difference. After all, some forty years of hostility was not likely to change quickly. To everyone's surprise, we had a very energizing first session. People spoke openly and freely. They began to relax. This led the plant president to speak more directly than he would have otherwise. He later said that he thought to himself, We are really getting somewhere now, so I should really tell them the truth. He told the group that man-hours per ton needed to be reduced. It was, in his mind, a simple statement of the manufacturing and competitive facts. Competitors' plants were more efficient.

The union heard this comment as a betrayal. They were being told, in code, they thought, that some of the people in the plant would lose their jobs. One way to reduce man-hours per ton of steel is to have fewer men making the steel! They "went ballistic" and reacted, much as they always had. One steelworker fired a remark right at the president:

> I feel pissed off and pissed on. I was very optimistic at the first meeting. I haven't heard anything new [today], except a lot of criticism . . . I was real optimistic . . . all I heard today is bullshit.

They listened to the conversation from this point of disturbance for the next few hours, triggered and reactive and unable to hear anything new. Disturbance of this sort usually leads people to listen in a way that is self-confirming: They look for evidence that they are right and that others are wrong.

But there is another step you can take in listening. You can start to see what you have been missing. You can "follow the disturbance"—you can learn to listen for the sources of the difficulty, whether it is in you or others.

Instead of looking for evidence that confirms your point of view, you can look for what *disconfirms* it, what challenges it. Gradually, this happened with the steelworkers. The managers began to understand the betrayal that the steelworkers felt by the comment about worked hours per ton. The steelworkers realized they had imposed their history on the managers—blaming this generation for things the previous managers had done. The managers, in turn, began to see the extent of the frustration and pain that the steelworkers had known. This brought up its own exasperation:

> How do you get by all the pain and all the patterns and all the hurt and all the mistrust that's built up over the years, that weren't necessarily created by anyone in this room specifically? I don't see us advancing to the next step unless we're able to do that, and it seems a monstrous job. I mean, I wouldn't have a clue. I sit here and hear what these guys are saying, and they've been hurt and abused. You hear some of the worst words that you can think of, and I'm saying to myself, How can we get beyond this? Realistically, can we get beyond this?

The asking of questions like this, impossible though it may seem, is an essential first step toward genuine change. Listening in this case becomes reflective: We begin to see how *others* are experiencing the world.

And then we make the most difficult step of all: We begin to connect what we do with what we say. Am I acting consistently, I might ask, with what I profess? In what ways am *I* behaving? In what ways am I doing to others the very things I claim they should not do?

We learn to listen for the gaps. *No one* acts consistently with their words. Some of us are more aware than others of how large this gap is, how systematic it is. Listening to our own actions, we begin to see what we have been doing to others. The result with the steelworkers was impressive. As the union president, walking out of the first gathering, said: "That was the first time we got together where no one got whupped!"

Listen Without Resistance

This is an approach developed by two colleagues, Sarita Chawla and Ken Murphy. It relates directly to the challenge of listening beyond the net of our thought, and even the disturbances we may feel. We can learn to listen in a way that recognizes and then puts aside the resistances and reactions that we feel to what someone else is saying. This may be better put as "listen *while noticing* resistance." The challenge here is to become conscious of the ways in which we project our opinions about others onto them, how we color or distort what is said without realizing it. If you watch, you may find that there is an almost irrepressible tape in your mind that plays, especially when you feel a reaction to another. It is in these moments that you face the challenge of simply watching what comes up. Watch, keeping in mind the phrase "Now this, and now this" as each opinion is heard.

Stand Still

Perhaps the simplest and most potent practice for listening is simply to be still. By being still in ourselves, quieting the inner chatter of our minds, we can open up to a way of being present and listening that cuts through everything. Think of this as calming the surface of the waters of our experience so that we can see below to the depths. As we learn to lift ourselves out of the net of thought, the conclusions we jump to, the disturbances of our heart and resistances of our mind, this surface sea of reactions can calm down. We discover that there is another world of possibility for listening. We can listen *from silence* within ourselves.

This practice is captured quite beautifully in a poem by

David Wagoner. He conveys advice given by a Native American elder to a child who might find himself lost in the woods. He is told to "stand still," that "the trees ahead and the bushes beside you are not lost."

To stand still is to come into contact with the wholeness that pervades everything, that is already here. It is to touch the aliveness of the universe. To be lost is to lose contact with this wholeness.

There are many traditions worldwide that encourage people to cultivate inner silence. Often this is done as an externally imposed renunciation of the world to achieve some end. But joyous release of inner noise is not the same as suppression of oneself! Silence is a state of being into which one can let go.

Listening from silence means listening for and receiving the meanings that well up from deep within us. These creative pulses may move in us, but often we are too busy to pay attention. Stand still.

QUESTIONS

- What am I feeling in my body?

- How does this feel?

- How is this affecting people?

- What are the different voices trying to convey?

- What voices are marginalized here?

PRACTICES

- Be aware of thought.

- Stick to the facts.

- Follow the disturbance.

- Listen without resistance.

- Stand still.

THE ART OF LISTENING TOGETHER

Listening is usually considered singular activity. But in dialogue one discovers a further dimension of listening: the ability not only to listen, but to *listen together* as a part of a larger whole.

This entails making a fundamental shift of perspective. It means taking into account not only what things look like from one's own perspective, but how they look and feel from the perspective of the whole web of relationships among the people concerned. This requires more than empathy, which might imply trying to put oneself in the other person's shoes while also sustaining one's own angle. Instead, we can enlarge our sense of ourselves—our sense of identity—so that we become what a colleague of mine once termed "an advocate for the whole."[11]

When people listen together, dialogue can sometimes evoke a deep and unusual experience of common understanding and communion. It is unusual because people come to realize that they do not need to know every detail of the personal histories of the individuals they are speaking with to have the feeling of profound connection. This is what is meant by a term coined by the early Christian communities at the beginning of the first millennium: *koinonia*. It means "impersonal fellowship." In this state, people connect very intimately with one another, but not intrusively.

To listen together is to do what people in Grand Junction gradually learned to do during the health-care dialogue project we conducted there: Make the transition from listening alone, as separate individuals and organizations, to listening as if one were a part of a larger whole.

Our initial meeting eventually brought this out very clearly. For many years people in the community had acted as if there were no underlying differences among them, thinking all the while to themselves that the intensity of their rivalry was troubling and seemingly out of place for health-care professionals. In our early sessions, people began to explore this contradiction and the impact this was having on their effectiveness.

For instance, an inquiry into the issue of physician contracting revealed the intensity of competition for good doctors and the economic dependencies the different hospitals all had on one another. However, they came to realize that their values for human compassion and care were at risk.

Subsequent dialogue sessions carried the conversation further. What began as a fragmented debate about who was to blame for the rivalry and paranoia in the system eventually became an honest inquiry into the personal sources of the trouble. One doctor, for instance, began to realize the degree to which he had contributed to the pain many were beginning to acknowledge.

> I am struck by the last couple of comments, how absolutely schizophrenic my behavior is—when it comes to care of a patient and my care of you. When I deal with patients, there's a [belief] that's hammered into you, that you never resolve a set of symptoms on the level of diagnosis. To jump to a diagnosis is a disasater. A chest pain can be a spider bite, an ulcer, pneumonia, or a heart attack. The minute I call it one or the other, I ignore the other possibilities. I don't deal with patients and medicine that way, yet I do deal with all of you that way.

His words encouraged people to step beyond thinking only about themselves and led them to inquire into what made sense for everyone. Becoming an advocate for the whole means listening not just for what *I* have done, but together, for the meaning that might have an impact on everyone.

The Grand Junction health-care inquiry, motivated at first, at least in part, by the hope of reducing the damaging effects of competition, evolved into an exploration of the nature of well-being itself, and what role the community was to play in establishing and sustaining health. Below the "seamless system" were a lot of overworked and pressured people sacrificed for the cause of good health.

It gradually became clear, for instance, that people held the belief that they were the last best hope for health for the community. But this responsibility was also one that few believed they could really uphold. Instead of discussing this, they did their best to assuage their sense of inadequacy. One way they did this was to purchase expensive technical equipment. The request for a more efficient collaboration came from the realization that costs were spiraling out of control and the federal government and/or the changing face of competition toward more managed care would greatly limit them. The group eventually began to meet together regularly to talk about the how to resolve technology needs in a way that suited everyone in the community, something that would never have been done jointly prior to the dialogue project there.

PRACTICES FOR CATALYZING LISTENING IN GROUPS

Listen for the Dilemmas

One of the reasons people struggle to say what they think is that they are in a dilemma. No matter what they say, they fear they'll be in trouble. For instance, note this conversation that took place among several leaders of business units in a consumer goods firm as they sought to design a companywide strategy, while at the same time taking into account their cross-divisional differences. All of these people had said on the one hand that they wanted the best outcome for the company overall. But they also privately believed that their own division's efforts must not be jeopardized, and they harbored views that others were out to take over, or take advantage of the situation. Listen as Fred, the leader of the task force, and Joe, one of the major players, interact (this is drawn from actual conversations and interviews).[12]

Fred's Unspoken Thoughts	What Fred and Joe Said
FRED: I know that Joe is going to hold out. Maybe I can flush him out a little.	FRED: Is everyone willing to commit to the outcomes of this task force?
FRED: Whatever that means.	JOE: I am very much committed to outcomes here. I would be willing to commit at any option, but only if I felt there was some good in it.
FRED: This guy is holding out. There is no way he will agree to anything we propose here if it runs counter to what he was already planning.	FRED: But you are not in favor of having us sell directly to the customers.
	JOE: As you know, we have built our entire business around creating and then selling through powerful channels [the suppliers to the end users]. Going direct would completely change our business. We cannot just go do that, and we will not.
FRED: This is hopeless.	FRED: Okay, let's try to get something defined that will meet all our needs.

Both Joe and Fred left this part of the conversation with the feeling that the same old impasse was likely to be sustained.

In situations like these, people typically fail to hear what the other actually intends. Often there is a fair degree of "noise" in the communication. Joe says he is open but also sends a mixed message. We are left guessing what he means. Fred pushes, but without inquiring into why Joe seems stuck.

We might look instead at what seems to have been the underlying dilemma in Joe's thinking. To oppose Fred in the way that he did *could* look like pure politics, which is what Fred attributes it to. But most people do not think to themselves, I will play this situation for what it is worth. Instead, they look out for their own agenda. If we asked ourselves What is Joe's underlying dilemma? we might consider that it was to protect the integrity of his own strategy as well as that of the whole group's efforts. Joe's dilemma is that to do anything else is to get him in trouble, either with the task force or with his boss. By digging in like this, he is announcing that he is in a kind of trap, though he does not know how to say this. If Joe does not take care of his agenda, he may lose. If he does, he believes he may also lose in the eyes of Fred and others. He is trapped, and no one is offering him an alternative.

By listening for and underscoring the underlying dilemma, you can learn a great deal about a situation and free people to own up both to what they intended and the impact they actually had. For instance, I asked Joe to tell us what he was concerned about, realizing he was not trying to be difficult or critical. He eventually admitted his dilemma and began joking about how he might have to steal other divisions' business. This eventually began to free things up.

In a conversation that you wish to turn into a dialogue, your own and the group's ability to be sensitive to—and name—the dilemmas people face can open doors.

THE DARK SIDE OF LISTENING

For all the wonderful qualities of listening and the fully engaged participation that can be evoked through it, there is also an underside to this practice. As mentioned before, we tend to think in ways that lead us away from wholeness and into fragmentation. Again, fragmented listening is *abstraction*, which literally means "extracting meaning from something." A part of me can listen and be fully participative while another part can abstract and fail to attend to what I hear—or attend only selectively. It is only by becoming aware of those parts of ourselves that *fail to listen*, even as we try hard to listen well, that we may break through to a new experience.

A part of me can, in other words, remain high on the ladder of inference, and so have perceptions not grounded in directly observable experience. Instead of listening without resistance, I listen but resist what I hear, selecting what I want and discounting what I do not want to hear. When we have an ax to grind with someone, we tend to hear the grinding of the axes, not what the other person has to say.

Instead of allowing a quality of stillness to pervade our listening, it is easy to be in motion, seeking to "grasp" or "take in" what is being said. Our listening becomes more intellectual. We are "here," others are "there." We try to "get" what they say. Our thought is doing the interpreting. We are separate from the person, and then the "transmission" model of listening prevails. Have I received from them what I needed to perceive rather than what they were actually saying? Listening in this sense objectifies the other person. It is possible to listen in this way, but we end up treating the other person as an object to manage not a being with whom we can create new possibilities.

What are we to do? The challenge is to become aware of

the fact that especially when we try hard to listen, we will often still have a part of us actively failing to do so. The key is to simply become aware of this, to make conscious just what we are doing. Awareness is curative; as we stand still, our listening can open us into frontiers we did not realize were there.[13]

Respecting

M ost of the time we see only single facets of people, flashes of light that come to us in this instance or that, revealing qualities we like and perhaps some we do not. We often see ourselves in this same way: the gradual revelation, sometimes over years, of a many-sided gem.

To be able to see a person as a whole being, we must learn another central element in the practice of dialogue: respect. Respect is not a passive act. To respect someone is look for the springs that feed the pool of their experience. The word comes from the Latin *respecere*, which means "to look again." Its most ancient roots mean "to observe." It involves a sense of honoring or deferring to someone. Where once we saw one aspect of a person, we look again and realize how much of them we had missed. This second look can let us take in more fully the fact that here before me is a living, breathing being.

At its core, the act of respect invites us to see others as *legitimate*. We may not like what they do or say or think, but we cannot deny their legitimacy as beings.[1] In Zulu, a South African language, the word *Sawu bona* is spoken when people greet one another and when they depart. It means "I see you." To the Zulus, being seen has more meaning than in Western cultures. It means that the person is in some real way brought more fully into existence by virtue of the fact that they are seen. As in most indigenous cultures, the memory of a sense of participation in nature has not been completely lost. To say "I see you" is to sustain you in this world.

A year into the steelworkers' and management dialogue, we met a significant crisis that revealed the power of respect. The union executive board was by now quite experienced with dialogue. Its members, on the other hand, were fearful that in learning dialogue they had lost their ability to attack management, and said so in those terms.

This came out in stark relief during discussions about the renewal of the labor contract between union and management. Historically, each such negotiation was intense for both sides. This time was particularly tough. The Kansas City, Missouri, plant in which we held the dialogues was a division of Armco, a large steel producer. Armco had decided that this division, which specialized in grinding media and steel wire, was incompatible with pursuing the stainless steel and other specialty markets in which it wished to compete, and put the division up for sale. It also made it clear that if the division was not sold within a set time, they would close it down and sell off the assets.

Shortly afterward a venture capital firm put up money to

help management buy itself out. Now suddenly the new contract was no longer only a labor agreement, but a symbol of the future of the plant. It had become clear that without a new contract, the deal for the buyout would collapse. The union's agreement became central to the future of the entire business.

That pressure took both management and union by surprise. People suddenly stopped seeing the negotiations as an opportunity to prove out the goodwill that had developed between union and management over the past year, but as a two-edged political battle. Management sought, under pressure from the venture capitalists, to have a new "business discipline," which really meant ensuring they would recover their initial investment from the company as quickly as possible. They also wanted to impose a rigorous new contract, asking for a wage freeze and greater employee responsibility for health benefits. No one calculated the impact of these moves on the container that held the union-management dialogue process.

Certain factions within the union felt themselves under similar pressure, and sought to find ways to capitalize on this situation to promote their own bid for leadership and show that the union could flex its muscles in its first serious vote under a new company.

All this combined to cause the union to turn down management's initial contract after an anxious and rushed vote. Now the pressure was on; the banks threatened to withdraw from the deal unless the union voted in favor of the contract. Management was caught because they could not tell union people what was behind the contract—how it meant the guarantee of their future and a likely substantial increase in wages over the next five years—for fear of being accused of unfair bargaining tactics.

In the midst of this we held a dialogue to talk through the situation. Many people predicted that the union would boycott the meeting. Instead, some forty people from both union and management came. In this meeting, the skills of a year of dialogue came to life in one of the most revealing truth-telling sessions I have ever seen.

Managers revealed their despair over the possibility of losing the opportunity to create a new company. Union people admitted they wanted the deal to fail simply because of their intense anger at the company for decades of perceived abuse. They also expressed their frustration with the process and their feelings of being caught between prohibitions about union-management negotiation and their deep desire to have others in the plant understand things in a new say. There were long silences and challenging exchanges in the meeting as people confronted years of difficult relations and betrayal.

Nonetheless, the polarization between management and union, perhaps now at its height, was held in a climate of respect that was quite astonishing. No one tried to convince anyone else of his position. There was no tone of accusation exchanged between managers and labor leaders. People tried to understand what was happening without resorting to blame. They asked themselves: Where had the unexpected dissatisfaction come from? Why were people in the plant angry and reactive? What had stopped people from seeing that there was a bigger picture here, while the promise of a new plant and new future hung in the balance? What had each party done that had kept them from seeing their mutual interdependence?

Later, people asked union officials to comment on their view of their differences with management. One union man said that he was troubled by the oversimplifications that everyone seemed to want to make—that either management or union was right. "It is just not that simple. It is striking to see how few people understand this now, and yet how clear it is to those of us who have been through this process."

This was an example of a dialogic inquiry in action, one in which deep polarizations and different positions were respected even under the enormous pressures of politics and emotional turmoil. After a year of sustained practice, this group of people, who had begun a pilot experiment to explore the value and impact of dialogue, found themselves applying it directly to their lives and their future.

This situation also revealed some of the limits of the work we had done. The delicacy of bringing about a new ecology, while profound to those who had participated, had not been successfully shared more widely. No one could say in a few words what had taken months to come to understand—especially given the politicized climate. The container was not yet large enough to hold the intensity of people who had had no contact at all in the process. This was to be a lesson and a question for the future: How could we bring new understanding more widely without necessarily requiring everyone to have an identical experience?

The union, after much late-night lobbying, eventually voted to approve the contract and the company, renamed GS Technologies, became independent. But the ratifying of the contract and the process of change in company ownership left some deep scars on people who somehow expected miraculous change and were not prepared for another cycle of investment and sacrifice.

RESPECT MEANS HONORING BOUNDARIES

Respect also means honoring people's boundaries to the point of protecting them. If you respect someone, you do not intrude. At the same time, if you respect someone, you do not withhold yourself or distance yourself from them. I have heard many people claim that they were respecting someone by leaving them alone, when in fact they were simply distancing themselves from something they did not want to deal with.

When we respect someone, we accept that they have things

to teach us. As this comment from a steelworker suggests, both sides felt this strongly at the steel mill in Kansas City:

> For the first time in my life here, I've seen management truly recognize that I was an individual; I was a need to this business; the union was a need to this business. The president of our union was a need to this business. I've seen the people in the union recognize that we need a plant president; we need the people in management doing what they're doing to make it all come together, rather than trying to get everything we can from one another, by lying and deceiving one another.

Discovering the depth of respect that managers and steelworkers, for example, could have for one another beneath all the political noise that had persisted for years was one of the single most transforming experiences for these people, one that they talk about to this day.

In the prisons where he runs weekly dialogues, Peter Garrett describes a culture that epitomizes the extremes of respect and disrespect. Prisoners' individual boundaries are continuously monitored and managed by others: the times for sleeping, eating, and recreation are all controlled by formal and stiff rules. These prisons use what they call a dispersal system to keep prisoners from becoming too powerful in any one setting. With less than one hour's notice, any prisoner can be moved to any one of the other prisons in the dispersal system, and often are. Prisoners who have taken part in dialogues in the prison each week for a year might one week simply not show up and never be heard from again.

And yet through the dialogue process a very different climate is evoked. In these settings a level of mutual respect and maturity is created that affects the people who visit it. The warden of one of the prisons, who had been skeptical of the dialogue work, visited one session. The prisoners had prepared themselves the week before for this visit. Initially, several of the prisoners wanted to confront the warden about prison conditions—to make him feel their anger. They talked this through to the point where, by the time he visited the session, they did not acknowledge his presence in any particular or special way. He simply joined the conversation like any other participant. The warden was impressed. Afterward, he commented: "This has been therapeutic for me personally." The climate of the dialogue had transformed a traditional authority relationship into one where there was much more mutual respect.

In his book *A Different Drummer* Scott Peck tells the story of a monastery that had fallen on difficult times. The order was dying. Only five monks were left, and were all over seventy years old. The abbot of the monastery, desperate for help, thought to speak to a rabbi who occasionally visited a hut near the monastery. The rabbi and the abbot commiserated about their lives and the loss of spirit that seemed to pervade everyone's experience. As the abbot left, the rabbi said: "I have no advice to give. The only thing I can tell you is that the Messiah is one of you." The abbot conveyed the rabbi's words to the monks. As they thought about his words, they began to consider which one the rabbi meant. They were suddenly faced with a profound choice: to take seriously the legitimacy and presence of the people now in their midst, or to discount these words. They looked at each other, thinking: Is it him? or him? or is it me? Gradually, they began to treat themselves and one another, says Peck, with "extraordinary respect," on the chance that one of them might be the Messiah. People around the monastery sensed a change, and slowly began coming again to visit. Soon the monastery was thriving again.

Treating the people around us with extraordinary respect means seeing them for the potential that they carry within them. I have heard another version of this story expressed as a practice: Treat the person next to you as a teacher. What is it that they have to teach you that you do not now know? Listening to them in this way, you discover things that might surprise you. This does not mean being blind to gaps in what they might say and what they do, nor does it mean being overly slavish in pointing out their faults.

Respect is, in this sense, looking for what is highest and best in a person and treating them as a mystery that you can never fully comprehend. They are a part of the whole, and, in a very particular sense, a part of us.

THE PRINCIPLE OF COHERENCE

There is an already existing wholeness to life. The universe is an undivided whole, whether we are able to perceive that or not. Embracing this principle in dialogue, I am more likely to look not for what needs to change, but what Humberto Maturana might say needs to be "conserved," that is, how the existing system works now and what aspects of it I wish to sustain. By looking for the coherence in difficult situations, I am able, when I am with people with whom I disagree, to pay attention to the underlying forces that have brought me and the others I am with to this pass. I learn to take seriously the possibility that what is happening is unfolding from a common source. In dialogue, I cultivate this in practice by developing my capacity for *respect*—for myself, for others, for difference, and for those in particular who oppose what I have to say.

Much of the science of the past few hundred years has consisted of competing proposals defining the notion of order. Each of them has had a kind of underlying coherence, though some support an image of the coherence as a set of interlocking parts, while others, such as the ideas now emerging in quantum physics, propose a coherence based on a very different sense of order—one where the world is not composed of separate and distinct parts that all interact according to a set of universal laws but, rather, is an "undivided whole."

The notion that the world consists of separate parts emerged from Descartes, who believed we could understand nature by thinking of it as a giant clock, a machine set in motion by God and then left to run. Descartes's ideas have led directly to the idea that the world *is* a machine. His image has been woven into the fabric of industrialization so that most of us take it to be real, not a metaphor—a defining feature of our world.

A hundred years later, the physics of Isaac Newton gave us a set of laws with which to predict the motion of all physical matter, from atoms to stars. Reality, from the view of Newtonian physics, consists of discrete particles whose forces could be measured precisely. As Danah Zohar has pointed out, this perspective has pervaded social and scientific thinking, leading to a preoccupation with mechanism, prediction, and control.[2]

Much social thinking has flowed directly from Newton's insights. Hobbes, Adam Smith, Freud, and even Karl Marx all postulated a set of universal laws that, if they were fully understood, would reveal the patterns and forces of human and social behavior. In organizations this thinking culminated in the idea of Frederick Taylor, the father of scientific management.[3] Taylor's ideas were drawn directly from Newton's mechanics. He divided jobs into pieces, microscopically assessing each movement and motion, leading to a modern revolution in the organization of work. The concept of the organization as a machine was the culmination of this way of thinking. And despite much talk to the contrary, functional, hierarchical organizations still dominate the organizational landscape. While the machine view has a kind of coherence to it, it is also a fragmentary perspective: It divides things up in order to understand them.

Physics today proposes a very different set of ideas. It holds that the observer and the observed *cannot* be separated. The new physics proposes that human beings are intimately part of the overall fabric of life. It suggests that the wholeness *of a situation* is the objective thing that directly influences behavior rather than of immutable laws that always apply everywhere, as the Newtonian theorists told us.

In one famous experiment, known as the double-slit experiment, physics showed this new notion of coherence quite powerfully. In the experiment, a beam of electrons is shot through two parallel slits, both of which are open, to a wall behind. The electrons pass through each slit and create an interference pattern on the back wall. As they do this, the electrons show a wave-like behavior. But when one slit is closed, something interesting happens: The light going through the other slit no longer spreads out. It acts like a group of particles, going through the slit and hitting the back wall in a focused pattern.

The electrons change their behavior, at times acting like waves, at other times acting like particles. According to classical or mechanistic physics, the patterns on the back wall should not change simply because one slit opens or closes. This is because the laws of mechanistic physics require that the two slits have some kind of physical interaction to influence each other. In fact, they do not. But the patterns change anyway. The underlying meaning of this experiment has been a source of considerable debate. But electrons are now no longer viewed as separately existing particles; they must somehow be considered parts of a larger whole.

Architect Christopher Alexander suggests that the electrons in the experiment behave differently according to the "structure of wholeness" in which they move. He maintains that this concept of wholeness need not seem a vague thing, but instead reveals great precision. According to Alexander, the two aspects of the double-slit experiment have different powers of "wholeness"; they confine space differently, and create different impacts as a result. Take a simple example proposed by Alexander: a blank page and a dot placed on an otherwise blank page:

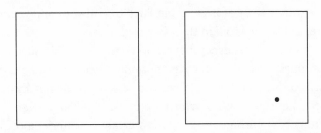

The dot on the page constrains the space of the page. The blank page is a "whole," actually it has many subwholes all blended together. The page with the dot suddenly now has several distinct subwholes: rectangles caught by the dot on the right side and underneath, and so on. The wholeness of the page has been modified.[4]

According to Alexander, the coherence we see is the relationship among the parts. We have been conditioned to see only parts, and to assume that the parts comprise the whole. But the holistic view suggests that the whole precedes the parts. Alexander endeavors to teach his architectural students to see the relative wholeness of any structure. The principle of coherence in dialogue teaches us to experience the wholeness or lack thereof in conversation.

Perceiving coherence in dialogue involves perceiving relative degrees of wholeness within conversations. Typically, most people do not know how to listen to the whole flow of a conversation; we select out pieces of it, aspects that matter to us or perhaps that irritate us. But we can learn to listen to the whole, and participate within the whole. This requires that we step back from the details, soften our focus, and hear what is going on in the overall space of the conversation. One steelworker in a dialogue described this well. Listening in the midst of a dialogue, he said, is like having "my ear attached to a funnel, and everything that everyone is saying is going in, and at some point—maybe in a few days—boom—I will understand it all."

Peter Garrett, who developed the process of dialogue in England with David Bohm, provides a vivid illustration of how to look for coherence in dialogue. In the dialogues he conducts in maximum security prisons in England, he works with some of the most serious offenders—serial murderers, serial rapists, felons of all sorts. I once asked him what the most important thing he had learned from his work. He said simply, "Inquiry and violence cannot coexist." He was speaking here of more than a set of conversational skills for inquiry; he was referring to the stance of deep respect and inclusion that must lie behind inquiry for it to have any real effect. And behind his stance is something else: an appreciation of the principle of coherence. By exploring what actually lies behind the sometimes horrendous actions of violent offenders, one finds a coherent story—a set of factors that almost inevitably seem to lead to the difficulties one can observe. These factors lie below the surface; they are often not readily apparent, but they can be found. Says Garrett: "The impulse behind intentions is pure, even though the intention may be distorted and the impact not what was intended. Inquiring deeply enough to reach the original impulse will always reveal wholesomeness. This provides the confidence to enter the loudest confrontation and the darkest territory without fear that it will get forever worse."[5]

PRACTICES FOR RESPECT

The core questions to help us *learn to respect* involve asking ourselves, How does what I am seeing and hearing here fit in some larger whole? How does this belong? What must be sustained here that others are missing? What is happening right now? The following are a set of practices designed to assist you to explore these questions.

Stand at the Hub

To respect someone, we must first remove our attention from the whir of activities all around us—as I said earlier, to stand still. This gives us perspective, something essential for coming to the point of accepting someone as they are.

Picture a spinning wheel. The hub seems to be moving slowly compared with the outer rim. In fact, at the very center it seems as if it is not moving at all. To the extent that our attention and focus is placed on the "outer rim," the daily, nonstop flow of activities and actions and events, everything will seem like it is moving too fast. If we can begin to shift our awareness to the "hub"—which might be thought of as the essence of things—we may find we have in fact more time than we imagined. Our ability to *perceive*, in other words, is a present-moment competence. It diminishes as we think about the past or worry about the future.

Centering

I have worked for some years now with a variety of practices that explore the physical dimensions of learning. Most of these derive from the martial arts. Almost all of them take seriously the notion that effectiveness means becoming centered—not fixed and rigid but fluid, like a branch in a tree. Rooted, but flexible.

Centering is the practice of finding the center of gravity, a point of balance, of quietness in yourself. This is not a placid state but a focused one. The following is an exercise in getting centered. To do this, you need to get ready for it. Take a minute to prepare yourself. Ready? Here we go . . .

Now, think for a moment about the shift you made inside yourself as you read the previous paragraph. What did you do to get ready? *That* is getting centered.[6] Before you walk into a big meeting, a high school dance, an important exam, the big presentation: Do you prepare yourself? Whatever you do represents your intuitive way of moving yourself in the direction of being grounded and centered.

There are two simple exercises two aikido masters, Richard Moon and Chris Thorsen, have developed that you might try with another person. First, stand up and have her push you very gently on one of your shoulders. Do you flop around like a wet noodle, or resist them? Focus your attention on your impulse in response. Then come to a more centered position in yourself, and see if you can let your center of gravity drop down to the point where you feel like you have literally grown roots. Have her push you again. This time, do not resist, but don't cave in either. Absorb the energy of her hand and remain intact. A little practice with this will bring out your ability to center more and more.

Second, sit quietly in a chair, feet flat on the ground, with nothing on your lap. Take a deep breath and another. Let yourself come to rest, breathing quietly, letting go of any tensions that you might feel, any thoughts that are floating through your mind. Call this state in which you now find yourself Level One. Now let yourself relax, and drop down to Level Three, several notches deeper in yourself. Notice your breathing. Then, after giving yourself another minute, drop to Level Five, even further down, even more quiet in yourself. Take a moment to reflect. What did you find? What did you like about this? Many people discover that they get calmer, more alert, more sensitive. These are some additional starting points for centering.[7]

Aikido is a martial art that seems particularly well suited to dialogue because it invites practitioners to become aware of and blend with the energies of one's "assailants," whether they are hostile individuals or challenging circumstances. One acts from this place of centeredness, constantly inquiring into circumstances, constantly alert to sustaining one's center. This is something that all practitioners continuously do. As Richard Moon points out, centering is an ongoing practice. It is not, he says, that the great masters of aikido never lose their center. They only discover it sooner and recover it faster than novices.

Listen as If It Were All in Me

Respect also implies taking seriously the fact that there is an underlying coherence in our world, and that we fit into this scene. We are participants, not observers. Accepting this means taking responsibility for ourselves. In this state, it is no longer possible simply to blame others for what happens. Our fingerprints are all over our world. The adage coined by Walt Kelly in a Pogo cartoon applies here: "We have met the enemy and it is us."

I was first introduced to a way to discover more about the underlying coherence of my world by Cliff Barry, who outlines a set of listening practices where one deliberately applies different lenses for listening. One lens that can reduce the temptation to blame and increase respect is to listen to others from the vantage point that says, "This, too, is *in me.*" Whatever the behavior we hear in another, whatever struggle we see in them, we can choose to look for how these same dynamics operate in *ourselves.* We may be tempted to say that a given behavior is all "theirs"—I do not have anything like that in me! Maybe so. But the courage to accept it as not only "out there," but also "in here," enables us to engage in the world in a very different way. If you can perceive it, it is also in you, you are bringing it forth whether you realize it or not. To maintain that it is separate from you is to fall prey to a pathology of thought: that there is a world independent of how you think about it and participate in it. The art of thinking together invites us to a different level of thought, to notice that for us to perceive something, it must somehow be in us, or it literally would not connect to anything in us. Even something that we feel is an enemy is connected to an image or perception in *us* of that enemy.

One of the more powerful, though challenging, practices for dialogue comes from using the disturbances one feels with others as a means of including those factors and providing them with space to be who and what they are. This is a kind of internal magic that involves no effort to "fix others," or tell them to change. It requires only a willingness to meet the difficulty outside of oneself *in* oneself.

In a dialogue I recently led, for example, a bright, very well educated Malaysian man spoke of his concerns about the utter lack of cultural awareness he found in management education programs led by North Americans. He held himself out, not as a participant himself, but as an expert commentator. His comments reflected the stance of an observer of the process: "This is all well and good, but you need to take into account how practical people would respond to what you are saying here. In particular, you need to take seriously the cultural differences between what is being said and how it would play out in other parts of the world. Have you thought about that?" His points were valid, I thought, and I acknowledged them, though I also noted how he distanced himself from the process.

As the dialogue deepened, others in the group began to speak more openly, talking about the questions they personally struggled with. The silences grew longer and more still. One woman expressed her deep appreciation of the silence and her sense of relief from having to have something to say all the time. She said this slowly, taking her time; her actions echoed the feeling she stated.

Immediately afterward, this same Malaysian gentleman began to speak again, very quickly, this time about the historical differences among the Asian Tiger economies. I could not figure out how to connect what he was saying to what had just been said. He was, it seemed, giving us an erudite lecture on cultural differences: "Now, you have to go back a while to really understand how this works," he began. "These cultural differences really matter. For instance, in . . ." He said that some cultures could feel left out of the kinds of experiences that people voiced here, that people would never express such things. He spoke as an expert, distancing himself from everyone, setting himself out as the one who understood what was happening and implying that others did not understand as well as he.

People's irritation with this man was palpable. The tension in the group began to rise. He was subtly accusing everyone of something and acting as if he were not guilty of it as well. The contrast in the comments was stark.

I then got an insight into what was happening. I suddenly saw that he was speaking about himself and his own sense of isolation in this group. He was not only lecturing us about others, he was making a plea to be understood. I could have pointed this out right then and there to the group; but instead, I listened to try to find these same feelings in myself: times when I have felt isolated, left out, excluded. I waited until I actually connected with these feelings in myself. When I did, I felt a kind of "click" that I had; suddenly what he was saying was no longer just him, it was me too. I then spoke, acknowledging this feeling and respecting him for raising it in the group. I asked others to reflect on ways that they, too, might have felt excluded somewhere. I pointed out my observation of his comments and asked him to start to speak from the first person, from his own experience. He did that for the first time all week. The tension in the room abated. People thanked him for speaking about his experience.

To listen in this way is to take seriously that what goes on around us exists not merely in others, it is also—however hard it is to see at the time—within us all as well. We get a clue about this most directly when we find ourselves irritated with others. We then know for sure that there is something in *us* too; it is in some ways already under our skin, or else we would not be feeling the disturbance! The challenge is to come to the point of acknowledging it.

Put differently, one of the secrets to the dialogic way of being is the willingness to forgive that which we see in another and come to the point where we can accept it as being in us. This implies coming to a place of respect both for others and for ourselves.

Make It Strange

Another practice for building respect involves highlighting what seems different or impossible to understand. We are often compelled to try to indicate to someone that we understand them. I want to propose a practice of generating respect that asks you to do the opposite.

Instead of assuming you understand someone, try this: *Make them strange.* In other words, look at them as if they were strange, incomprehensible, different from you, unique. Try to not assimilate them into a category you already have worked out. "Making strange" means seeing the other as Other, not at all like you. With this as a starting point, you have a way to begin to understand them in a new way.

One of the exercises that Edgar Schein uses in a course on change at MIT is what he calls the "empathy walk." I recommend you try this. Think of someone who is as different from you as you can imagine. Find such a person, spend up to two hours with him, and then write something about your experience. The students we have asked to try this have sought out a wide variety of people: homeless people, prostitutes, drug dealers, their own classmates, people with very different racial or religious backgrounds. Almost always the students discover—sometimes to their amazement—that they have many things in common with these people. They sometimes spend much more than two hours together. They look for what is strange and different and discover what is held in common.

RESPECTING

QUESTIONS

What is at risk in this situation?

Dominant preoccupation?

Conversation be drawn to include those who might be impacted?

PRACTICES

Stand at the hub

Centering

Listen as if it were all me

Making strange

Respect in Groups

Often differences that emerge in a conversation ruffle feathers and disturb things to the point where people can no longer act as if all were in agreement. The effort to cover up and regain a polite veneer often can be enormous. But to enable a dialogue, a group of people must learn to do something different: to respect the polarizations that arise without making any effort to "fix" them.

In a dialogue session several colleagues and I conducted in Red Lodge, Montana, a woman told us of her intense anger toward her husband. He had left her recently. But what incensed her most was that he had left her for a man. He had hidden from her for years the fact that he was gay. She said, "I know I am supposed to be tolerant. But this is just not right. There is something that is simply not right about these people." As she finished, I looked around the room to see two women looking at each other, trying to restrain themselves. They had not said much up to this point. Trying to remain calm, one of them said: "I am sorry, but my partner and I cannot simply sit by while you say these things. Please tell me what makes you so sure you are right." Her partner was the other woman. These two gay women were deeply hurt by the insinuation that there was something wrong with them.

Over the next few moments these three women said what they felt and thought, both about the original comment and about how it felt to be talking together now. No one else in the circle reacted to what they were saying or tried to correct or "help" them. They simply provided a quiet space of reflection. It eventually became clear that there were two very different points of view in the room and that neither required the other to change. What surprised everyone most was the fact that both views had been exposed quite openly, and yet no one had then come forward to negate the other. The three women sat after the session for some time talking energetically together. Later they reported back to the group that they had found the experience quite profound—they had not shifted their views, but they now had a sense of mutual respect and understanding. The content of their conversation didn't matter as much as the feeling it generated.

PRACTICES FOR CATALYZING
RESPECT IN GROUPS

Support the People who Challenge

Making deliberate space for people who have a different point of view is vital to learning to share in dialogue. Respectfully encouraging people to speak can bring about a balance in the conversational ecology that otherwise might not have occurred. This requires a willingness to hold the space open for inquiry once new perspectives come out.

This can seem a crazy move in a setting where people are angry or on the warpath. But someone must find a way to integrate these voices or they inevitably will interrupt and seek to destroy the gathering.

Learn to Hold Tension

One of the most challenging things a group can learn in a dialogue is to hold the tension that arises and *not react to it*. Typically, when faced with this kind of cross-current in the conversational ecology, people begin to "vote" on which person or perspective they feel is "right." This relieves the tension for them, but, ironically, intensifies it for the rest of the group, since this reduces the space in which a new understanding can emerge. One of the group competencies of dialogue is the capacity to sustain respect for all the perspectives that arise, long enough to inquire into them.

Related to this is the acceptance of the multiplicity of voices that we find within ourselves and in expression through others. A dialogue with a group of people can begin to be a mirror of the different things that go on inside everyone. As these voices emerge, we can choose either to reject them or recognize that they may have some relevance and place "in here," in me. Whether we like to admit it or not, we all have many different voices in ourselves—some of which we have inherited from places we no longer recall, some of which we created for ourselves.

I have a friend who used to run a two-acre organic farm. He said he always grew enough for the insects *and* the people! Managing the tensions within ourselves is a bit like this. We make room for all the perspectives and voices without trying to get rid of any of it.

Holding tension means accepting without intensifying the deep divisions that we sometimes feel within ourselves.

THE DARK SIDE OF RESPECT

When we do not respect, we impose on others. For instance, in one dialogue session one man began to speak at length about Buddhism and how it connected to dialogue. A woman who was a professional facilitator apparently felt he was speaking in a way that was inappropriate and began to "facilitate" him. She felt the lecture the group had received from this participant was wrong. She stepped in to try to stop it. Ironically, in so doing she herself did what she was accusing the other of doing—lecturing him and the group on how best to behave. She shifted from being a participant to being an expert but did not have the permission of anyone to do this. This jolted the group, although at the time they did not know quite what to do. The woman had removed herself from the process and evidently had an angry tone to her words. Others began to get angry with her, claiming that she had no right to behave that way.

A wildfire of judgment erupted in the group. People

blurted out comments, charging each other with misdeeds, without reflecting either on the impact this had on others or why they thought it. Once the circle of respect was broken, people's interpretations of what was happening and what should have been happening, according to their particular internal model of "dialogue," came into conflict.

People began to advocate their point of view. Some felt that the "official" facilitator should intervene to stop the interaction. Others felt he should not. The person being "facilitated" was confused; the unofficial facilitator was fed up with what she felt was a lack of direction and so she stepped in, in part, she said later, to show people how things might be handled.

The projection of many different opinions and points of view all at the same time often evokes the opposite of respect. It brings out the experience of conversational *violence*. This is the shadow, the opposite, of respect. In these moments there is a breakdown of the kind of mutual respect people aspire to have.

The loss of respect manifests in a simple way: My assessment that what you are doing should not be happening. The source of the trouble lies in my frame: My belief causes me immediately to look for a way to change you, to help you to see the error of your ways. It causes me to avoid looking at my own behavior and how I might be contributing. People on the receiving end of this attitude experience violence—the imposition of a point of view with little or no understanding.

Remaining aware of those parts of us that *do not* respect others may be the most instructive thing we can do to help become aware of how to deepen our capacity for respect. As before, noticing the times when you seem to be doing the opposite of the practices listed above can be quite helpful. For instance, notice times when you are not standing at the hub of your world but are clearly revolving around the periphery of it, perhaps feeling tossed around. This is very likely to be a moment when you will be unable to respect what others are saying and doing. When you are uncentered and therefore unaccepting of yourself and where you are standing, you are also unlikely to be able to do this for others. You might notice times when you are listening to someone and thinking, This is all about *them*. This has nothing to do with me. That moment might also be a clue to reflect more deeply on your own defenses. Finally, you might notice moments when you think you understand someone else well, when you believe there is nothing new to learn. The more confident you are about this, the more likely it is that you are not fully able to respect what is different about that person, or new in the situation, that you have not previously understood.

Suspending

When we listen to someone speak, we face a critical choice. If we begin to form an opinion we can do one of two things: we can choose to defend our view and resist theirs. First we can try to get the other person to understand and accept the "right" way to see things (ours!). We can look for evidence to support our view that they are mistaken, and discount evidence that may point to flaws in our own logic. This produces what one *New York Times* editorial writer called "serial monologues" rather than dialogue.

Or, we can learn to *suspend our opinion* and the certainty that lies behind it. Suspension means that we neither suppress what we think nor advocate it with unilateral conviction. Rather, we display our thinking in a way that lets us and others see and understand it. We simply acknowledge and observe our thoughts and feelings as they arise without being compelled to act on them. This can release a tremendous amount of creative energy.

DEFINING SUSPENSION

To suspend is to change direction, to stop, step back, see things with new eyes. This is perhaps one of the deepest challenges human beings face—especially once they have staked out a position. It is difficult in part because we tend very quickly to identify what we say with who we are. We feel that when someone attacks our idea, they are attacking us. So to give up our idea is almost like commiting a kind of suicide. But nonnegotiable positions are like rocks in the stream of dialogue: They dam it up. One of the central processes for enabling us to enter into dialogue is the practice of suspension, the art of loosening our grip and gaining perspective.

In one of our dialogues with workers and managers, a union leader said, "We need to suspend this word *union*. When you hear it you say 'Ugh.' When we hear it we say 'Ahhh.' Why is that?" This man had broken with the tradition of constantly defending his union and opposing management, probing more deeply into the underlying assumptions people held. The innocence and clarity of his question opened up a rich vein of conversation.

The word *suspend* comes from a Latin root *suspendere*, which means "to hang below." But its most ancient root is the Indo-European *(s)pen*, which means "to draw, stretch, or spin." From this root we get the words *spider* and *spinner*. To suspend something is to spin it out so that it can be seen, like a web between two beams in a barn.

The absence of suspension, as I have indicated earlier, is certainty. The word *certainty* comes from a root that means "to determine" or "to distinguish." It has come to mean a rigidity about the distinction we have made. Some ideas have absolute certainty or necessity attached to them—they carry a nonnegotiability to them. These "noble certainties" are part of everyone's experience and are one of the limits to dialogue. What are your "noble certainties"? What makes you so darned sure you are right? Only by asking such questions will you be able to practice suspension.

Access Your Ignorance

This points to yet another dimension of suspension, which I borrow from my colleague Edgar Schein at MIT: *Access your ignorance.* Most conversations are conducted by people who know what they think and why they think it. These people cannot get to dialogue. Dialogue is characterized by people who surprise themselves by what they say. They do not have all of their thoughts worked out in advance but are willing to be influenced by the conversation itself. They come with questions to which they do not yet have answers. And they do not demand answers of others.

I was once called in by a CEO to "diagnose" his organization. After a long series of interviews with people throughout his organization, I reported to him, "I've finally found the problem with the organization."

He was obviously excited by the news. "What is it?" he asked.

I took a deep breath. "It's you." And then I explained how everyone had looked to him for leadership but found him to be less genuine than they would have liked, and too enthusiastic about everything. He left no room for anyone to say what they thought, to challenge his views.

There was a moment of shocked silence before he asked me to go. But he kept thinking about what I had said. Later he described to me the internal transition that followed: "It took me a while to realize that this was in fact helpful news. In telling me about my behavior, it was my *certainties* that you were talking about. I had missed many things because of what I was so certain of. This was news I hated to hear, but it really helped me start to look again."

To access your ignorance is to recognize and embrace things you do not already know. The range of possibilities before you opens dramatically. This can be scary. But fear can be a helpful rather than a hurtful element in suspension. It is like the feeling you get when you peer over a large cliff at the vast expanse around you. You may feel fear, but you also feel exhilaration at the new perspective. The willingness to engage in this can change your life.

NATURAL BRIDGE

Some years ago a friend of mine and I were traveling through Oregon, his native state. We decided to visit a place called Natural Bridge, an ancient intersection of water and rock formed by the flow of lava across a large river. The lava had covered the rock and forced the river underground for about three hundred yards. In places, the water would emerge in a series of natural Jacuzzis before disappearing again underground. My friend and I went up to one large round pool of flowing water and stood at the edge. I could tell he was thinking about jumping in for a swim. I said to him, "Let's wait and watch." We stepped back and had lunch. Later we walked back over to the spot. I had grabbed a stick to throw in the water. Slightly below this pool was another one about eight feet wide. The water flowed over the edge of the first pool and drained into the lower one. I could also see an underground hole in the rock connecting the two pools. I threw the stick in to see where it went. But just as I did this, my friend jumped in the pool. The stick got sucked downward and disappeared; it did not come out into the lower pool. Neither did my friend.

It is in moments like these that time stops. I began counting the seconds. I knew he was underwater, now under the rock. I was standing above, in the sunlight, thinking about my friend drowning below me. I began counting the seconds: "ten, eleven, twelve." But there was no sign of him. "Twenty, twenty-one, twenty-two." At nearly two minutes I found myself fighting the thought of his picture in the newspaper obituary.

A few seconds later, and over a hundred yards away, I heard a splash and saw my friend emerge upright from the rock, alive and triumphant. He had been sucked down below, tried to get back to the pool above where the light was, and was gradually drawn into the darkness. He finally gave in and began to swim under the water. Ahead of him he saw nothing but blackness; behind him, the slowly dimming light. Suddenly off to his right he saw a small patch of light through the water, and he swam for it. It was a very narrow hole in the rock, just wide enough for him to slip out and through.

We were both relieved and shocked. We walked around without talking, not knowing what to say. Embracing death and life in a place where water flowed under the rock, we both had experienced a profound turning point: his beneath the rock, turning away from the light and letting go into the void, the blackness, which turned out to be a choice that saved his life. Mine above the rock, letting go of a dear friend—an encounter with death's wind, the shock of being able to do absolutely nothing.

This forever changed our friendship—changed the meaning of it for me and so changed our ways of being together. Suddenly we were in a kind of immediacy of aliveness and connection with life in a way that had not been so before. This sense has never left us, now some twenty years later. This experience forced us to *suspend* our habitual ways of being together. It put everything on hold; but more important, it gave us perspective, insight, and ultimately understanding.

FROZEN GREASE AND FROZEN FRAMES

We may not all be faced with life-threatening situations that require us to step back and see things from another perspective. But opportunities to suspend our certainties and remain fluid present themselves every day, moments in which we can practice suspension.

Once while I was driving at sixty miles an hour with a friend on a road through the middle of some Wisconsin cornfields, racing to catch a plane, the hood of the car we were in suddenly popped up and caught on the safety hook. It seemed as if it might fly open at any moment. We stopped and tried to slam the hood down, but it would not stay shut, constantly popping up and catching. The danger seemed apparent: Driving along the road, the hood could suddenly fly completely open, breaking the windshield and causing an accident. We were stuck. Nothing we did seemed to work. All I could see was a broken hood, inconvenience and malfunction, and the chance of missing my plane. I tried bending the latch slightly so that the hook could catch the edge. No luck.

We managed to find a mechanic. He stared at the hood for a moment and then walked back to his shop. I thought he would come back with a wrench and try to bend the mechanism back into place. He came back with a can of lubricant, sprayed it on the hood lock, and pressed the hood down. It shut and stayed closed. "It's been real cold over the past few days," he said. "The grease froze."

The same situation produced very different interpretations for both of us. He saw temperature effects where I saw mechanism. He saw a simple solution where I saw the possibility of having to dismantle the entire latch and replace it. My interpretation kept me stuck. His freed us to get on our way. His experience enabled him to see this situation from a different point of view. This is the "muscle" of suspension in action.

Staked out in a point of view, we remain frozen, unable to

move. The first step in suspension is to step back. Seamus Heaney, the Irish poet, conjures this when he talks about the parable of Jesus drawing in the sand. Jesus tried in this story to divert people's attention, buying time for perceptions to clear, for new options to be seen:

> Debate doesn't really change things. It gets you bogged down. If you can address or reopen the subject with something new, something from a different angle, then there is some hope. In Northern Ireland, for example, a new metaphor for the way we are positioned, a new language, would create a new possibility. I'm convinced of that. So when I invoke Jesus writing in the sand, it's as an example of this kind of diverting newness. He does something that takes the eyes away from the obsession of the moment. It's a bit like a magical dance. People are suddenly gazing at something else and pausing for a moment.[1]

Often the last thing we wish to do when the stakes are high is to pause, to look with new eyes, to refocus. Our obsessions blind us. To stand above the pool of your own perceived possibilities is the art of suspension.

HOLDING THE LIGHTNING

Suspending your assumptions in this way can force you to handle a great deal of intensity. David Bohm once told the story of how he, while attending a dialogue in Sweden, found himself forming a criticism in his mind about another person in the room. He wanted to interrupt this criticism, but to do so in a way that could let him see its nature and structure. He did not want to just let it go on unchecked, nor did he wish to suppress it. As he watched his own reactions, he said he felt like a bolt of lightning was moving in his body: Containing and reflecting on the energy of criticism brought up great intensity in him. To suspend criticism is to observe its motion, to take back into yourself the force you might otherwise put off onto others around you. If you neither suppress this energy, disavowing it (what, me critical?), nor express it (those idiots deserve what they get), you are left with having to hold it in yourself and explore its meaning and dimensions. This can be quite uncomfortable, which may be why it is rarely done. But it can lead to enormous insight, for instance, about the pervasive habits of judgment we can impose on others. The very act of inquiring into one's reactions in this way produces a change: To observe one's own thoughts and feelings is to bring into them a perspective and attention that can transform them.

REFLECTION IN ACTION

The kind of thinking I am speaking about here is something we do *while* acting. Educator Donald Schön, in his renowned series of books on professional effectiveness, once described this capacity as "reflection-in-action": the ability to see what is happening as it is happening. Schön spent much of his career arguing that this kind of ability was not only an intimate part of what we call spontaneity, but necessary to it. Reflecting in this way means we are able to free ourselves from habitual ways of responding and stay fresh and alive.[2]

Seeing one's own thought in this way is a little like opening the mind's factory door and looking at the processes inside. Typically, we are aware only of the products of this factory, our thoughts. We are not all that aware of how our thoughts are produced. Suspension is the act of looking at these thoughts.

TYPES OF SUSPENSION

In dialogue we can divide suspension into two types, one of which leads to the other. *Suspension I* is to disclose, to make available for yourself and others the contents of your consciousness so you may see what is going on. Many psychological techniques, psychodrama being perhaps one of the most prominent, help people to externalize their thoughts and the "voices" in their minds so that they may see themselves more clearly. To do this, you must locate, name, and then display for others what you are aware of, as Bohm did by describing his experience to his colleague in the example above.[3]

An opportunity for this kind of suspension arose during a critical dialogue with the steelworkers. The division in which these people worked was in the process of being sold; suddenly the labor contract between union and management had become an important political bargaining chip in the process of the sale. Usually all labor contracts are negotiated through the international union, who sent representatives and tried to get roughly equal terms for all contracts. Typically, the corporate leadership would also attempt to dictate terms to the plant and division leadership.

In this rare case, both plant and union leadership were concerned that the contract would become a political football, and that the corporate leadership and the international union would not comprehend the kind of progress being made in the dialogues. The union president told management, "I personally want to do a contract with the people in this room, not [others]. We know what we need." And the plant president agreed:

> Well, if you talk about ideal negotiations, ideally it would be the people in the room who know really what is best. The union people know what is best for the membership here and we think we know what is best for the plant.

This led the union members to react with concern: Did this mean the international union was going to be cut out of the picture? But unlike other conversations, where management and union would polarize and propose only competing ideas, this time the union people openly admitted the potential for misinterpretation their newfound alignment with management might stir. Said one union man:

> I think that was a fear out in the mill, to do it locally, without international help. You know, we're sitting here talking and someone's gonna misinterpret this that you're gonna negotiate the contract without the international, that's what it sounds like. And if it gets down to the mill, we'll cover for you for a while, but we can't hold 'em off for that long. [laughter]

Here a union man offered a perspective, both on the current conversation and on its likely impact beyond this group. This forced everyone to examine the matter. They were suspending the idea of negotiating without the international's imposition, an enormously hot issue, considering its pros and cons.

It had not always been possible to do this. In one of the first meetings I asked if the union people would like to review the list of managers proposed for the dialogue, and if the managers would like to do the same. People reacted almost violently: "We don't tell them what to do and they don't tell us what to do." The "brotherhood" of the union also meant they would take a closed-rank approach to most problems. Controversial matters were always to be raised outside the hearing of management. But here, in this dialogue, union people were speaking about ways their own actions could be taken, and doing that in front of managers.

There is another level to the practice of suspension (*suspension II*). In this we become aware of the processes that generate that thought.

To suspend in this way is to move upstream—to make ourselves aware that our thoughts do not simply arise from nowhere but have an origin of a very particular and deterministic sort.

For example, I might become aware of anger that I have toward someone. I can become aware that I am "thinking anger"—that is, thoughts come to my mind like, They have no right to treat me this way. How dare she? Who does she think she is? and so on. As I look at this, I begin to see that all of this is in fact simply a stream of thought that is being triggered by a set of impulses within me. In a very real sense, I am *causing* this line of thoughts to flow. "They" are not doing anything to me. It is emerging strictly from within me, in particular from my inner ecology and the memories I have about these experiences.

By observing my thought processes in this way, I transform them. This is one of the central transformational vehicles of dialogue.

THE PRINCIPLE OF AWARENESS

Underlying the practice of suspension is the principle of awareness. To be aware is to allow our attention to broaden and expand, to include more and more of our immediate experience. The central idea here is that we are capable of coming to understand what is happening as it is happening. The mechanistic notion of the universe, which does not see human beings as participants in the whole, discounts knowledge that can be consciously gained by a first-person observer. But in a worldview emerging within cognitive science, philosophy, and the humanities, first-person knowledge is highly relevant. This view holds all aspects of experience have an "interpretive" element. It says, in other words, that human beings experience the world through the structures of their consciousness, not "directly."

BIOLOGY AND THE AWARE UNIVERSE

For instance, two South American biologists, Humberto Maturana and Francisco Varela, have led a frontal assault on this "representative" theory of cognition that most of us still believe—that there is a world "out there," and that our brain makes pictures in our minds of that world. This leads us to listen with a "transmission" theory of communication in mind. This is the "if I speak loud enough they'll understand what I'm saying" school of communication. Listening in this world means turning up the volume.

Maturana and Varela argue that our biology of cognition simply does not work this way. They say it is more complex and somewhat more strange sounding: "Based on what I hear, and how my personal biology and past history work, this is the world of experience I choose for the moment to live within." They say we do not simply observe the "world," we actively create our experience of it through the structure of our nervous system and consciousness combined with stimuli from the environment. The world is very much already in us in the sense that we have thousands of years of evolution guiding and determining how our nervous systems work. But we also have our entire social history, which is also in us and which also deeply influences our perception. The world participates in us, and we in the world.

These ideas are particularly relevant to cultivating awareness in dialogue because through them we may come to the realization that we cannot simply "make" change happen as if we were separate from the thing we seek to change. It may be that only by entering into a dialogic relationship with the situation that we seek to change may we discover the ways in which the existing structures affect us and might evolve. This implies, practically speaking, that you would not seek to "manage" an organization but, rather, cultivate the conditions under which it might evolve and change.

Rather than seeking the "levers" for change, or the "tools" to "drive" change—images that flow from a mechanistic worldview—you would seek to inquire into the way the system works, the principles that guide it, and the underlying coherence within it.

PROPRIOCEPTION

In dialogue we can apply these insights in a very particular way: cultivating an awareness of the nature of the ecology of our thought. Try this: Raise your arm for a moment. Shut your eyes and move your arm around. You can tell where it is at any moment. This is because you have the capacity for proprioception, a self-perception at the physical level. Proprioception is a long word that simply means "self-perception."

David Bohm tells the story of a woman who lost this capacity. She was suddenly awakened one night by an attacker. The more she fought off the attack, the more intense it became. Eventually, she struggled over to turn the light on, and when she did, she realized that she was striking herself with one hand and fending her arm off with the other. She had lost her unconscious awareness of her arm.

Bohm goes on to suggest that we have lost proprioception, or self-awareness, at the level of our *thought*. The idea here is that just as we have an impulse to move our arm, we also have impulses to move our minds. While we are aware of the impulse at a physical level, we usually are not so aware of what might lie behind our mental processes. In fact it seems to us that our thoughts just "appear." I am suggesting that this is not so. Suspension can give us access, enabling us to perceive the impulses that lie behind everyday thought.

To get a sense of this, try reflecting for a moment about a time when you really wanted something. It does not matter what it was. Now ask yourself, if you actually got what you wanted, what did that give you? Go beyond the immediate answers. Ask, what else did this fulfill; or if you did not get it, what was left empty in you? Then ask, why did you want it? These can be challenging questions to explore but can put you in touch with the underlying impulse, which may not be all that obviously connected to the object of your desire.

PRACTICES FOR SUSPENSION

Learning to suspend, which is at the heart of the process of dialogue, is a discipline in itself. There are a number of practices that can help you learn how to suspend. All of them begin by inviting us to stop and ask: How is this working? What is going on here? How does this problem work? Suspension asks us to put on hold the temptation to fix, correct, or problem-solve what we see so that we can begin to *inquire into* what we observe. For those of us addicted to problem solving, this can be a challenging skill to develop.

The following are a set of practices and principles to develop suspension.

Suspend Certainty

Suspension requires that we relax our grip on certainty. As we see that our thought is just a medium by which we can understand the world, we realize that thoughts are in a very real sense "things." They have a particular shape, size, depth, and density. Normally, we experience our thoughts as inner maps of outer experiences. But they are also deeply a part of what we see and how we see it. Like film director Kurosawa's famous film *Rashomon*, in which a man is robbed and the story is told several times over from the perspectives of the different characters— there are many different views of reality.

How do you let go of the conviction you have about something? You might begin by asking yourself, Why are you so damned sure about this? What is leading you to hold on to it so intensely? What could the payoff be to you? What would happen if you let it go? What is at risk if you do? What might you lose? What do you fear you would lose?

Mine for the Questions

Most of us live in a world where it is unsafe to say "I don't know." In both our professions and our families, we are supposed to have answers to problems. I know of many companies where the engineers are seriously penalized if they report a problem or ask a question for which they do not yet have the answer. Naturally, they do not report these things, which only leads to delays and a lack of coordination. This is no climate in which to foster genuine inquiry.

Instead of good answers, we need good questions. The power of dialogue emerges in the cultivation, in ourselves, as well as in others, of questions for which we do not have answers. Identifying one good question can be vastly more significant than offering many partial answers.

In cultivating a dialogic stance, I encourage people to develop a capacity to "mine for the questions." By this I mean to look for the really important, hard questions that keep people up nights and go to the heart of our concerns. Each of us, I have found, has several questions that are at the very center of our lives. You might try reflecting on what questions live within you.

Finding good questions is not always easy. What immediately comes to mind is not always relevant. When people ask me to help them solve their problems, the first thing I do is listen for the quality of the questions they are asking themselves.

I listen in particular for the degree of self-reflection in the questions. To what extent, I ask myself, do they see their own part in what they are exploring? To what degree do they attribute their problems to sources outside of themselves?

To do this implies that we actually know what a question is. An estimated forty percent of all questions that people utter are really statements in disguise. Another forty percent are really judgments in disguise: "Do you really think she deserved that raise?" Only a small percentage of "inquiries" are genuine questions. Real questions are often notable for the silence that follows their utterance. People may not know the answer! In fact, it becomes clear that finding an answer too quickly is not necessarily a wise goal.

President Clinton, at one point in his year-long program of race dialogues, turned to one of the participants and asked him if he was in favor of the kind of affirmative action that produced Colin Powell. He was asking the other person to tell him where he stood. But he pushed the person he was addressing into a very difficult bind. Does the other party say no, he is not in favor of the affirmative action that produced a Colin Powell—and run the risk of looking absurd? Or does he say yes, implying that Powell needed affirmative action to succeed? Does he challenge the President's question itself? Some difficult dilemmas arose in this moment, which neither Clinton nor the person questioned seemed to recognize or articulate. As a result, the conversation froze.

More generally, we should ask, what does getting *any* kind of answer do to move a conversation forward? This kind of exchange distances the questioner from the conversation, keeping his or her own views hidden and therefore inaccessible. Such questions also imply that there is a right answer, and that the questioner already knows what that right answer is.

Finding a question is one thing. Allowing oneself to tolerate the tension that arises with its articulation is another. This ability to let oneself see what emerges instead of leaping out of the discomfort of an unanswered question is crucial. The poet Rilke begs us

> to be patient toward all that is unsolved in your heart
> and to try to love the *questions* themselves like locked
> rooms and like books that are written in a very foreign
> tongue. Do not now seek the answers, which cannot be
> given you because you would not be able to live them.
> And the point is, to live everything. *Live* the questions
> now. Perhaps you will then gradually, without noticing
> it, live along some distant day into the answer.[4]

To mine for questions is to cultivate the suspension of answers and to open the way for the dialogic way of being.

Seek the Order Between

The idea that we must take a position in order to get our view across is seemingly built into our culture. This is the essence of "good debate." While it is popular, it greatly limits the potential intelligence and inquiry we might obtain from a conversation—particularly one with tough issues. One way to develop suspension is to look for what David Bohm called the "order between" the extremes. This does not mean looking for compromise so much as looking for the unresolved issues around which people are polarizing.

This is difficult, because the positions that people voice are always partial, always limited, and almost always call up the opposite point of view. Thinking positionally polarizes. It tends to lead us down a path that says things are either this *or* that. To find the order between we must recognize that positions in this sense are always false, because they are pieces from a whole cloth. We have many such examples. A notorious one is the phrase "mind and heart." The words imply that the two are distinct and separate. But—they are distinct only in thought, though our language leads us to think of them as clearly differentiable. More genuine probing asks us to suspend polarizing our differences and look for what exists between the extremes. Inevitably, there is a range of questions that neither position can embrace or react to. In the Clinton race dialogues, for instance, the issues that might come to light might have to do with America's unresolved relationship with its history of slavery and the treatment of blacks in subsequent years. What is the relationship between affirmative action and no affirmative action? Perhaps this could lead us into an inquiry about why we are having the conversation in the first place. Suspension is the art of finding the "order between" the positions that people take.

Try Frame Experiments

Suspension is also the art of trying to see people in a different light. The term "frame experiment," coined by Don Schön, refers to a way of bringing a different perspective to the fore and trying it out on a situation to see what we might learn. For example, a senior manager in a major consumer company was known for being a bully. Every time the senior group would talk about difficult strategic issues, he would take over the conversation, reveal his "superior" knowledge, and intimidate people. Even the CEO felt stymied by this fellow; he clearly knew a great deal, perhaps more than anyone else at the table. But his ways of working were destroying the spirit of the top team and limiting its ability to lead. Another manager particularly was having difficulty with this situation, and was prepared to either challenge it openly or leave the company.

A colleague of mine began to coach this second fellow. She suggested that he see the first manager not as a bully, and instead see him as a protector of the culture of the organization. This was met with some incredulity at first. But the second manager tried it. They traveled together on the company plane, relatively tight quarters! Afterward, the second manager said to me, "You know, he wasn't actually as bad as I had thought. We had a very good conversation." Sometimes the change comes because you put on new glasses and not because the world outside of you changes all that much. You can learn to see things that were there all the time but overlooked by you.

Externalize Thought

Another critical practice to develop suspension involves externalizing thought. What does this mean? In some of our workshops we do an exercise where people who do not know each other are asked to come up with a dilemma they face for which they have no clear solution. They then "borrow" two other people and ask them to represent the two sides of this dilemma, the two sides they picture in their mind. These two people stand up, face each other, and replay the thoughts rumbling around in the other person's head. For example, a woman stood up once and said, "My dilemma is, do we go to his parents for Christmas or mine?" Everyone laughed, recognizing the challenge. "Every time this comes up, we have a huge fight. If we go to his, my parents are disappointed and I feel I have caved in. If we go to mine, I feel guilty that I have imposed my parents on him. I am stuck."

This person found two others who quickly got in the spirit. One began, speaking as the woman: "You know, I want my parents to see their grandkids. We do not see them very often as it is. And my husband gets his way most of the time." The other person replied, also speaking as this woman: "Is this really fair? Am I imposing this on my husband? Maybe we should have Christmas at our home and have everyone come to us! But that would be even crazier." The conversation got quite heated, and apparently quite realistic, according to our initial volunteer.

Everyone in the group tried this exercise using their own examples. Another woman debated with herself about whether to promote a younger employee to a senior position. She was torn, because this younger man was her friend, someone she had mentored. But she was not certain about his abilities and feared she might bias the decision inappropriately. Many reported being somewhat stunned that strangers could seem to understand exactly what was going on in their heads, as if they had read their intimate diaries. "They knew exactly what to say!" "I saw myself very clearly, and I told them only the smallest bit of detail." You can try this yourself by finding two people to display the different voices in your head, or you might simply write down the different perspectives, stepping back to see them both and how you feel about each. A process like dialogue can help us to see that there are aspects of all of us in each one of us: I am in the world, and the world is in me. What is needed today, I believe, is not individual transformation, but a shift of a completely different order: a process of dialogue that can help individuals experience firsthand the degree to which the world is in them and how responsible *they* are for their experience. The challenges people in organizations face, for instance, are not merely personal, they are systemic—in a way they are everywhere and nowhere. They are in this sense in all of us. But we share much more than we might realize or like to admit; we share a common ecology or network of thought.

Ask: What Am I Missing?

Perhaps one of the most powerful ways to suspend thought is to ask the questions. What is it that I am or we are systematically leaving out of this conversation? What are we ignoring completely or failing to pay sufficient attention to? Inevitably, some see this more clearly than others do, and so this practice is often best cultivated with a group of people. To reflect in such a way that encourages us to ask this question greatly increases the chances for learning and growth.

This practice can take many forms. You might ask yourself at the end of a day or at the end of a meeting, What is it that I did not do, or left out somehow? Reflect on the results you got (and the results you did not get). Then ask yourself why you got the results you did and what you might have done that you were unaware of at the time that encourages this.[5]

Ask: How Does the Problem Work?

One of the great temptations many people face is that of trying to "fix" or correct what they imagine to be wrong or problematic with themselves, with others, with the world. This is especially common when it comes to a special someone who is driving you up the wall. We can see so clearly how, if that person would only act differently, things would be so much better. Especially for us.

Yet leaping in with advice on how others can improve themselves is not always welcome. Many think of change in mechanistic terms: The "machine" is broken, someone needs to fix it. Their central question is What can I do to fix this? This kind of thinking reinforces fragmentation. When someone arrives with an attitude that says "Hello! I am here to change you" (or, the marginally more subtle "I am here to help you change") it's not surprising why people shy away from them.

Suspension involves asking a very different question: How does this problem or situation work? In other words, what are the forces at work that have produced this problem in this way in the first place? It is framed with the realization that even if you helped the person change to alleviate today's problem, the odds are low that you would have helped them when they came to face tomorrow's. In fact, you may well have weakened their capacity to address the issue for themselves.

Asking How does the problem work? opens an inquiry into the problem itself. You're really asking, How have things come to be this way? Why this way and not some other way? What impact does it have? How do people feel about it?

QUESTIONS

What leads me to view things as I do?

What is the question beneath the question?

What themes, patterns, links, do I perceive underneath what is being said?

In what alternative ways can I perceive or frame these things?

PRACTICES

Suspend certainty.

Seek the order between.

Try frame experiments.

Externalize thought.

Ask; What am I missing? How does the problem work?

SUSPENSION IN GROUPS

Collective suspension means raising to the surface issues that impact everyone in a way that all can reflect on them. Suspension at the group level, like at the individual level, has to do with interrupting the habitual functions of memory and inviting a fresh response.

Group memories hold enormous sway and are not easily

released. For instance, one high-tech company I worked in found it enormously threatening to have someone propose an alternative approach to a strategy. This company has been quite successful, and as a result quite unwilling to move off its familiar path. "That is not how we do it here," one man complained to his team after I had explained the idea. "This is making me very nervous," he said. I said, "The problem you are facing is really much tougher than any you have handled before, by your own admission. What is it about this approach that makes you nervous?" "We have not used it before," he replied.

Most groups will have a number of critical issues that limit their effectiveness—issues that they are unable, for whatever reasons, to see clearly. Much of the time the ecology of a group is such that it is impossible for much reflection in action to take place. Things happen too fast. The pressure to produce results is too great. The fear that arises in people at the thought of slowing down the process is too overwhelming.

Interrupting these habitual patterns can be quite powerful. In the presentation made by steelworkers and managers to the management conference I mentioned earlier about their dialogue experience, a union participant said, "We have learned to question fundamental categories and labels that we have applied to each other." One manager in the audience raised his hand and said, "Can you give us an example?" "Yes," the union member said. "Labels like *management* and *union.*" The manager's jaw dropped. He had never heard a union man so willing to refrain from defending the union to look at it objectively.

Collective suspension is the practice of shifting the ecology of a group so that it can begin to see it has alternatives, to understand that it no longer needs to be limited to a single point of view. A group can develop this ability over time by talking together. It can also be assisted by a facilitator.

PRACTICES FOR CATALYZING
SUSPENSION IN GROUPS

Create a Clearness Committee

Invented by the Quakers many years ago, this process consists of having a group of people, selected by you, ask you questions about a subject that you identify as important. The group's job is not to provide you with answers, only questions. Having a group of people ask you questions over a hour or two can be enormously illuminating; people frequently discover that what they thought was essential was peripheral, and vice versa.

Sensing the System

For many people, participating in a group conversation—especially one where there are more than eight people, can be quite distracting, even overwhelming. A practice that is well worth cultivating is one where you learn to think of the people in a meeting as aspects of a single whole.[6] You approach this group with a curiosity about its collective behavior. You can ask yourself, How is this group as a whole behaving? How is what is now happening impacting the least powerful person in the group? the silent ones? the strong ones?

Learn not to personalize every emotion but to look around and see what is happening with others. Ask the question What is this group seeking to "conserve"—to sustain? Biologist Humberto Maturana shares this question as he looks at the evolution of social systems. We must look not only at what is changing, he suggests, but at what stays the same, or is being "conserved." We can do this in a group dialogue by asking the same question.

THE DARK SIDE OF SUSPENSION

While a part of us may be willing to be open and to explore other perspectives, to step into the other guy's shoes, there is also a part of us that has no interest in this whatsoever. "I like my opinions," this part of us says. "And often I am right!" Acknowledging that we hold to what are certain about, and that we may be quite unwilling to relinquish these things, gives us a sense of where we stand. It can also tell us how flexible we are and uncover the choices that we face if we are to suspend our reactions. If I am unable to step back from what I think, I remain invested in it, certain—perhaps to the point of nonnegotiability.

The shadow of suspension is that part of us that wishes to be certain. It is also the part that tends to see *others* as certain: "They are *so* opinionated." But to make such a claim is a contradiction: We are being opinionated about *their* being opinionated! We do to others in this sense what we abhor in ourselves, and often fail to notice it. When two people, or two groups of people, meet who are both full of certainty in this sense, conflict is inevitable. The absolute inviolable status of Jerusalem to the Israelis leads them to say they shall never partition the city. Yet this conflicts with the absolute necessity of the Palestinians—that Jerusalem be acknowledged as part of their heritage. The inability to step back from this perspective prevents suspension, and genuine resolution.

When do you hold only certainty? When do you look only for answers, not questions? Can you recall a time when you were unable to see things from any other point of view? Or when you realized you never asked yourself, "What am I missing?" These questions will give you a sense of those times when you are not able to suspend your thought, and may help you to activate this ability.

Voicing

To speak your voice is perhaps one of the most challenging aspects of genuine dialogue. Speaking your voice has to do with revealing what is true for you regardless of other influences that might be brought to bear. "Courageous speech," says poet David Whyte in his book *The Heart Aroused,* "has always held us in awe." It does so, he suggests, because it is so revealing of our inner lives.

Finding your voice in dialogue means learning to ask a simple question: What needs to be expressed now? To do this you need to know how to listen not only to your internal emotional reactions and impulses—or to the many images of how you think you should behave—but to yourself.

For many of us this is no small feat. We have been inundated with numerous messages about how we ought to behave, what we ought to say, in all the different circumstances of our lives. To discover what *we* think and feel, independent of these things, requires courage.

This is true in part because our authentic voice is not a rehash of others' words. So we are unlikely to find someone else speaking what we ourselves need to say. We may sometimes find others saying things with which we resonate. Think for a minute of someone you truly admire. Now consider, what about him or her is it that you find so attractive? You may find that it has to do with the fact that their expression is authentic and unique. They reveal themselves. This experiment can show you something about yourself, because you are unlikely to notice qualities you admire in others unless they are already present in you in some form, at least. This person you admire carries an aspect of your voice, temporarily holding it for you as you find your way back to it.

As we begin to embody our own genuine expression, we find our voice has magic in it. Consider the magic word itself: *abracadabra*. It comes from an ancient Middle Eastern language, Aramaic, thought to have been spoken from around the seventh century B.C. to the seventh century A.D. The phrase is said to come from the Kabbalistic tradition, a form of Jewish mysticism. It was the incantation used to remind the Kabbalists of the power of their speech. *Abra* comes from the Aramaic verb *bra* meaning to create. *Ca* translated to "as." *Dabra* is the first person of the verb *daber*, "to speak." In other words, *abracadabra* literally means "I create as I speak." Magic![1]

Speaking our voice can transform our circumstances. At an annual meeting of MIT's Center for Organizational Learning, five managers and five union steelworkers talked about what they had learned after six months of dialogue. A group of about 125 managers from leading companies around the United States listened to them. That the managers and union workers were able to sit to- gether and talk openly about respectfully of one another about what they had achieved was enormously impressive. After all, here were two groups that had mistrusted each other for decades; now they were thinking together. They spoke freely and unrehearsed. More than one person said later that tears came to his eyes.

Toward the end of the presentation, one manager from a high-tech industry challenged their apparent success: "You seem to have your team working well here. But what about shocks from the wider system? The price of steel, the price of scrap metal, the environment? How do you plan to overcome that hurdle?" No one replied for a long while. Then Conrad, the vice president of the local union said, "Well, we don't really have a plan. We just take things one step at a time."

He went on. "You know, sitting up here has been very un- comfortable for us. We do not usually do presentations like this. We were not sure what would happen. But now I see that we have a container that is large enough even to include all of you." There was no bluster or defensiveness in his words; he simply drew a larger circle. Our authentic voice can set a new order of things, open new possibilities. It comes out even more clearly in dialogue, where the challenge is to speak the new word. And to do so at that very moment. Conrad took the "external shock" of the high-tech manager's comment to the group and included it in the same fash- ion they were including and dealing with all their problems.

Our organizations give us many mixed messages about ex- pressing our own voice. On the one hand, we hear of endless "empowerment" programs, transformation initiatives, and de- velopment plans in companies large and small. On the other hand, we are expected to toe the line and defer to the authority figures who reign supreme. Corporations are in many ways one of the last bastions of feudalism.

Despite the democratic climate in which most modern

corporations have arisen and function, in many ways life within them is a direct denial of the freedoms that guarantee their survival. A former company president, a woman CEO colleague of mine who emigrated from then-Communist Yugoslavia when she was a twenty-three-year-old engineer, tells a poignant story of the paradox she discovered in her quest for her voice:

> When I was working in an organization there, under Tito, it was acceptable to say more or less anything you wanted to your boss. After all, you had a job for life. What could he do? But you must never, ever say anything bad about the president of the country. It was not only injurious to your immediate health, you could get locked up and disappear. People did, all the time. Your words of dissent would be viewed the same as pulling a gun on the president. So I came to America, the land of free speech and democracy, looking for new opportunity. And can you imagine what I found? You could say anything you wanted about the president of the country. But God forbid you say anything bad about your boss! Is that free speech? Is that democracy?

SELF-TRUST AND VOICE

It takes determination to speak your own voice. The pressures that arise both from within yourself and from your organization often seem designed to sap your energy. The antidote is self-trust. Only as you learn to take seriously the possibility that what you think might be in fact valid for others do you find the backbone and confidence to share it. In his marvelous essay called "Self-Reliance," Ralph Waldo Emerson prods us to take this step:

A man should learn to detect and watch that gleam of light which flashes across his mind from within more than the lustre of the firmament of bards and sages. Yet he dismisses without notice his own thought, because it is his. In every work of genius we recognize our own rejected thoughts: they come back to us with a certain alienated majesty.

The journey to finding and speaking your voice entails feeling the confidence that what you are thinking is valid, and fits. Emerson continues:

Great works of art have not more affecting lesson for us than this. They teach us to abide by our spontaneous impression with good-humored inflexibility then most when the whole cry of voices is on the other side. Else tomorrow a stranger will say with masterly good sense precisely what we have thought and felt all the time, and we shall be forced to take with shame our own opinion from another.[2]

Finding and speaking one's voice requires first a willingness to be still. Daring to be quiet can seem like an enormous risk in a world that values articulate speech. But to speak our voice we may have to learn to refrain from speaking, and listen. Not every word that comes to us needs to be spoken. In fact, learning to choose consciously what we do and do not say can establish a great level of control and stability in our lives.

Many people feel "pressure" to speak. Containing and holding that pressure, something can form within you. Let what is in you take shape before giving words to it. It is like letting a picture develop; you do not want a partially formed picture but a whole one. Sometimes the cycle of development will be quite fast. Sometimes it will take longer.

Speaking one's voice also requires a willingness to trust the emptiness—the sense of not knowing what to do or say—that sometimes appears first. One of the reasons people chatter away is that they are lonely. They are afraid of silences; they fear that there is not a creative space in them but an empty void. There may be creative pauses, spaces into which new energy has not yet rushed and filled. But a little patience will be rewarding. What is often most lacking in us is the confidence that what does appear actually has merit, is worth saying—that we are worth listening to.

Such speaking requires a leap into the void. This presumes courage, a willingness to enter into the dark forest of one's own lack of understanding. Often the voice that is genuinely ours is not well developed. We may be an expert at mimicking others but not speaking for ourselves. In dialogue this emerges as the willingness to speak in the circle without knowing what you will say. More than a gimmick, this is the very motion required to unleash our locked-up energies. Fear often reigns. To leap into a moment of silence with a thought that is not well formed or one that is potentially controversial, whose utterance might change relationships, terrifies. In these moments we can easily retreat into planned speech, the things we have said before. We can cover our tracks through practiced routine, or we can practice speaking without knowing in advance what we are going to say.

Finding and then speaking your voice also means finding the right words. Yet most of our words are designed to sustain our separation. When we speak words that come from a place of wholeness and actually articulate that wholeness, we can sometimes feel as if they are not entirely our own. This may be because we are speaking from a part of ourselves that is unfamiliar, one that is larger than we might have realized—one that is connected to a much larger field of awareness and attention. If we rise up to speak in these ways, sometimes the smaller parts of ourselves can feel nervous or concerned. But the integration of all the different aspects of oneself is a part of the discovery process of a dialogue.

One of the most common experiences people have in dialogue is the discovery that the whole is somehow larger than the parts. Now, this is not something that we are typically trained to expect or understand. Despite a plethora of words about synergy, we are generally inexperienced when it arises and unaware of how to sustain an ecology that lets it continue.

Paradoxically, we may hear our own voice most powerfully when we are with a group of others in dialogue. There is a deeply communal dimension to speaking together that is typically lost on us. If I speak, it is often to make *my* point, to indicate my superiority, to claim my ground. Often I lie in wait in meetings, like a hunter looking for his prey, ready to spring out at the first moment of silence. My gun is loaded with preestablished thoughts. I take aim and fire, the context irrelevant, my bullet and its release all that matter to me.

Dialogue offers us another possibility, which is to discover that in speaking I can create. My voice is not simply something that reveals my thought, or even parts of myself; it literally can bring forth a world, conjure an image. But this kind of speaking requires that I learn to listen for the distant thunder that may ultimately turn out to be my own voice waiting to be spoken. This sometimes occurs as the feeling of being tapped on the shoulder by destiny. Suddenly I have the sense that everyone is waiting for me, that it is somehow my turn, that I have something for others that must come out. Often I find people who have this experience look around anxiously for someone else to fill their shoes, to do this job for them. "They can't have meant me." Yet this inner call can be answered only by you, and in answering it one finds one's own voice and one's own authority. Everything else pales by comparison.

THE PRINCIPLE OF UNFOLDMENT

Behind the practice of speaking your voice is another principle for dialogue. This principle encourages us to remain aware of the *constant potential waiting to unfold through and around us.* By doing so I am able to take seriously the possibility that there is something to listen to.

Bohm's notion of the implicate order is one development in science that correlates with this principle and illuminates it. The implicate order is based on a premise about the nature of "unfoldment and enfoldment," where reality unfolds from a patterned invisible level into the visible world that we see, and then folds back up again into the invisible state. Reality consists both of a surface level "explicate order," which has a relative independence, like the individual notes of a piece of music, and a deeper implicate order out of which the explicate flows. As David Peat, Bohm's biographer, indicates, Bohm "proposed that the reality we see about us (the explicate order) is no more than the surface appearance of something far deeper (the implicate order) . . . the ground of the cosmos is not elementary particles, but pure process, a flowing movement of the whole." The implicate unfolds, both in an external sense and in thought, to produce the explicate world we experience.

Earlier in his career Bohm developed the first equations to explain the state of matter called plasma. A plasma functions in a collective fashion, as a whole. Yet it is made of individual particles, each of which moves freely and individually. When viewed close up, it appears as a random movement of particles, moving freely. Bohm was able to create two sets of equations, one to explain the collective behavior, and the other to explain the free individual movement. He then went on to show that the two descriptions were part of a single whole, and that each is enfolded in the other. This was the genesis of his idea of an

"implicate order," in which there is both an underlying wholeness and relative independence of the external parts.

As I mentioned in Chapter 2, Bohm gave a particularly
striking image of how this might work in nature. A seed, he
said, is more like an aperture through which reality unfolds, not
merely the source of the tree. This perspective challenges our
ordinary perceptions; it prods us to see the world with new
eyes. Bohm expanded his view, saying Nature itself could be
constantly unfolding and folding back up again:

> If you were to look at this on a long scale, of say fifty
> or one hundred years, there would be changes, you
> would see that trees were in different positions. And
> you might think that a tree had moved across this
> space from one place to another. In fact, what hap-
> pened is that one tree has enfolded into the ground
> and another tree has taken its place. Now, that is the
> picture I would like to suggest of the fundamental par-
> ticles, the electrons and protons and so on—quarks,
> according to the latest theory that make up all matter.
> The evidence from quantum mechanics would suggest
> that these particles are not little balls which are per-
> manent and just cross space like a billiard ball, but
> rather they are constantly unfolding and folding back
> and unfolding again in a slightly different position. . . .
> This happens very fast so it will appear continuous
> and constant to us on the large scale.[3]

The implicate order unfolds into an explicate, relatively differentiated order, which is not separate from the
implicate. There is separation without separateness. Bohm compared the explicate order to the patterns in a river. The swirls in
the river are distinct forms, and in some cases can have high de-

grees of stability. But these patterns emerged from and are an integral part of the totality of the system of the water.

Thought and the Implicate Order

Of particular importance to dialogue is the linkage Bohm began to make between the implicate order and the processes of thought itself. What if ideas, perceptions, which appear as distinct things to us were themselves the explicate version of some more implicate order? This corresponded well to my own subjective experience. It is possible to have a relatively abstract idea, like beauty, but when one tries to grasp it, one realizes that it is too subtle, is in fact comprised of a much broader range of tacit perceptions that one can know but cannot precisely define.

A central point here is that everything that is emerging is doing so from a common source. Behind the complexity of the explicate, external world is a process of unfoldment that is proceeding everywhere in the same way. I find that as we look for this principle in operation in a dialogue, we can, for instance, see a common thread of conversation emerging through several people at once.

There is always a larger cycle unfolding in and through me, whether I am aware of it or not. I can become aware of it, and give voice to it, as I accept responsibility for myself and for my connection to this larger implicate order. In this sense "vision"—an overused word in business and organizations—could be understood as the capacity to see this larger creative cycle. The application in dialogue of this principle begins with the practice of *voicing*, of listening for and speaking my authentic voice, which ultimately flows from the implicate order.

LEARNING TO FIND YOUR VOICE

There are specific practices that you can use to develop your capacity for voice:

Ask: What Is My Music—and Who Will Play It?

My colleague Michael Jones, who now makes his career as a successful improvisational pianist, having sold over 1.5 million CDs, was once asked a very penetrating question by a complete stranger. Earlier, Michael left music to work as a consultant in Toronto. Yet he kept his music alive, finding time during the breaks at the seminars he led to play the piano. People often commented to him that they recalled the music more than the content of the seminars! Once, while playing, an older man came up to him and they began to speak. The man asked about his work and what the music was that he had just played. "That was an arrangement of 'Moon River'," Michael said. "No, before that" said the old man. "That was some of my own music," Michael replied. The man then said, "You're wasting your time with 'Moon River'." He then continued, asking Michael, "Who will play your music if you don't do it yourself?"

We might each ask ourselves this question. Who will play *my* music if I don't play it myself? People often say it is hard to know what their music is, no less find the courage to offer it. Sometimes we know what we would express but require the courage to bring it out. The resolve that wells up from within us first to find out what our music is, and then to give ourselves the permission to give it, is the molten core energy of your voice.

Overcome Self-Censorship

Imagining what you might do is a first step on this journey. We all have a tendency to self-censorship, for withholding what we think for fear of upsetting others or disturbing the order of things. But finding our music involves listening in a deep way to what we may not have dared voice. The practice here entails a continuous willingness to ask yourself, What do I most long to create in the world? And why do I long to create it? Setting aside all the counterforces that would tend to dismiss this question as impractical or irrelevant is an enormous part of this process. But holding Michael's simple question in your heart can go a long way toward opening doors you would not expect to open. Finally, we must also ask ourselves what might be at risk if you do not bring it out, as well as if you do? What choices are you making *now* about how much of your voice you express?[4]

Jump into the Void

One way to get a feel for this experience is to step into an improvisational spirit in conversation. In our workshops we invite people to try this. Michael Jones plays a piece of music from memory, and then at some point seeks to shift into improvisation. We ask participants to see if they can notice when the change occurs. Afterward we ask people to see if they can continue by speaking from the same place that the music came from. People are surprised to find that they do not have all that much to say at first.

The reason for this, I believe, is that we know how to speak from memory, but we are less experienced when we have to think in the moment, without a preplanned notion of what we should say. We develop a repertoire, a way of working that lets us handle situations. But suspending this, we must think again. To speak spontaneously and improvisationally requires a willingness not to know what one is going to say before one says it. Jumping into this void can be quite scary but is tremendously powerful training for finding and expressing your voice. Without planning things out, parts of you that you may not be familiar with are free to speak. And what comes out is often not at all what you expect.

Sometimes in a dialogue a feeling may arise in you that seems to bring pressure to speak and yet one's mind may be blank. I am learning to recognize these moments as precursors to creative expression (not just invitations to sheer terror), where the pressure builds in me and, at times, can emerge through words.

In these moments of emptiness, it is as though someone had tapped me on the shoulder and is asking me to participate. When I do say something, I then find I had something to say that fits with what is happening, but that is not entirely predefined by me. I hear myself articulating something that I sense is present in others.

Ask: What Do You Want to Be Known For?

One of my Ph.D. dissertation advisers, Chris Argyris, once asked me a question very similar to the one posed to Michael Jones. Unlike others who had spoken to me about my work, Chris did not begin with my written proposal or the academic references that he thought I should follow. He simply asked, "What do you want to be known for?" He was asking me, What is my music? This cut through the fog and let me speak what I had made a forbidden subject for myself—what I truly cared most about. In that moment I realized that it is not only the "dark" and unsavory aspects of oneself that get repressed, it is also the golden parts, the noble aspirations. The answer for me lay in seeking to uncover the reasons human beings subvert their own intentions—why despite a lot of good intentions we have a world that is not what it might be—and proposing a way to overcome this pattern of thinking and interacting.

VOICING

QUESTIONS:

What needs to be expressed here? By you? By others? By the whole?

Designed with intention, what purpose would this pattern serve?

Animating this conversation, relationship, system?

Trying to emerge? What is it?

PRACTICES:

Ask: Who will play my music?

Overcome Self-Censorship?

Jump into the void?

Ask: What do you want to be known for?

Speak the forbidden?

FINDING VOICE IN A GROUP

The voice of a group differs from that of an individual. In every group one can ask the questions, "What is it that people together are endeavoring to say here? What is it that they want to say all together?" This is *not* the same as assuming that everyone says the same thing, or even that they agree on critical matters. It is a matter of listening for an emerging story or voice that seems to capture more than what any one person is able to articulate, and saying that.

The voice of a group of people is a function of the emerging story among them. The narrative voice, the voice of the storytellers, is unlike that of the rational, analytic mind. It does not break things up or categorize. It makes distinctions, but these are always seen as part of a larger weave. So, for instance, the steel-workers had a forty-year-long story of abuse and difficulty at the hand of management. Management had a similar story about child-ish steelworkers, untrustworthy people for whom management wanted only what was best. After a year of dialogue, when the union president was able to say "You notice? We are not talking about the past as much. Something has changed here," he was ac-knowledging the shift in collective voice, the change in the under-lying story that had gripped him and his colleagues.

This is in fact the other major feature of the emergence of a collective voice: the realization that the collectively held images that everyone had sustained, must dissolve. Doctors in Grand Junction admitted that they were uncomfortable having to sustain a charade of composure continuously, in the face of disease and death. They acknowledged that some of the costs of health care were attributable to this fear, assuaged by steady investments in technology that was not in fact always necessary or that con-tributed only marginally to effectiveness while adding enormously to costs. Senior administrators admitted to not having a clear sense of how to organize their systems despite the pressure to act as if they knew just what they were doing. The community as a whole confronted, though did not resolve, the realization that they were in the disease-care business, not the health care business.

PRACTICES FOR CATALYZING
THE COLLECTIVE VOICE IN A GROUP

Let the Sound Cascade

The sounds in any conversation have a powerful impact on what is intended and stated. One practice, developed by Risa Kaparo, is to let someone speak and then to listen as the sound of his voice cascades into silence. People typically notice that there is a notable change in the meaning of what they heard as they wait a moment or two and make space to let the meaning bloom. Often, of course, the energy in the conversation is such that speaking quickly is the norm, and waiting is seen as awkward or even impolite. Giving a moment of space is a practice that a group could choose to adopt as the norm.

The idea here is to make space for what is seeking to be spoken to come through. To free this kind of space is to enable what the poet Rilke speaks of as uncontrived words: "I believe in all that has never yet been spoken. I want to free what waits within me so that what no one has dared to wish for may for once spring clear without my contriving."

Speak to (and from) the Center

In dialogues that seem to flow powerfully, people begin to realize that they are speaking to the common pool of meaning being created by all the people together and not to each other as individuals. They are seeking to gather a new quality of meaning and understanding together. In a dialogue, people are not just interacting, but creating together.

To be aware of the challenge of speaking to the center enables the collective voice of a group to emerge more quickly. This can be quite awkward if people use it as a strategy, as a rote step. It may help to think of the "center" here as the center of each person, the center of meaning emerging in and through everyone. The center of the circle can be seen as a reminder of this emerging, invisible fact.

People in groups quite often concentrate on the circumference of a circle, and this is the orientation of most group-dynamics approaches—they explore the nature of the interpersonal and shared assumptions and patterns of relationship among people.

Yet it is the center that is most important.[5] By literally looking only to the center, you may be able to break the habit of focusing only on interpersonal relationships. One must come to the point of listening fully to the center of each person.

THE DARK SIDE OF VOICING

One of the most challenging moments I have ever had occurred in an early dialogue session we held. We had gathered some forty people together to reflect and think about Peter Senge's new book, *The Fifth Discipline,* which had just been published. During the dialogue, a woman began to speak about how she felt about the injustices of the world, both toward herself and toward others. She spoke vigorously. She was very articulate. And she was very long-winded. After an initial ten-minute monologue, I began to get uncomfortable. I felt she was dominating the conversation and seemed not to notice that this was the case. Others were looking annoyed.

I nodded my head as I listened, silently thanking her for her words, hoping she would recognize my signal as a cue for her to stop. She did not. She continued to speak for another twenty-five minutes, almost forty in total. People, growing impatient, would try to ask her questions and engage her in conversation. She would thank them, say that what they were saying reminded her of another point, continue on. It was infuriating and deeply challenging. The content of what she was saying was that no one ever really made room to listen, either to her or to others. So to try to stop her was to do the very thing she was nearly pleading not to have done in the world. On the other hand, she had so alienated people that I thought we might have a riot.

Why is this kind of thing infuriating to many people? Why did the group respond as it did, where people felt angry but were unwilling to say that? I believe it is because this woman and the group touched the shadow of finding your voice in a way that impacted everyone. She represented for everyone that part of us that feels, on the one hand, silenced, unheard, and often unable to speak, and, on the other, the part that does not know when to stop, that *must* be heard, even to the point of dominating everyone around us. The dialogue seemed open and inviting, and so she seized the moment. The group then had the challenge of deciding how to receive her efforts to express her voice, and generally took the stance that what was happening was wrong and should have been stopped.

There are two aspects to the darker dimensions of our voice. When our voice is underdeveloped, we are too quiet, unable to bring out what we think in a way that lets us create what we want. When it is overinflated, all we know how to do is speak, occupying enormous territory, crowding out others. Neither extreme represents balance, revealing our true voice. Learning to speak your voice entails acknowledging those aspects of yourself that participate in both extremes.

One reason we get caught in these extremes is that we live out of an image about what we think we are and should be. I met a lawyer the other day who was quite senior in his profession. He exuded "lawyerness." He introduced himself as an attorney. He began speaking about his important work and some of the well-known people with whom he worked. I began to feel a bit insignificant! I realized I was interacting with a role, not a person. I had the sense that this person was so deeply involved in sustaining his persona that finding his center was nearly impossible.

Idolatry emerges as we create and sustain images of ourselves and our worlds without realizing that this is what we are doing. We become addicted to a certain view of ourselves: We need to notice that we are doing this in order to overcome it. We can begin by asking ourselves, What voice is speaking now? Is it mine? Or one I inherited or absorbed from others?

PREDICTIVE

INTUITION

In retrospect, it all seemed to be ill-fated. Yet when Madeleine Albright went to Ohio State in Columbus in the autumn of 1997 for a town hall meeting to explain the Clinton administration's reasons for bombing Iraq, she had no reason to suspect what lay ahead. Her intent was to explain that the extraordinary and consistent violations by Iraq of the UN resolutions regarding inspections of potential sites for biological, chemical, and nuclear weapons manufacture required a serious response. But what she found was a crowd that challenged her every move.

Perhaps if the White House had thought more clearly about history, about war protesting, about Kent State, said the handlers later, it would have gone differently. Or perhaps the event just needed to be better orchestrated. Some thought that if President Clinton himself had been there, the teacher who felt criticized might have been hugged rather than insulted, the vociferous and questioning students mollified, the hecklers acknowledged but not yielded to. The great communicator could have managed this one easily. But bringing Clinton out in public for this kind of showing was seen as ill timed, given the sex scandal swirling around him. And there was every reason to think, in retrospect, that Clinton would have faced the same hostility from the crowd.

Furthermore, even if he had "controlled" the crowd, having Clinton in Columbus would have been counterproductive. Despite his good intentions, someone with skills like his can give everyone a pleasant feeling but may unwittingly cover over the fact that people are not actually coming together. Instead, they are just complying with the authority or charisma of the leader. It can be a substitute for awareness and for the hard work required to actually think together, which requires that we suspend our positions and listen to what others have to say.

It took everyone by surprise when Albright was heckled as she tried to explain why more bombing of Iraq was necessary. But what is more of a surprise was that the administration expected a "town hall" meeting to be a stage on which its message could be made clear and "sold." Whatever happened to the promise of the town hall meeting, where there might be a free exchange of ideas, where people might listen and think together? This, however, did not seem to be on the agenda.

People still gather all over New England to exercise this relatively rare form of democracy. In the small towns where the annual town meeting still takes place, virtually everyone goes. Only town citizens can vote. In Hanover, New Hampshire, where I went to college, the town hall sessions were a subject of fascination and some amusement to the students. It seemed so old-fashioned to us. In reality these meetings, too, were highly orchestrated and predetermined. But most of the time things got said and debated in the open that would never otherwise have been. The structure of genuinely democratic participation was still present, even if it was not always executed well.

But we have lost our respect, by and large, for public forums like this—precisely because they almost always turn into one-sided exchanges or shouting matches. Many people insist that such shouting matches are a good thing. We would not have learned about the mood of the country without the heckling that shocked Madeleine Albright. And besides, they say conflict is fun. It is also often unavoidable and necessary. One must stand up to nonsense. In this sense, the town hall meeting worked as it should have: Differences emerged, people learned, policy was influenced.

At the same time, our conversational repertoire as human beings seems shockingly narrow. Under pressure we are often not capable of doing anything *except* argue. Public discourse is almost always reduced to the kind of exchange in which discussion, not dialogue, prevails. The dominant stance is one of blame, not reflection or responsibility. People typically walk away having learned to resent such forums. But they do not learn about what they might have done differently, what they did to cause the results they got, or how to do something differently next time. They became reinforced in their fragmentation and separation.

In short, the problem exists because people use these meetings as an opportunity to get their ideas across as strongly as possible and sway everyone in their direction. This is like trying to make music by having many notes all running together with no space between them. No space, no music. You could argue that the point here is not to make music, it is to win. While that may be true, it is a limited viewpoint ensuring that everyone else will try to do the same, repeating the old habits of thinking alone that sustain polarization.

In Columbus, several sets of forces stood in the way of a free and open flow. For instance, people took an oppositional stance, resisted the formal structure of the gathering, and were unwilling to abide by the "rules of exchange" set up by the organizers. At the same time, the way Albright and her staff read those forces and responded to them turned a town hall meeting into an oppositional debate. They did not create a setting in which to hold the intensities that emerged. They opposed the opposition, tried to divert attention, advocated their opinions, and failed to inquire into the nature of the underlying distress of the crowd. The pressures of the situation resulted in a breakdown. However, Albright and her staff did not see the breakdown as an opportunity for learning, merely as evidence of the volatility of the issues.

Albright and the others responded in a way that actually reinforced the very dynamics they said they wanted to defuse: The stated intention of the town hall meeting was to create a way for people to learn about the administration's policies and invite greater understanding and acceptance.

SEEING STRUCTURES

This part of the book explores the reasons for the difficulties that arose, and asks the questions What might Albright and her team have said or done to alter these dynamics? Could they have developed an intuition that would have led them to be able to predict the reactions that arose in the face-to-face dynamics of the conversation and make moves to address it? And if so, how might they have done it?

Doing so requires developing an ability to think strategically about the kinds of generic differences people have, the common and predictable misunderstandings they are likely to get into, and the ways they tend to reinforce within one another the negative patterns they say they want to change. It requires in particular an ability to have "predictive intuition"—which in this context means the capacity to perceive the face-to-face "structures" of interaction: those forces operative within any setting that tend to guide behavior. While the ambition to produce dialogue is a noble one, most often it is the inability to accurately predict and perceive the kinds of limits people face that is their downfall. It rapidly becomes clear that having an atmosphere and intention conducive to dialogue—a dialogic way of being—

and some of the skills described in the chapters above—is necessary but not sufficient for actually having dialogue.

The capacity for predictive intuition can give people the leverage they seek. It is possible to respond to these forces in a different way, one that is conducive to dialogue and that directly meets antilearning forces like these and responds to them in a fashion that transforms them. To do so requires that we understand more precisely how and why people interact as they do. Then it is possible to respond creatively and catalyze dialogue.

There are many different systems of thought that seek to help people develop what I am calling predictive intuition. The following chapters explore aspects of several such systems as illustrations of what is required. But it is important to state at the outset that the point here is not to become enamored with a particular system, but with the result that system can produce: a capacity to perceive and name what is happening as it is happening. The systems themselves are scaffolding for developing predictive intuition. The point of these systems, in my view, is to develop your intuition, not to become overly locked into the system itself. Then you have the capability of applying this knowledge to achieve a variety of results.

If I spent the many years required to learn the martial art of aikido, I might then have developed what we could call "physical awareness." I would have the ability to stay in charge of myself, and to recover my centering quickly if I lost it, despite pressure. I might be able to manage stress more effectively. I would probably be able to take care of myself if I got mugged. And I might be able to apply this awareness and understanding to business problems I faced. Developing this physical awareness enables me to produce a wide variety of different results, in different domains. The same is true for predictive intuition.

As I develop it, I become able to foresee more clearly the kinds of difficulties that might lurk in complex settings where the stakes are high, and find a way through them.

Also, similar to what might take place in aikido, I might initially make the mistake of thinking I knew more than I did, imagining that because I knew a few techniques, I could handle a high-intensity exchange, when I could not. Or I might stop learning and begin to rely on the few techniques I knew worked, hoping they would apply in all circumstances, never having actually developed my own intuition. Instead, I would continue to borrow from the understanding of others, an understanding that had been condensed into a technique. My practice would in this case likely seem rigid, full of jargon, inauthentic.

While there are perils to developing predictive intuition, there is also an enormous need. Settings like the one Albright encountered are the norm. Understanding how to meet these, and develop dialogue within them, is a very valuable gift.

I cover two different dimensions of predictive intuition in the next few chapters. The first explores ways we can learn to detect gaps between what people intend and what they do, and how we can understand problematic "patterns of action," and the impact of each of these on dialogue. The previous part of the book explored the four practices and new capacities for behavior we must use to bring about dialogue. Now we can see how to anticipate whether these four practices are actively present, how they fit together, and what to do if they are not. The second dimension of predictive intuition examines how hidden but powerful structures of interaction can neutralize dialogue, and how to begin to anticipate and overcome these.

This part also explores what it takes to practice the art of thinking together in small and large groups of people—in families, in business teams, in large or what we call "median-sized" groups of up to forty people, and even in very large groups of three hundred people or more. Many people feel intimidated in large groups—even groups beyond fifteen people. Most of us are used to the family-sized groups of less than eight, the size that human beings have lived in and worked in for millennia.

Patterns

of Action

PUTTING THE FOUR PRACTICES
INTO ACTION: FINDING THE GAPS

One starting point for developing predictive intuition is to explore more carefully the gaps between what people intend to do and what they actually do. This has been the focus of the work of Chris Argyris and Donald Achön for many years. Argyris and Schön pioneered the development of a *science of action*—a way of understanding why what we do is not always what we intend, or even what we are aware of, and of learning how to close these gaps. Their work shows that human beings produce the kinds of errors described above consistently as long as they remain un-aware of the rules that govern their behavior. We *are* aware, say Argyris and Schön, of what we believe and intend to accomplish. You may have well-developed theories of what you should do to lead effectively, for instance, or formulate strategy. But if we watch what you actually do, we will likely find a gap.

This is more than saying there is a gap between our "walk" and our "talk." Argyris and Schön claim we operate by two sets of rules, one governing what we hold to be true, and the other gov-erning what we actually do. Most people are unaware when they are creating a gap like this, and so continue to do so.

The implications of this misperception are rather serious. It means most change and leadership efforts have built into them a series of inner contradictions that typically go unnamed and therefore unaddressed. Examples abound.[1]

The recent reengineering movement within corporations epitomizes this problem. Thomas Davenport, one of the founders of the process, has written that reengineering "didn't start out as a code word for mindless corporate bloodshed. It wasn't supposed to be the last grasp of Industrial Age Management."[2] Yet in a recent survey, CSC Index's "State of Reengineering Report" reported that seventy-three percent of the companies that participated in the study said they were using reengineering to eliminate jobs, and sixty-seven percent said that reengineering efforts produced "mediocre, marginal, or failed results."[3] Reengineering started out as an ideal solution to a modern business problem: how to link technological and computer-based shifts in the ways people worked with the insights of the Total Quality Movement.

By combining these, a new change process was born. Yet its impact has not been what was intended. Despite growing to a $51 billion industry, the reengineering movement "ignored people," which is to say, it ignored the systemic effects that the interactions between people create within organizations.

Reengineering created fear and was resisted. Few people wanted to "be reengineered" or to work in a reengineered organization. At its base it failed to ask what it was about how we were *originally* operating that created the need to be "reengineered" in the first place. What led us not to see this before or, if we saw it, to act on it? How can we be certain that the actions we are now taking are not simply a recreation of the past?

What is even more puzzling is that efforts to make a difference on this score often makes matters worse. Argyris has recently written that the "empowerment" programs have rarely, if ever, achieved anything more than "external" commitment rather than the genuine internal commitment that their designers espouse.[4]

INNER CONTRADICTIONS
IN CORPORATE CHANGE

I studied the efforts of a major Fortune 500 corporation to create greater partnership between its employees and its managers. While the company's intention was sensible and hard to argue against, the way it was "rolled out" contained numerous inner contradictions. Everyone in this organization was asked to have regular conversations with his or her manager. But "regular" in this context meant a mandatory conversation every quarter with a predefined set of objectives and measures. What began as a way to create openings between people became a rigid and routinized process. People soon began to go through the motions because they had to. They took the attitude, as so many people do inside large organizations, that "this too shall pass." The organization's actions were at odds with its intentions, yet getting people to not only realize this but do something about it has proved very difficult. Many senior managers in this organization have seen an analysis of the dilemmas of this process but have been reluctant, until very recently, to make changes.

What can be done about inconsistent and problematic action of this sort? One way to move beyond these limited-action dynamics is to do what I have begun to do here—name the difficulty. As the author of the *Inner Game of Tennis*, Tim Galway, has put it: "Awareness is curative." As people become more conscious of the ways in which they unintentionally undermine themselves, they begin to make changes to reduce these difficulties.

As many people have now begun to realize, it is possible to develop a very different set of skills for handling circumstances like these. People like Argyris have inspired a generation of practitioners who now teach these skills to people around the world.[5] There are now several good books on this subject, including Senge's *The Fifth Discipline, The Fifth Discipline Fieldbook*, and Peter Schwartz's *The Skilled Facilitator*.

DETECTING PATTERNS
OF ADVOCACY AND INQUIRY

At the core of producing a set of actions that can truly bring about change is what Argyris calls "balancing advocacy and inquiry." *Advocacy* means speaking what you think, speaking for a point of view. *Inquiry* means looking into what you do not yet know, what you do not yet understand, or seeking to discover what others see and understand that may differ from your point of view. It is the art of asking genuine questions, ones that seek to understand the rules that govern why people do what they do as much as to challenge what they do. As I noted earlier, most people do not actually have questions in mind when their sentences end in question marks!

While easier said than done, balancing advocacy and inquiry means stating clearly and confidently what one thinks and why one thinks it, while at the same time being open to being wrong. It means encouraging others to challenge our views, and to explore what might stop them from doing so. Typically, we have more advocacy than inquiry—a manager tells his staff what to do and how to do it. Most conversations you get into, I predict, are dominantly advocacy. I have explored this skill now in thousands of cases, and for the past twenty-five years Argyris has studied many thousands more, and there seems to be a very high degree of reliability for this finding: especially under pressure, human beings resort to unilateral advocacy of their position. Genuine inquiry is in short supply.

There *are* settings in which inquiry prevails over advocacy. Unfortunate caricatures of this include the aggressive lawyer leading his witness: The lawyer asks questions he already knows the answers to (or hopes he knows), or the person who asks warm, caring questions, never ruffling a feather, though making it quite clear who is in charge. I had one very senior manager from a large corporation object strongly to something a colleague of mine proposed in a consulting engagement we were conducting for his boss. "Do you think he really *meant* to propose that solution?" he asked me. The implied message was clear: My colleague had proposed the *wrong* thing.

Bringing advocacy and inquiry together implies learning how to make explicit the thinking that leads you to say what you say. This goes against much of the social training most people receive. Most of us learn to cover up this thinking for fear that it will embarrass someone. A colleague told me the following story. One day he was in the office of his boss, the CEO of the company. My colleague had been weighing for months whether or not to leave the company. He had decided not to leave, because there were clear contractual limits restricting his control of his investment in the company if he left before the company was sold.

To my colleague's surprise, the CEO announced, "Well, I really need someone to do the XYZ job, but you are not that person, so we are stuck." My colleague said, "Wait a minute; in other words, you feel that the only way to get this other job done is for me to stop doing my job, because they conflict? The fact is, I am not sure I want to say. Unfortunately, the conditions for my leaving the company are not favorable right now." The CEO replied, "Well, what can we do to change that?" And they had a very straightforward conversation that led to my colleague leaving in such a way that he did not lose any of his investment in the company. Afterward the CEO was a little stunned by the whole thing. "Did we really say what we thought? That was far less painful than I had anticipated."

The pain arises from the cover-ups and the cover-up of the cover-ups. This case was easier, admittedly, since my colleague was open to leaving under the right conditions. But my colleague and the CEO could have easily completely missed one another. Instead, they both said what they wanted to say.

The Link Between the Dialogue
Practices and Advocacy and Inquiry

The dialogue practices described in the last part of the book give a sense of how this might be done. There is a direct connection between voice and respect. This is the "line of action," or *advocacy*. If we speak our own voice, not what we think we should say, and do it respectfully, we are advocating in a productive way. It is the best way to make our view as clear as we can to someone else.

One must listen in a serious way, not just to others' words, but to our own reactions to their words, and to the impulses that arise within us that make us want to react. As we do this we must also suspend our reactions and our assumptions about what others say. In other words, balancing advocacy and inquiry means putting into practice the four qualities described earlier.

These four practices are the key elements of the stance we must take in order to advocate and inquire effectively. If any one of them is missing, we are likely to have imbalance. Remember the plant manager who spoke "directly" and "openly" within the steel mill we worked in about the changing economics of the business he was in. His words were heard as an attack by the union. He was speaking his own voice as best he knew how. But beneath his words it was evident that he had little respect for the steelworkers. His private attributions about them were that they were incapable of taking responsibility for themselves and were more like children than adults. While he never said this publicly, his actions conveyed it quite clearly. During this same conversation, for example, he claimed he found people talking on the phone inside the plant, taking long breaks, doing things he "would never have found in the plant he first managed." This incensed the steelworkers, who felt the plant manager was taking things out of context and judging them unfairly.

Argyris's discipline, "action inquiry," would have asked this manager to state more directly what he thought about the steelworkers and why he thought it—what had led him to the conclusions that they were untrustworthy. While challenging, it would have been helpful to the steelworkers, who showed themselves to be quite capable of responding to fair exchanges like this. It would have also been helpful to the plant manager, who might have let his own view be changed. His fundamental lack of respect revealed his inability to see them as people. This fueled his inability to see that he, too, missed things, including the impact he had on the steelworkers, that led them to withdraw from him, not tell him everything they knew and seek to bait him at every opportunity.

The plant manager's problem lay in the fact that he was unwilling to be changed, that he was certain of his view. Because of this, no technique for conversation would have made any difference.

To get more effective inquiry, we must both listen and suspend. In this case, the plant manager listened for evidence that he was right, and remained certain he was right. This, in turn, closed down the inquiry process.

KANTOR'S FOUR PLAYER SYSTEM

Typically, a conversation appears as a hodgepodge of perspectives and sentiments, one voice speaking after another. Sometimes people interrupt or differ. Sometimes they stay silent. And sometimes they agree, supporting what is said and defending the speaker. But it is possible to see more than this in a group conversation.

David Kantor, through his work as a clinician in the field of family systems therapy, has developed a powerful theory that suggests that conversations reflect innate structures that only partly stem from the individual's needs. They also reflect the unspoken needs of the group and the situation. To Kantor, people take a stance not because they intend to, but because the conversation needs someone to fill that role. By using Kantor's powerful model, and other such models, we can become attuned to these hidden imperatives—and we can build an intuitive ability to predict how the conversation "wants" to play out. This also gives us the tools to change the dynamic. At first glance it seems as if there's no overriding pattern to this: People come with different agendas. But what if there were a way to recognize the structure of conversations so you could predict what will happen next? Kantor's model reveals four fundamentally different kinds of action within a group.

These four kinds of action are relatively easily distinguished, and can apply in an enormous variety of settings.

When someone makes a *move;* they are initiating an action. They carry, at least for the moment, the focus of the conversation.

Another person listening to this initial proposal might agree and want to support what is being said. This person says so, and symbolically comes close to the first person. The second person could be said to be *following* the first. A third person, watching these two agree, may think to him- or herself, There is something not quite right with this picture. He or she steps in and *opposes* them, challenging what they are saying or proposing. Symbolically, this third person might stand between the first two. Finally, a fourth person, who has been observing the entire situation, and who has the advantage of having one foot in and one foot out of the circumstance, describes from his perspective what he has seen and heard. This person may propose a way of thinking and seeing that expands everyone's vision, and could be called a *bystander*. He or she adds a valuable dimension to the conversation. The term *bystander* here does not necessarily mean someone who is uninvolved or silent. Bystanders can speak, but they provide perspective instead of taking a stand.

A healthy conversation, argues Kantor, consists of all four of these actions being used in balance. None is left out. And all the people in the conversation find themselves free to occupy *any* of the four positions at any time. They are not found by informal and unspoken rules imposed either by the system or by themselves. Of course, in most conversations we find a mix of different energies. Someone might observe and then make a move. Or they might seem to follow and then oppose: "I like what you are saying, but I have a problem with it. . . ."

We can see all of these quite clearly in the following example. In the film *Dances With Wolves*, Kevin Costner, playing a Union soldier, takes over a remote fort located in the midst of Native People's territory. (According to several North American Native elders, this film is a fairly accurate depiction of the culture and of the Native Peoples.)

Costner lights an enormous fire, and the smoke that billows from the fort alerts the Native People that a white man is present; as they say, only a white man would announce his presence in so clumsy a fashion. Shortly afterward twenty or so Native elders hold a conversation circle in a tepee, where they speak about Costner's arrival and its potential ramifications on their ways of living. This conversation, you must realize, represents a cultural crisis of a high order—a potential threat to their territory and their existence. But unlike a typical board of directors in a corporation facing a similar threat, these people do not panic or begin to attack one another. They maintain a steady and reflective inquiry that is both passionate and intelligent. Here there are no flip charts or meeting agendas; there is only the gentle smoke from a smoldering fire in the center of the circle. Some stand as they speak, others do not. But throughout, there is a rich sense of respect and listening. In the scene outlined below, the young warrior named Wind In His Hair speaks with Kicking Bird, who is an older veteran of the wars with the white man:

Wind In His Hair: I do not care for this talk about a white man. Whatever he is, he is not Sioux and that makes him less. When I hear that more whites are coming I want to laugh.

Kicking Bird: *(holding up his hand to quiet the group)* Wind In His Hair's words are strong and I have heard them. It's true the whites are a poor race and hard to understand. But make no mistake—the whites are coming.

Wind In His Hair: *(standing)* Kicking Bird is always looking ahead and that is good. But this man is nothing to us. I will take some men. We will shoot some arrows into this man. If he truly has medicine, he will not be hurt. If he has no medicine, he will be dead.

Medicine Man: *(seated, quiet, he waits, and then speaks)* No man can tell another what to do. But killing a white man is a delicate matter. If you kill one, more are sure to come.

Chief: *(also seated, raises his hand, speaks very slowly, calmly)* It is easy to become confused by these questions. It's hard to know what to do. We should talk about this some more.

Several very different points of view are expressed, without anyone feeling the need to rise up and change anyone else's point of view. We typically do not see this: Two points of view cannot generally live side by side for long.

Wind In His Hair begins by making a *move*. The group as a whole *follows* him, nodding in agreement and listening intently. Kicking Bird *follows* at first, but then *opposes*, challenging the direction in which the conversation goes, and making a final punctuating *move:* "I think this is a person with which treaties might be struck." The group *follows* him now.

Wind In His Hair *follows* this, and then *opposes* the white man, escalating the conversation. The Medicine Man *opposes* Wind In His Hair: "No man can tell another what to do" and then *bystands,* commenting on the impact shooting arrows into a white man is likely to have. Finally, the chief speaks, again *bystanding* and then *moving:* He proposes that they suspend their thinking about this problem.

The sequence of actions is nearly perfectly balanced. Each of the four dynamics is present. No single dynamic is overly present; each one keeps the others in balance. The two dominant actors engage in a sequence of moving and opposing. But there are others in the group who oppose, or follow, and, ultimately, who bystand both of them and the entire conversation, lifting it to new levels. Typically, this is not what happens: When two people are caught in a move/oppose "he said, she said" conversation, others head for cover and go silent. In this case they do not. Other people make strong counterbalancing moves that are respected and held by all. This leads to a sense of balance and listening.

Very commonly we see "mixed moves." People make a move in one voice but have another message underneath. For instance, I may say: "Let's go to the beach today," but underneath I may also be saying "And let's *not* do what you wanted to do." I am moving with one voice and opposing with another, all in the same breath. People listen very carefully for such intentions. One critical step in learning dialogue is to become conscious of the tone we are using as we take the actions we do. This "noise" triggers reactions and may prevent us from allowing a deeper level of inquiry to open up.

Typically, we find that some of the four positions in a conversation are silenced, or, as Kantor calls them, "disabled." A disabled bystander sees what is happening in a group but doesn't do anything about it. A disabled opposer cannot offer correction to or challenge what is happening. Any system that silences bystanders and opposers is by definition in trouble, according to this theory. Vital information will not be shared and people will go underground with their views.

Each of us has what might be considered strong moves, ones we do well, and weak moves that we do poorly. I once found myself witnessing a verbal jousting match between two colleagues. I wanted to do what I felt was needed, which was to bystand the whole thing—to ask questions, to provide another view. Instead, I joined the fray. I was so angered by what one of them was saying that I could not help but follow the other, almost as if "the enemy of my enemy was my friend." I was a weak bystander in this case.

Finally, one can also be "stuck" in one of these four roles. When we are stuck we repeat a move that would be better changed. I love to speak in front of groups of people about ideas. I get a sense of energy and excitement from this, and find myself making moves, initiating new ideas. Then I introduce more ideas, and more, until the space is flooded! A stuck mover needs colleagues around who will remind him to slow down and make space.

What are your strengths and weaknesses? Are you able, particularly in high-stakes circumstances, to play one of these four roles well? Which one of the four roles needs toning and strengthening? Which gets you in trouble?

These four action positions, while valuable on their own, become extremely powerful guides for understanding the nature of action in dialogue as one links them to the underlying practices that lie behind them. Each position—move, follow, oppose, and bystand—has a dialogue "practice" that corresponds to it. For *move* it is the quality of truthfulness and voice; for *follow*, listening; for *oppose*, respect; and for *bystand*, suspension. The quality of action is greatly influenced by the degree to which these four qualities are present.

Toward the close of a dialogue session that we held recently, one man—we'll call him Frank—began to feel carried away by his experience. He said that he felt something very powerful had happened to him over the several days the thirty of us had spent together.

> We couldn't really break away. We didn't want to leave each other, there was something that was happening there that felt like we were thinking together. . . . And I compare that against when my vice president would call me and say, "I need you to give a twenty-minute presentation about something that at least two people would be interested in listening to for twenty minutes." So I thought that I would spend more time comparing and maybe it wouldn't have been as coherent, or as authentic as I felt last night.
>
> I feel a sense of rhythm with this kind of intimate group, and a sense of that we know how to dance to-

gether, and that we've developed a sense of intelligence where we're not bumping into each other. . . .

But his emergent sense of connection troubled him. In particular, he was worried about returning to work:

> Am I going to be able to tap into some of this truth that I have found very recently? I guess that that worries me a little bit. I mean the first conversation that I will have when I get back home most likely will be with my wife. And I'm actually kind of worried about that conversation. I mean I am worried about that first sentence.

A woman in the group, Mary Jo, with a long South Texas drawl, paused a moment and then responded:

> This isn't an [overly] opposing voice but I've had a few problems of thinking of this as "love in the cottage." I guess that is kind of a very prim expression. "We're all so happy together, and we're all . . ." I guess I don't feel the same way. Frank, you know that this is some sort of wonderful place that when I leave I'll feel totally different.

The sequence of an initial, heartfelt, tender statement followed by a more direct challenge might have created a difficult moment. Yet the climate of the dialogue changed these dynamics. Mary Jo's statement had a great deal of *respect* in it; it was not condemning Frank; she was just expressing a different point of view, a clean opposition, challenging for the purpose of testing and deepening what was happening.

This opened a series of other interactions: Someone immediately followed, saying that like Mary Jo, he had been uncomfortable with Frank's words. Another man then added:

> You know, I really appreciated Frank's comment and Mary Jo's. I don't feel a particular compulsion to have to either reconcile the two or pick one. At least in this environment I've got feelings of both. And that's just fine.

There was a moment of quiet. People seemed to be searching for words. The ordinary experience of different points of view creating polarization had instead, in this case, quite clearly enriched everyone. It was as if it took a moment for everyone to absorb this fact. People then spoke quite slowly and deliberately.

After several days of work, the group had begun to create a climate in which it was possible to lay out seemingly opposing viewpoints and have enough perspective to see that there was room for both, and that by hearing both, everyone was able to learn. No one felt the need to correct either person, cover up the apparent differences, or "take care" of anyone. This made it easier for them to accomplish all four forms of dialogic behavior: suspending, voicing, listening, and respecting. Balanced action in a dialogue consists of the way people in conversations make their point of view, combined with character and being present. When all of these elements are in balance and present, dialogue is possible.

LISTENING FOR THE UNDERLYING INTENT

A starting point for this is to notice which of Kantor's four-player actions a person is using, and listen for the underlying intention behind it. Kantor shows that often there are some generic "intentions" beneath each of the actions, and suggests typical ways these get misinterpreted.

For example, a woman in a course I was facilitating sat through a conversation about musical improvisation and dialogue with growing impatience: "I cannot for the life of me see the relevance of any of this." She finally snapped. She was known in her group as someone who often said things like this. She often "opposed" what was being said in the conversation. In fact, she sent two messages, one that conveyed her inability to see a connection, and the other, her belief that there was no connection *anyone* could find—the ideas themselves and the people conveying it were flawed.

People who oppose in this fashion often seem critical, complaining, divisive, difficult. And often they are! And yet their intention is rarely any of this. When we react and attribute nasty motives to them, we miss the valuable information that they are trying to bring into the picture. Knowing something of this, I asked this woman to say more about her reaction, about what had led her to it. Gradually, it came out that she felt personally incompetent regarding music, and that her sister had tormented her with her own musical ability for years, leading the woman to hate it and all it represented. This woman's underlying intent was really one of self-protection as much as it was an effort to maintain her own integrity as she listened.

Each of the four-player actions described by Kantor also has a generic set of "intentions" behind it. Understanding what there are, we can learn to set aside our reactions to the noise of another's communication and listen for what they are really trying to say. For instance, here are some of the ways opposers are heard and what they intend:

OPPOSER INTENDS	But sometimes comes across as	
Courage	**But**	Critical
Integrity	**sometimes**	Complaining
Correction	**comes**	Blaming
Protection	**across**	Attacking
Survival	**as**	Contrary

Someone looking to correct their understanding could be heard by us as critical. This is unfortunate, since it might lead us to discount them and therefore not learn from them.

Similarly, someone who dominantly carries mover energy might come across as dictatorial—or even scattered, if all they ever did was propose things and never follow up on anything. Someone who is strong at following but weak at the other player roles might come across as weak and unable to stand on her own. And a good bystander might seem aloof and distanced.

In each case, the challenge in dialogue is to go beyond the appearance and the baggage that might be attached to a particular action, and look for the underlying intention. What was the person trying to do? What was *I* trying to do? This can also be reversed: How do I come across? Why was my intention, which was clear to me, so badly misheard by others? Here are all the positions, what they intend, and how they tend to come across:[6]

		But	
	Direction	**But**	Omnipotent
MOVER	Discipline	**sometimes**	Impatient
INTENDS	Commitment	**comes**	Indecisive
	Perfection	**across as**	Scattered
	Clarity		Dictatorial
	Completion	**But**	Placating
	Compassion	**sometimes**	Indecisive
FOLLOWER	Loyalty	**comes**	Pliant
INTENDS	Service	**across as**	Wishy-washy
	Continuity		Over-accommodating

	Correction	**But**	Critical
OPPOSER	Courage	**sometimes**	Competitive
INTENDS	Protection	**comes**	Blaming
	Integrity	**across as**	Attacking
	Survival		Contrary

	Perspective	**But**	Disengaged
BYSTANDER	Patience	**sometimes**	Judgmental
INTENDS	Preservation	**comes**	Deserting
	Moderation	**across as**	Withdrawn
	Self-Reflection		Silent

At the heart of the art of thinking together is an exploration of the underlying motives and intentions of the people concerned. The central spirit behind this approach is *forgiveness*—a stance that looks to the motives that a person intended regardless of how their actions appear. This does not mean we disregard action. But we may come to the point of understanding action far better with this approach.

Overcoming

Structural Traps

To take our exploration of predictive intuition further, we must develop another level of awareness. This involves understanding how the forces within a setting operate to produce certain results. My favorite image of the importance of this was captured in a cartoon, where two fish swim in a blender that has yet to be turned on. The one fish says to the other, "And they expect us to relax!"

The blender is a vivid example of a structure that determines the behavior (and anxiety level) of the fish.[1] Are there such factors present in your dialogue setting? The expectation others have around budget time, for instance, that you will ask for more money than you expect to get. This is an example of a generic structure that guides the way many people operate in creating and approving budgets.

DEFINING STRUCTURE

When we think of "structure," many of us picture an organizational chart or the layout of a building or an architectural blueprint. Structure usually refers to the physical arrangement of things. Biologists say that all physical things have a basic structure—an arrangement of the physical components of matter. But when it comes to social structures—in this case, interactions between people in a dialogue—structure means something else.

I define *structure* in human conversation and interactions as "the set of frameworks, habits, and conditions that compel people to act as they do."[2] These structures govern the way we think and act. They are relatively stable: We can predict the way an individual or group will tend to behave once we know the structures that guide them. These structures are composed of the quality, content, and timeliness of the information being conveyed. This includes the goals, incentives, costs, and feedback that motivate or constrain behavior.[3]

For example, the CEO of an organization I studied for several years initiated a new way of interacting with his direct reports. In his view, having all eight of these people involved in every decision was unwieldy and created a bottleneck. So he decided to meet with people in smaller subgroups. This made several of the people in this team think that he did not trust them, although they were afraid to say so. After all, they thought to themselves, he already does not trust me enough to value my participation. In the next meeting of the full group, the CEO asked whether people liked the new arrangement, and whether any of them were having trouble with it. Thinking the CEO did not trust them, they all avoided the subject, saying nothing negative. The CEO took their absence of objections to mean assent, and continued the process. Eventually, the group erupted. The CEO was shocked. "We tried to tell you," his direct reports said.

These people were caught in a structure of interaction that was mutually self-reinforcing and self-fulfilling. The CEO's actions led others to act cautiously, which in turn led the CEO to feel confirmed in his thinking. This is a relatively common feedback process that occurs often in teams. Nobody, including the CEO, wanted to create an impasse and explosion. Yet almost anyone in that situation would find it impossible to avoid one. This is an example of what Kantor calls a "structural trap."

DIAGNOSING STRUCTURAL TRAPS

A structural trap is a condition where one part of the system requires people to act in one way, while another part of the organization requires them to do something else that directly contradicts this. This is because different subsystems of any organization often have very different assumptions and ideas about what is wrong and what needs correction, and tend not to communicate well to one another. The net effect is that people feel their efforts to produce change are constantly being undermined and neutralized despite many well-intentioned efforts to reverse the decline.

For instance, senior managers in a division of a well-known industrial equipment company I know were deeply frustrated with their lack of progress. They were entrepreneurs who had virtually invented their industry, and had led it for many years. They had several highly successful local operating businesses around the world.

But now new competitors were entering. Their global

market share had eroded significantly, profitability was down, and their once-unchallenged dominance now lost. Yet every effort to regain leadership had failed. The senior managers reflected on what they needed to do, and developed clear ideas about what actions were required. They would agree on a change, only to find some months later that nothing had been done.

The cause lay in the fact that this was a highly individualistic group where every leader took responsibility to effect change, while at the same time furiously working to make his part of the organization successful. They launched numerous uncoordinated change efforts, many of which overlapped. More critically, these change efforts had deeply embedded inner contradictions. Everyone agreed, for instance, that they needed to dramatically overhaul their centralized manufacturing process, shifting to a "lean" production system that had very limited inventory and very fast turnaround times. But this required that the division's local operating businesses give up some of their control and that everyone manage from a common forecasting system.

It turned out that each local business had a phantom forecasting system in addition to the "official" one that actually guided their decisions. The local businesses believed they had to compete with each other for manufacturing resources. To make their actual needs known by sharing their private forecasts meant they might not be able to meet their customer's requests, harming their local profitability. The local managers were measured and rewarded on the basis of their local, not companywide, performance, a system tightly controlled by yet another part of the organization. The local managers were caught: To help the overall business, they might suffer individually. But to protect their local efforts would cause them all to fail in the long run, as competitors continued their assault, making the very changes they were resisting. Everyone agreed that they needed a new system. But in practice, people were reluctant to act.

This kind of trap often goes unspoken and undiscussed. In this case, the problems were endlessly analyzed and seemingly well understood, but no one could seem to bring all the players together in the same room to talk about their different assumptions and dilemmas. As a result, problems persist, sometimes for years.

Structural traps like these can cripple an organization. The way to manage these traps, I believe, is to engage in dialogue about them. To do this, it is helpful to have a language for mapping and understanding the traps and the forces that sustain them.

Kantor has developed a way of diagnosing traps like these. His theory, which he calls "structural dynamics," originated out of an attempt to integrate two divergent streams within family-systems therapy: the idea of "systems" components, or the ways the different elements of a system are composed; and the idea of psychodynamics, the internal life of the people and their aims, neuroses, and development.

Kantor's system uses terms that have been known for many years. Their value is that, one, his is a very forgiving model. There is no good or bad here. Each has a use, a positive contribution to make, and a limiting dimension. The challenge is to understand how this works in practice.[4] Second, the language Kantor has created is very *usable*. People have found that it helps them to understand themselves and why they get in trouble communicating with others, and it helps them to understand others and why their efforts are sometimes met with blank stares. Third, and most important as it relates to dialogue, it names some of the central ways human beings fragment themselves.

Kantor approaches this by articulating a variety of different levels on which people interact, all simultaneously affecting them, all combining and shifting moment by moment. Two of these levels are particularly important for dialogue.

■ People speak three different languages when they express themselves: the languages of affect (or feeling), meaning, and power. Yet this fact often goes unnoticed, leading to confusion and miscommunication not unlike those of translation across any two languages. Speaking louder, or attributing the other person just does not "get it," are common errors when facing these "language" breakdowns.

■ Distinct from this first layer are three different lenses that guide people to different preferred ways of organizing power and relationships within any system: open, closed, and random "system paradigms." These preferences guide our thinking and feeling whether we are aware of them or not. Becoming aware of another person's and our own preference can give us an enormous advantage in understanding and communicating well.

Understanding these levels can help us suspend fragmentation. Only by including all the elements of the whole can we actually experience wholeness.

THE LANGUAGES OF FEELING, MEANING, AND POWER

The tragic death of Diana the Princess of Wales brought a wide range of reactions from people around the world. Some spoke of their *feelings* of shock, grief, anger, compassion. The prime minister of England worried publicly for Diana's children. Many spoke about the need to take *action:* to stop drunk driving and to reform the predatory behavior of the photographers who pursue the rich and famous to obtain a photo that can fetch a high price. Still others were more reflective, asking questions like "What does this mean for England and the relationship between the press and the rest of us?" "What is the *significance* of the enormous public outpouring of emotion from a country and people not known for doing this?" "What are the implications of this for the status of royal family in England?"

One can hear in this different reactions stimulated by the same event. One spoke the language of the heart, of feelings. Another spoke the language of action and change—what I call the language of action, or *power:* "What are we going to *do* here?" these people asked. A third inquired into the broader implications of the event and its aftermath. This is called the language of *meaning:* "What does this mean for England?"

The primary concern for people who speak the language of feeling is "Are we taking care of the people and how they feel?" People who speak this language tend to see the world first as a network of relationships, and are attuned as much to the tone that gets expressed as the content of the expression. One is likely to hear people who speak this language reporting on how they feel, inquiring into how others feel, expecting this level of experience to be taken seriously.

A group of senior educational leaders I know spends a great deal of time thinking about the dysfunctions of the state education system in which they work. They are determined to make a change in it. But if you listen to their words, they do not talk only about taking action. They constantly refer to the children, to the needs of children, and to the pain they feel when racial prejudices in voters blind them, preventing them from voting to spend money to improve inner-city schools. Their primary orientation is in how it feels to be a teacher, how it feels to be a child in an underfunded system, and how they could take care of the needs of all the constituencies for which they feel responsible.

In the language of *meaning*, people express interest in the ideas, values, theory, and philosophy behind what is happening. They are often passionate about ideas, or have a clear set of principles that they wish to have known and followed. Or they may simply explore ideas to the exclusion of concerns about action or feeling. The social scientist and philosopher Donald Schön was as fine an exemplar of someone who spoke the language of meaning as anyone I have known. Don personified the spirit of inquiry. Writing our doctoral dissertations under his guidance was both a wonderful and painful experience. Every time my fellow students and I would go to him, we would cringe as we discovered the myriad questions that we had not asked, the numerous holes in our arguments, the fascinating new ground that was not yet clarified. Don would listen by shutting his eyes as we spoke, sit silently, and then would summarize what he had heard. Inevitably, he grasped it in a way that went far beyond what we said, and pointed out the high standard to which we could be thinking though typically were not yet! He was a clear mirror, one that revealed depths that begged for exploration, and that showed us why stopping short, and being superficial, were simply inadequate.

Finally, there are many people who are uninterested in feeling or meaning—they just want to know what we are going to *do*. This Kantor calls the language of *power*. By *power* Kantor does not mean authority, he simply means the energy to get things done. A manager I know, a former navy commander, exemplifies the language of power. This man is utterly focused on action and on leadership—on being prepared to take responsibility to make things happen. There is always a sense when you describe things to him that he is asking the question "So what?" This comes across not as a put-down but as an urge to connect language to action.

He takes his responsibility very seriously. This for him trans-

lates as a requirement to confront people who are not, in his esti-
mation, doing their job. For instance, members of a senior management team will often speak privately about the difficulties they
have with their boss. This man will confront the boss, saying, are
you aware of this? What do you intend to do about it? In a firm
but kind way he indicates a complete unwillingness to tolerate
avoiding these issues. Consultants often take their future in their
hands when they confront their client. This man sees it as his job,
and believes that they should be equally forthright about confronting him about anything they see that they do not like.

People speak from these different "language domains" all
the time, depending on the circumstances, the people present,
and their internal makeup. The domains are not always used in
their "pure" form; one usually hears a mix, depending on the
situation. The point here is not to provide a universal system to
label one another but, rather, a means to transcend the differences in language in face-to-face dialogues.

These are in fact truly different languages: Communication
across them carries the same difficulties that translation between
any two languages carries. People speaking the language of feeling
tend to be discounted by people who speak the language of action
and power. Asking such people to reflect about the meaning of
things can often evoke the reaction that you are being too "intellectual." And asking questions about how to take action may feel
premature to those communicating via the language of feeling or
meaning.

What Language Are You Speaking?

Understanding which language you and others are speaking is
vital to engaging in genuine dialogue. The fragmentation of our
language is one of the most debilitating factors in an attempt to
conduct genuine dialogue. People who advocate "dialogue" typ-

ically tend to use the language of meaning or, at times, the language of feeling and the heart; this can evoke a strong negative reaction in people who see talk as a luxury, as a prelude but not a worthy substitute for action.

I recently heard a group of managers and corporate change consultants talking about how they reflect on what they do. One man urged people to think about the actions they hoped to take, the impediments that they saw, and the role they saw themselves playing in the process. A woman began to question his approach, saying she felt there was a completely different way to see things, one that took into account how people felt, what stories they told about their situation, what personal relevance it all had, and what impact it had on them. The man had used the language of power, of efficiency; the woman was listening and responding in the language of feeling.

Often these differences can produce significant communication breakdowns. Two people speaking different languages tend to hear the other as simply missing the essential point. Such breakdowns typically lead to an "advocacy war," where one person tries to convince the other of his way of seeing things. If you want to reach someone, you must learn to speak to her in a language she can understand, and listen to her in the language she is speaking.

These language differences show up at the organizational level as well. For instance, people in human resources often speak the languages of feeling or meaning—their preoccupation is with taking care of people. But the majority of the people to whom they report speak the language of power. The responsibilities of a line manager often come down to a "numbers" game—his organization must achieve financial goals that match shareholder expectations. The line manager of necessity is focused on action and power. People who speak to him in the language of feeling are often seen as "not getting it." In order to compensate, one sometimes sees HR managers adopting power language, often without the familiarity necessary to do so—and so losing credibility.

Breakdowns happen in many other ways too. Scientists and researchers often speak the language of meaning: They seek to understand underlying causes. Managers speak the language of power and want to get something done. But knowing that meaning is important to the researchers under them could help to bridge differences.

Fred Simon, a former senior line manager at Ford, made this shift in a dramatic way. Looking back on his experience with the MIT Organizational Learning Center, he said that he had been, in his own terms, very much a skeptic on "having a bunch of academics come in and mess around with his business." At the same time, he realized the significance of changing the way people behaved. Simon was the program manager of the team developing Lincoln Continentals at Ford, including a new model that was intended to be launched three and a half years into the future. The fear of making errors within Ford was such that engineers responsible for building the new car were unlikely to share news of problems that they had discovered in the new car design until they also had a solution. But their delays delayed others who depended on them as well, slowing down the entire development process. Within Ford any discussion of this was cast in the language of power—of getting things done as quickly as possible.

Simon gave his team leaders tools and an atmosphere in which it was possible to share *meaning*—to reflect on what was working and not working—without being punished. This enabled the competitive pressures across teams to diminish. People learned. And they found a way to detect and reduce errors much more quickly than before. As a result, they broke numerous records on their way to producing the new car. By learning together they produced prototypes on schedule, giving them enough time to test-drive the prototype and give engineers feedback on the final design—something that had never been done before.

Listen for the Language Differences

You can listen for Kantor's three languages to help shift the conversational ecology. Most conversations seem to use a dominant language. For instance, intense negotiations typically operate in the power domain. People are concerned with actions, results, and the moves of the other side. To gain leverage and open up new options, you can inquire into and explore the other two domains. How do people feel here? Has anyone asked them? In a management-union conflict, the union might fear being a victim of management's whims. This could easily lead them to oppose—despite what they think or say. They assume the situation is unfair and unbalanced. The question in their minds might be, Will this situation *ever* change? Moves by either party to recognize and respond to this could open new doors. You might ask yourself, for instance, What is the underlying meaning of this situation for me and others? What is the meaning of this conversation for you?

NEGOTIATING DIFFERENCE:
SYSTEM PARADIGMS

In June 1997, Robert McNamara, Secretary of Defense under Lyndon Johnson, led an important trip to Vietnam. Organized by James Blight of Brown University, McNamara's goal was to speak openly about and learn from the errors of the Vietnam War, perhaps to prevent future conflicts. McNamara had stated openly that he was increasingly convinced that the war—and the loss of life it entailed—was not necessary. In an interview, he said, "Human beings have to examine their failures. We've got to acquaint people with how dangerous it is for political leaders to behave the way we did."[5]

Attending with McNamara were military, diplomatic, and political leaders from both Vietnam and the United States who were involved in the conflict, as well as a group of historians from the United States. Their intention was to try to make sense of what they called the "missed opportunities" in the war. McNamara had already expressed his sense that the tragedy of this war was based on a set of mistaken assumptions and moves, and in the meeting he continued to reinforce these points. He was hopeful that the Vietnamese would also "come clean" about their thinking and admit their errors.

But it was not to be. The Americans left with the impression that they were more forthcoming in admitting their errors than the Vietnamese. The Vietnamese did not respond to specific requests about what they had done wrong. At the end of the event in a press conference, the leader of the Vietnamese delegation said, speaking of the war: "The opportunities were missed by the United States side, not by the Vietnamese side." In reflecting on the gathering, it was evident that both sides did not fully see how to take advantage of the situation.

From a perspective like David Kantor's, however, what becomes clear is that these two peoples were living out of two very different kinds of mind-sets, and that this was at least partially responsible for the breakdowns, both historically and in this meeting. The Americans wanted an "open" exchange that took individual responsibility and culpability seriously, that reflected together about what had happened. The Vietnamese took a more "closed" approach, wanting everyone to understand not individual actions but a long-standing history and context, the traditional sources of decisions, the pattern of events, and the lines of authority that led to those decisions and events. These two structures—the open paradigm and the closed paradigm—are present in many different settings. People who use one paradigm often fail to talk well to people using the other. Seeing how they work can be illuminating.

The Americans had wanted the meeting to focus on the period of McNamara's term—1961 to 1968. The Americans wanted to talk about the events at the time, and about the decisions that might have gone differently—decisions that were in the hands of individual leaders and policy makers. The Vietnamese disagreed. They wanted to reach back to 1945 and before, to display their understanding of how their five hundred-year-old effort to achieve and sustain independence was not supported by a country that they believed would be most likely to do so—America. The Vietnamese wanted, and I suspect still want, Americans to understand the extreme betrayal they felt by a country that should have supported them but chose instead to prosecute a vicious war against them. The Americans wanted absolution and a chance to learn.

There were other differences. The Americans wanted to share information quite openly. Bolstered in part by the opening of previously closed archives in the former Soviet Union, they hoped that a similar degree of disclosure would occur in Vietnam. They provided volumes of data. But the Vietnamese delayed and then proved unwilling to fulfill agreements made in advance of the meeting about sharing archival information about policy making at the time of the war, and about having CNN broadcast the event. They were uncertain about the value of opening the proceeding as widely in the media as the Americans seemed keen to do.

People's actions followed their framework. The Vietnamese received the Americans' requests by withdrawing, by becoming "stone statues" one American participant described them. This led to increasing doubts on the part of the Americans about the willingness of the Vietnamese to be open *as they defined openness,* and so they pushed harder to get them to open up. This self-reinforcing cycle was in part driven by a different sense of what counted as openness. For the Americans, such openness was about honesty, confession, and learning; for the Vietnamese, "openness" meant moving forward, consolidating, and clarifying public images of themselves and their intentions with past transgressions—and creating a platform for future interactions.

Open, Closed, and Random System Paradigms

The contrasting approaches here represent two of what Kantor defines as a set of three different "system paradigms" that exist both in families and larger social organizations.[6] These paradigms are really different ways of setting boundaries, governing, and organizing power and decision making. It is vital to stress that in this model, *each* of these has value and is "good," and each has limits to its effectiveness.

The Americans who went to Vietnam expected an open-systems approach to the meeting; an open-system values communication. An open system's work gets done, in fact, through open deliberation and exploration of each individual's needs. Its ambition is to balance the good of the individual with the good of the whole. The expectation of an open-system approach is that it shall respect the individuals and the challenges they face, and from that sense of participation grow a sense of responsibility. Community grows out of this deliberative respect for the individual.

In theory (if not in reality) a deliberative body like the United States Senate is an open system: It seeks to resolve differences through a process of open exchange. Perhaps the most striking open system recently is the Internet. So far at least, the inability to control the Internet by any single node or perspective has made it a unique open system.

Open systems value learning and adaptation through participation. The ideas about learning organizations developed by Peter Senge and others are a good example of an open-system approach. The vast majority of "new thinking" in the management world advocates an open-system approach. But while they advocate one thing, they often do another. Most such systems retain a firm closed-system underside, to the dismay of their employees. This leads employees to speak disparagingly about the "program of the month," and take a "this too shall pass" attitude toward management innovations that proclaim an open-system value set.

The Vietnamese, in contrast, have a very different cultural paradigm. They preferred—in this meeting at least—what Kantor calls a closed-system paradigm. Closed systems value tradition. They place community and history first and the individual second. A closed system regulates the life of its members, particularly the time and space within which people work. A closed system values and respects the network or fabric of relationships within which people operate. It takes as its relevant measure the whole stretch of times, not just a single incident.

The Vietnamese, in this paradigm, needed to remain loyal to their legacy and their history and wished that others would understand this and be open to considering this. Their history was particularly complex. It carried several very different forces within it: the communal and collective habit of the Asian culture, the pressure from the hierarchical, culture of communism, and the effort to attain freedom in the face of a long line of invaders and oppressors. "Our habit is to keep secrets in order to defend ourselves," said Vietnamese organizer Nguyen Co Thach.

The closed-system paradigm tends to refine and defends the historical legacy. American-style candor, on the other hand, takes the view that there are important leverage points in an individual's or an institution's actions. To the Vietnamese, this misread and misunderstood the larger context. And what is worse, confronting an individual's behavior directly can often seem just too frank and insulting for an Asian culture closely manages face-to-face relationships and that places family and traditional associations above the individual. It is important to see that this does not mean they were unwilling to talk; rather, they needed to retain their way of approaching the problem. When it began to seem that their approach would not be understood, this was likely seen as further evidence of the gap that led to the conflict in the first place.

A closed system also respects position and place, and expect others to do the same. The military is organized around this notion, though in recent years some branches of the United States military has begun to experiment with other approaches. To some degree, every organization is a closed system in this sense. Closed systems have what might be called a "positive" view of freedom. They propose a way of seeing the world that they deem to be the "right" and valid way. From this follows the expectation that everyone will be a constructive part of an overall single endeavor. In many closed families, one finds "locked doors, careful scrutiny of strangers in the neighborhood, parental control over the media, supervised excursions, and unlisted telephone numbers."

One sees this in many corporations too. For example, one institution I know of has a practice of circulating to all three hundred of its headquarters employees a list each week of the travel and attendance schedule of every senior officer of the foundation. They strive to know where everyone is at all times. This is a closed-system approach because it seeks to fit each person within a particular context of time and place and, by implication, with the work of the organization. Space, time, and energy are all regulated.

There is also a third paradigm, what Kantor calls a *random* system. The music of jazz musicians is a wonderful example of a system that is "random," by which Kantor means simply that exploration is done by improvisation. I have a colleague who operates in a random fashion quite often; it is perhaps this element of his character—the expression of his creative energies—that is such a source of consternation to his associates. He is ready to "seize the day" at all times. He will make agreements in one set of circumstances, only to find later that there are new factors that he had not anticipated and so change his prior agreements. Sometimes he operates within a very precise and controlled parameter, in a closed-system mode. At other times he will be very open and collaborative, expecting to encounter differences and conflicts, and determined to learn from them. One cannot predict how he will act on any one day!

I have another friend who is both well known and enormously creative, but whose house looks as if a tornado has struck it. Moreover, his house reflects his internal state—a blinding swirl of things piled everywhere. He does not seem to care; in fact he revels in this apparent chaos. His house is a very rich place, full of artifacts from travels, books half written, gifts, objects of all kinds. There is no apparent order here—to mortal minds anyway—though it is clear that this kind of creative space enables him to flourish and create without feeling the press of formal and conventional ways of doing things.

In a random system, individuals determine their own definitions of space and time. In short, as Kantor puts it, one is encouraged and permitted "to do your own thing." A person operating in a random system lives out of the present moment, emerging creatively from it.

The term *random* may sound pejorative. To some people it seems disordered, chaotic, unfriendly perhaps—again, depending on the type of system one prefers. It is important to understand that the term *random* system, particularly as it applies to social systems, does not mean it *lacks* order. In *Science, Order, and Creativity,* David Bohm and David Peat suggest that a "random order," however chaotic, is in fact a special kind of order, one that draws from a larger context; it is what they call orders of an "infinite degree":

> This may appear to be a curious step to take, since chance and randomness are generally thought of as being equal to total disorder (the absence of any order at all). . . . But here is it proposed that whatever happens must take place in some order so that the notion of a "total lack of order" has no real meaning.

A random-system paradigm is one in which people are in one way or another attuned to "orders of infinite degree": they listen for possibilities that go beyond finite systems and bring back things that enrich the rest of us.

Random systems are characteristics of any fiercely individualistic culture. Academic institutions—indeed, most professional organizations—are notoriously difficult to manage for this very reason. A layer of closed-system administration is typically greatly resisted by random or open-system thinkers, for instance. People become academics in large part because of their individualism, and the independence they can achieve from hierarchical organizations.

All three paradigms offer powerful and useful ways of functioning, and all three have a "shadow" side, a dark side, as well. With any situation, people and organizations tend to prefer one of these paradigms over the others. The challenge in a dialogue is to create a setting in which *all three can begin to talk together* in a fashion that is respectful, that sees the limits of the others' approach, and yet does not condemn it for its limits. Dialogue searches for a language of inquiry that includes and transcends differences such as ones I will explore here. At the same time, understanding the underside of each of these paradigms as well as its gifts is vital if we are to meet one another on equal ground.

FLAWS AND LIMITS IN OPEN, CLOSED, AND RANDOM SYSTEMS

Closed Systems

The flaws in a closed-system structure have to do with the ways it creates errors, the impasses it can reach, and the form of tyranny it can take. One typical error of a closed system is that it seals itself off from the external world—it becomes a system of "insular purity."[7] This impasse in the extreme can encourage it to remain the same at all costs, becoming isolated; people in such settings tend to feel stifled. The closed system's form of tyranny is repression. These systems limit the differentiation of their members, and people in authority in closed systems acquire unchallengeable control.

One major corporation that I recently studied illustrates the limitations that can arise from this approach. The company was controlled by a single, extremely bright, autocratic leader. All major decisions in the organization flowed through him. Nothing of any consequence could be done without his knowing about it. Among many other things, he was the R&D department, the resource allocation committee, the reward and compensation committee.

In a small organization this can be workable. In this organization, however, which had over twenty thousand employees and grossed more than $8 billion per year, the situation was not tenable. In his organization he was always right. The majority of the senior people in the organization took the view that any new idea or proposal he did not agree with was wrong, and that perspective rippled down through the rest of the company. "You would get yelled at," said one manager we spoke to. "You would get whacked," said another. This became a kind of operating mentality within this company, to the point where product development teams would constantly ask, "Have you shown it to him yet?" This would systematically keep him from seeing things until the very last minute. The impact this CEO had on the other senior leaders of the organization was nothing short of devastating.

This was a closed system gone terribly wrong, and such examples lead many people to reject these systems out of hand. The central limiting factor of a closed system is that it tends to be blind to and unable to move with emergent possibilities. Its values are embedded in the well-established traditions of the past; in a pinch, it is to these values that the organization remains loyal rather than new options.

OVERVIEW OF CLOSED SYSTEMS

Core Purpose: Stability through tradition and lineage

Characteristics: Hierarchy, formal authority, "control over"

Leadership: Manages for the good of the whole

Limits: Tyranny of tradition, blindness to emergent change

Open Systems

The fundamental limits to an open system are the result of confusion over boundaries: There is disconnection and division as outsiders become privy to internal processes. People are forced to extremes. The core limit of an open system is the "tyranny of process." Meetings and decision making can go on endlessly, with no one ever deciding anything for fear of excluding someone.

One environmental organization I worked with felt it vital that they make decisions in an open fashion. But since there were many differences among them, openness became a kind of endless pursuit of everyone's issues. They lacked an ability to differentiate among types or strategies of openness.

This was a group deeply committed to having what they termed a "fair" model of decision making, by which they meant open. They had initially run their organization by insisting that every individual, regardless of seniority, would have an equal say in all policy decisions. This broke down quickly as it became evident that some people had no understanding of the purpose of the organization. They gradually moved to a representative system, where employees voted for a council that then governed the organization. Then they hired a COO, who was responsible for keeping order in an otherwise unruly (in their terms) system. They are, as a group, still wrestling with the optimum form of governance but aspire to finding a way to make an open model work.

An open system, ironically enough, can be a very poor climate for ideas. At its worst it includes too much, and so is afraid to cut out or seriously explore options not based on facts, or that lack rigorous thought. The open system is openly tolerant, in other words, of all points of view. At the extreme this is incoherent, since it leads such systems to be tolerant of people who are intolerant, and who would destroy it.

OVERVIEW OF OPEN SYSTEMS
Core Purpose: Learning through participation

Characteristics: Democracy, pluralism, collaboration

Leadership: Balance the good of the whole with the good of the individual

Limits: Tyranny of the process

Random Systems

The flaw of random systems is that they can decay into anarchy. In such a system nothing is allowed to remain constant, and individuals become the primary focus of the system. This can produce fragmentation. Kantor writes:

> Life becomes careless, scattered, and incomplete. Members fail to attain satisfactory relationships. The people and their movements neither mesh nor serve as counterpoints to one another. Instead, other members are experienced as totally independent entities, making no vital connection with one another, each getting in the other's way.[8]

These features were characteristic, for instance, of Apple Computer. Apple was full of enormously creative people who were actively pursuing their particular agenda. There was very little focus, and as a result very little capacity to make choices and so stay competitive. These same characteristics produced some spectacular successes: initial enormous growth, leading-edge technology and design, and many wonderful new ways of both running a company and bringing a product to market. At the same time, it also produced many unhappy people, from customers to developers to suppliers, who experienced a constant sense of shifting sands, of things never quite stabilizing. Another interesting flaw in a random system is that it tends to swing toward a closed paradigm. Lurking beneath many seemingly random, creative individuals is a highly closed system person. For instance, there were ways in which Apple operated as a closed system. Most notoriously, Apple kept its operating system proprietary for many years, refusing to let others copy it or use it. Many have argued that this closed architecture approach greatly limited Apple's ability to expand, and may have been the decisive factor in making it only a niche player in comparison to Microsoft.

OVERVIEW OF RANDOM SYSTEMS

Core Purpose: Exploration through improvisation

Characteristics: Creativity not constrained by formal structures

Leadership: Rapid innovation

Limits: Tyranny of anarchy

CHANGING THE STRUCTURES IN DIALOGUE

The steelworkers' union-management dialogues outlined earlier are a good example of how these system paradigms interact in complex ways, and how this way of thinking can suggest alternative kinds of actions.

Management claimed to be willing to participate in a dialogue—which they understood to mean talking openly about their differences, the culture and the problems they needed to solve. But they thought that the union would not be as open; their culture was more closed to outside influences, controlling through tradition and hierarchy—in other words, a closed system. Despite the union's claims to support democratic principles, management believed that the union would be unwilling or unable to reason openly about the economic difficulties the business faced. Management feared that any conversation of this sort would just be seen as subterfuge to get the union to agree to more concessions. The union, on the other hand, had a symmetrical belief: They saw management as closed, hierarchical, and unwilling to reason openly about their underlying assumptions, need for control, and beliefs about "steelworkers." The greatest difficulties in communication, they felt, were not between management and union but between senior management and middle management, where direct hierarchical authority by one group over the other had led to a great measure of mistrust.

Both management and union believed themselves to be open and so agreed to a dialogue, which seemed to hold the promise of openness. But under stress, particularly at first, both tended to be insular, unwilling to remain reflective or suspend their beliefs. Part of the challenge in this setting was helping each side to see how the other heard them, and how inconsistent their beliefs about themselves were with how they presented themselves. The gap between the openness they professed and the closedness they practiced created a set of dilemmas that, once discussible, began to be resolved.

Dialogue Is Not Only an Open System

At first glance, the work of dialogue seems to promote a dominantly open-system approach. Dialogue usually includes some form of open exchange among people. Many writers and practitioners portray dialogue as a form of people speaking openly together. This framing tends to alienate people who enter systems inclined toward either a closed or random approach. Many managers, for instance, use a closed approach, and therefore find dialogue to be "too soft," not something that practical people will find compelling. Yet dialogue's potential and aim, I would suggest, is to help create a climate of inquiry among all these elements. All of them are present as ideals and ambitions in most systems. Discovering ways to enable people from different systems to inquire together would allow a new form of interaction that would not be limited to or constrained by any of them.

It is possible to combine the different languages of communication and system paradigms to provide a much richer picture of the ways people can interact. For instance, the Vietnamese were closed in meaning; they had a view of history that they felt was important to acknowledge. The Americans were open in meaning; they wanted to share responsibility and accountability and were tolerant of multiple perspectives, curious to bring out differences. The Americans, notably McNamara, were open in feeling—McNamara expressed his regret and feelings about the war very directly. The Vietnamese were closed in feeling: "stone statues." The Americans were open in power, wanting to share responsibility for organizing and arranging the meeting. The Vietnamese were closed in power, resisting input and wanting to hold to a particular way of operating.

Understanding these differences and, most important, not trying to change the other's structures might have allowed a different way of thinking. The Americans, for instance, might have said to the Vietnamese, "Tell us more about your history and how it has affected you. Help inform us of the ways you believe we are likely to misunderstand the significance of its impact."

It is also true that this might not have created an opening. People can continue to choose not to participate, especially if they feel deeply mistrustful of the other. But it is possible to come to at least understand the sources of the mistrust, and the degree to which they are structurally determined. It makes very little sense to encourage a closed-system manager, for example, to adopt wholeheartedly an open-system approach. He or she is likely to see it as too open, lacking control, lacking clear lines of accountability. But the person's paradigm can be respected and understood, and this can enable a very different way of thinking together.

The value of this structural language is that it can enable us to recognize the way someone is operating and appreciate the worldview that it stems from rather than trying to make someone conform to our way of thinking. In a given impasse, ask yourself, Am I open in meaning? Is the person I am speaking with? Or is he closed? How does my way of working in power mesh with his? How important is affect to each of us?

Each approach has strengths and blind spots. Ultimately, dialogue can open the door for a rare kind of inquiry, one that enables all three ways of operating to be present together, and to learn from each other. By giving names to the other approaches, it is possible to transcend the tendency toward ignoring or discrediting them. That way, when the stakes go up, people won't simply feel they have been misunderstood.

APPLYING PREDICTIVE INTUITION

Mapping Systems

Developing predictive intuition means creating ways to understand and anticipate the situation you face, and the likely ways the human beings involved will react. To bring about dialogue, we must recognize the location and sources of breakdowns that would prevent dialogue. These breakdowns often arise over differences in the languages people speak, the system paradigms they prefer, and the unintended impacts of the actions they take. These breakdowns will also tend to occur at key interfaces in the system, that is, in places where people who need one another to act must interact, and where they are not always in complete agreement.

One of the most potent ways to refine your predictive intuition is to make a map of the system that you are seeing. A "map" in this sense is an external representation, usually in words or pictures or both, of the issues people face. One creates a map of a system in order to raise awareness of the underlying structures in memory that guide the behavior of a group or system, and the self-defeating actions that flow from these structures. Maps like these can take a number of different formats. They can be built from preexisting frameworks or invented online in the moment.

In the Grand Junction dialogues we ran, for instance, one of our early steps involved helping people to reflect on what had been happening in their community for the past few years. I did this by creating jointly with them a map of their system that began by outlining some of the dilemmas they faced—for example, the desire to support alternative forms of medical treatment, and their fear that doing so would invoke scorn and loss of credibility. It became clear that this in turn could have serious economic consequences; the hospitals needed to contain costs, on the one hand, and yet provide care to everyone who needed it, on the other. The group gradually added other features of the story—including strategies for how they coped with these problems and assumptions that underlay what they were doing—all of which they surfaced and mapped out with remarkable good humor. Coping strategies they listed included everything from rationalizing that the system is not so bad to changing job titles (and so avoiding issues) to blaming the person they worked for.

This particular map was a simple feedback system: It showed people the ways by which their behavior had produced the very results that they did not like or want. And yet they saw that they were the ones taking action: There was no one else to blame. They suspended their tendency to blame others, instead taking responsibility for their actions.

Look for the Parallels

A second kind of map, and way of exercising predictive intuition, is to learn to reflect on-line, in the moment, about what is happening in a conversation. This is especially important in dialogue, because a dialogue group is a mirror of the people who participate in it. Whatever the content of a conversation, people will tend to mirror it in the way they talk. The challenge in a dialogue is to learn to suspend what is happening so that we can see this mirroring structure at work.

In one dialogue we held, a group of managers began talking about the "bad" culture in their company, about how hierarchical it was, how it excluded people, how focused it was on power, on what was "right" and "wrong." People traced their difficulties to others who were not present in their dialogue session. But they were condemning others in much the same way they claimed the culture condemned them and made life hard for them, without realizing they were doing so. The hierarchical, right/wrong culture was being vividly displayed in that room, though the people were all speaking about other situations, elsewhere.

When we mapped and then explored this contradiction in the dialogue, people were shocked to see their own behavior, and felt that there was a vital though enormously challenging hurdle to climb to begin to understand how this worked.

Developing predictive intuition, we can begin to perceive how the structures of our interactions guide behavior. As we learn to see these structures, we can greatly increase the likelihood and quality of dialogue.

A R C H I T E C T U R E

O F   T H E   I N V I S I B L E

If you walk into Chartres Cathedral in France, you are immediately struck by the beauty and quiet of the place. Alive and sacred, it makes you feel dwarfed in its immensity. Chartres has a sense of wholeness to it, though you may be hard pressed to say exactly why. In part this is because there are centers of focus in this building—not just one, but many throughout the building—which draw your attention and energy, make you feel comfortable and at home, give you a sense of the ground beneath your feet. Even with the various foci, there is an overall sense of cohesion to the setting.

The same feeling may be evoked when you talk with a close and truly supportive friend about something that matters to you both. You may find yourself taking a deep breath, relaxing, feeling gratitude. You gain perspective, a new outlook, a fresh start. Things come clear in this kind of exchange—precisely because there is now a central element to the conversation—your common interests and concerns.

By contrast, think about what it is like to walk into a meeting where people have just broken off an argument. You may be struck by the tension in the room. Most people naturally contract, withdraw, protect themselves. The feeling is more one of fragmentation than unification. This is a conversation without a center.

In each case, the feelings give you a sense of a distinct "atmosphere"—a quality that is discernible, though not always glaringly obvious. It is the difference between a romantic dinner conversation and a chat on a subway platform just as a train comes screaming into the station. This difference is based partly on the nature of the physical arrangement of things, and includes the noise level, the smells, the sense of space.

The underlying feeling you experience relates to more than just physical arrangement or even the associations you bring to each setting. It is a function of the quality of energy, experience, and *aliveness* that each setting gives rise to. It is determined, in each case, by a very precise set of conditions. This is no abstract notion. These feelings are real, and are consistently experienced by wide numbers of people. In other words, while we may have our own visceral sense about a place, it is possible to validate our perception with others who are there.

Each of these settings evokes a different quality of what I shall call a "field of conversation." In physics, a field, is "any system of variables that vary in some systematic fashion through space."[1] For instance, iron filings line up around a magnetic field, distributed in a systematic fashion around the poles of a magnet. It is these overall spatial patterns of concentrated energy that allow different kinds of patterns to appear.

CONVERSATIONAL FIELDS

Conversations have fields too. A field of conversation is made up of the atmosphere, energy, and memories of the people who are interacting. When you talk and interact with people, much of your experience is at first colored in fact by your memory of them, of people like them, of circumstances and feelings that we have had previously. These memories provide a base of experience from which to think and talk. Embedded in these memories are energy and feelings as well as prejudices and blindnesses.

Think of a person with whom you are presently having difficulty. If you were suddenly to come upon her unannounced, you would no doubt fairly quickly recall all the thoughts you have about her, and all the negative feelings you have been harboring. The encounter might be tense. The "field," or space between you, would be filled with the history of your reactions. Words that you each might speak would come, initially at least, from this atmosphere. Fields like these are powerful, because the memories have an emotional charge to them and tend to work quickly, seamlessly, automatically. They create an atmosphere in which it is hard to change.

Yet being aware of fields of conversation gives us some ability to influence things beyond what we normally can do. We can be very deliberate about creating settings that alter the "field" in which the conversation takes place. We can begin by becoming conscious of the "field" we have within ourselves—the qualities of character and energy that are within us. We can then evoke new qualities from others, just as the facilitator in Chechnya did by telling the story about his mother. It may even become possible to realize that these fields change in character over time, and that mapping the qualities of fields can help our practical efforts.

Physicist David Bohm once compared conversations to the field behavior of a superconductor. In a superconductor, electrons moving through a wire are cooled to the point where they no longer collide or create heat through resistance. Instead, after reaching an optimally low temperature, they begin to act like parts of a coherent whole, moving around obstacles like ballet dancers on a stage. Under these conditions the electrons flow with virtually no friction. They have both high intensity and high "intelligence" as they naturally align themselves with an invisible pattern. Similarly, when we are in dialogue and are thinking together in a coordinated fashion, we are like the cool intensity of these fields of electrons. Rather than seeing our conversations as the crashing and careening of billiard balls, individuals may come to see and feel them as *fields* in which a sense of wholeness can appear, intensify, and diminish in intensity again.[2]

The idea that social "fields" are an important determinant in the quality of our thinking, acting, and conversation represents an important evolutionary step in how human beings think about society and organizations. It is as important as the earlier shift in the 1940s, with the movement from a linear to a systems view of the world. The explosion of systems thinking in almost every subject of human endeavor is enormously powerful.[3]

The work that my colleagues and I have been doing over the past fifteen years with dialogue, in social and organizational settings, suggests that there is another important change in the offing, from systems thinking to *field-based* thinking. In a way this is a return, from a different vantage point, of a much older tradition in social science started by Kurt Lewin. Lewin was a psychologist who saw "fields" as a kind of life space made up of the forces acting on a person. He conducted very rigorous analyses of this, using complex mathematics, though his attempts were not widely followed.[4]

The concept of fields in dialogue is somewhat different from the way Lewin described them. He was concerned with the field of the events, feelings, and thoughts that an individual builds around him or herself during a lifetime. But in dialogue we look at the dynamic fields that arise in each moment, continually shifting, among groups of people and large organizations. Where a system is a set of inter-related and interdependent elements, a field of conversation derives from the ideas, thoughts, and quality of attention of the people involved here and now. It includes not only the interpersonal forces but the force of the ideas at work. The ideas and memory patterns they evoke carry energy and atmosphere, and are charged, to the point where people form elaborate neuropsychological internal reactions to them. For instance, a conversation between two baseball fans can evoke in each a whole host of memories, associations, physical sensations, emotional reactions, and sense of belonging with one another. The body, mind, and emotions are all involved. The "field" they create by sharing memories predisposes the way they see each other. Similarly, when it comes to making change in businesses or organizations, creating evocative fields can provide important leverage points for change.

For example, several people I worked with were recently trying to reform California's health and safety education program for children. They lamented the excessive competition they saw between state agencies and social service nonprofit organizations. Everyone claimed to care about the children, they noted, but the groups viciously fought one another for funding and recognition. Traditional efforts to change this ongoing, self-perpetuating mess had failed.

As we spoke together, it became apparent that there was an underlying, hidden set of factors at play. The protagonists began to realize that an atmosphere of isolation prevailed in themselves, in government agencies, and in those running the social programs. Isolation led to mistrust, which in turn reinforced the structure of "independent agendas" and competition. The atmosphere of isolation and loneliness influenced people's thinking and actions, though they had not initially realized it. Seeing this, they realized they had many new opportunities for addressing the problems between these agencies, but only if they could change the discourse now, staying conscious of their own tendencies for isolation, and the ways they reinforced this in others.[5]

My colleagues and I have explored the nature of these fields as they form within individuals, groups, and larger social settings like organizations and communities in depth. I think we are just now on the cutting edge of this subject. We have found that people who wish to innovate or develop new knowledge, who seek effective strategic choice making or who are engaged in organizational learning efforts, must come to see their work as functions of the quality of these fields rather than as the product of individual action or willpower alone. In fact, we have found that *without* an awareness of fields and their qualities, most such efforts unwittingly create resistance and cause unintended consequences that may be greater than the problems they set out to solve.

In the course of this part of the book I describe our discoveries, so far, about the underlying architecture of these fields: the ways they form, differentiate, collapse, and emerge; the principles that govern them and methods to manage within them. We have developed practices that you can use to develop a field that will tend to produce dialogue as well as make you aware of those that tend to inhibit or destroy it. I also suggest an approach to change that links the individual, the group, or team and the larger system, and shows how we might begin to develop a coherent approach to learning that pervades each level. Thinking this way points to an entirely new kind of leadership—one that is based on the capacity to evoke, hold, and embody such fields. This means developing in-depth knowledge of the ways that fields engender behavior, both in day-to-day life and in the emotionally high-stakes and high-stress episodes that occur from time to time in every business.

T E N

Setting

the Container

In the summer of 1993 five thousand people from nearly every religious tradition in the world met in Chicago for a gathering held only once each century—the Parliament of World Religions. Turbans and crosses, feathers and flowing robes, naked chests, conservative suits, and blue jeans all mingled together under one roof. One of the key meetings within this conference consisted of a group of 250 leaders from the various religions around the world. According to one of my colleagues, when these leaders sat together in silence, their dignity and stature seemed immense. They displayed a level of respect for one another that was consistent with the aims of the gathering.

They lived up to the behavior that we might expect from our religious leaders. "They did silence well," noted my colleague.

This was particularly evident in a brief ritual that occurred between one of the Native American elders and the Dalai Lama. Early in the conference, this Native American elder, who was in a wheelchair, was quietly moved over to be near the chair of the Dalai Lama. This created something of a stir. It was unplanned and unexpected; it broke the flow of the carefully orchestrated event. From within his coat, the Native American elder slowly removed a long peace pipe. He lit it, took a puff, and then passed it to the Dalai Lama. The No Smoking signs in this Chicago meeting hall glared down at them. People who were there said the room shimmered as these two leaders sat together. All eyes were fixed upon them. The Dalai Lama took a puff from the pipe, and gently passed it back to the elder. All were aware that they were witnessing an "unofficial" but significant moment; it was suddenly clear that the Native Americans were the authentic hosts of the event. They had once lived on the very spot where the conference hall was erected. The majestic silence of the ceremony reminded everyone in the room of their stature and understanding, and of their ability to convey an enormous amount of energy and intensity in a few simple gestures. What is striking about this incident is its genuineness. There was no pretense, just a quiet, respectful exchange between two revered elders.

This quality of authenticity is at the core of the dialogic state. But it presents a challenge. It cannot be faked; such exchanges must be genuine. One can try them on, experiment with them. But gaining genuine understanding requires work. Alexis de Toqueville, the great chronicler of American culture and life, once gave a very pointed description of the work required:

A great man has said that *ignorance lies at both ends of knowledge.* Perhaps it would have been truer to say that deep conviction lies at both ends, with doubt in the middle. In fact, one can distinguish three distinct and often successive stages of human understanding. A man may hold a firm belief which he has adopted without plumbing it. He doubts when objections strike him. Often he succeeds in resolving those doubts, and then he again begins to believe. This time he does not grasp the truth as if by chance or in the dark, but sees it face-to-face and is guided forwards by its light. . . . One may count on it that the majority of mankind will always stop short in one of [the first two] conditions: they will either believe without knowing or will not know precisely what to believe. But only a few persevering people will ever attain to that deliberate and self-justified type of conviction born of knowledge and springing up in the very midst of doubt [italics in original].[1]

Doubt and confusion are the flaming swords at the gate of true understanding. It would be far easier if there were a less intense route! As far as I know, there is not. But the opportunity lies in choosing not to be discouraged by this but to trust it. I am less sanguine than de Toqueville about people's abilities to come to genuine understanding. I find the willingness to go into the unknown is made easier when one realizes that it is the same as trusting oneself. "Trust thyself," Emerson once put it; "Every heart vibrates to that iron string."

A mechanistic way of seeing would lead us astray here. A set of "practices" for dialogue could begin to sound a lot like a set of simple rules. It is this very way of thinking *itself* that I am asking you to reconsider.

FOUR PRACTICES AND CREATING
THE CONTAINER

As I have intimated, perhaps one of the most important dimensions of dialogue concerns the atmosphere, or "field," in which it occurs. A field is the quality of shared meaning and energy that can emerge among a group of people.

We cannot manufacture a "field." But we can create conditions under which a rich field for interaction is more likely to appear. These conditions make up what we have called the *container* for dialogue, in which deep and transformative listening becomes possible. You cannot work "on" a field. But you can create a "container."

A "container" is a vessel, a setting in which the intensities of human activity can safely emerge. The active experience of people listening, respecting one another, suspending their judgments, and speaking their own voice are four key aspects of the container for dialogue. As I noted in the first chapter, often the missing ingredient for those who try to listen to one another is not just their individual effort, but a setting where it is possible to hear one another and speak safely together.

When I first introduced to the steelworkers the idea of a container, they understood it immediately. In fact, they coined a term for it—they called it a "cauldron." A steel mill has built into it a very graphic illustration of a container: enormous vats of 3,000-degree, white-hot molten steel in a room the size of two football fields, over 100 feet high.

The image of the container is very old. One finds references to it in the Kabbalah, the Jewish mystical texts; in the writings of the alchemists; and in modern times in some of the work of psychologists looking to create what they call a "holding space" for the emotional intensity of a family.[2]

The Holy Grail, the image from the myth of King Arthur, was

supposedly the chalice that was used by Jesus at the Last Supper. The word *grail* comes from the French *graille,* which means "great container." The *graille* was a common soup container. The word also has the same root as *corral*—a round, containing enclosure—and also *kraal*—a Zulu word meaning "an enclosure of huts and cattle." According to Laurens van der Post, a novelist and unique elder to this age, these roots reveal the magic of this term and the universal quest behind it. The container is

> round, forming the circle which has always been magical and an enclosure of life, sacred because it is an image of wholeness, something which contains all. . . . This is more evidence that the search for a divine container, to be divinely contained, is African as well. It is most moving that even the words show how unending and universal is the quest for spirit to be contained in wholeness. . . . When a Zulu in time becomes wise and resolved so that he becomes an *Induma*—a headman and advisor to the King—he wears a circle of metal or ivory around his head to indicate he is whole.[3]

The container is the circle that holds all, that is a symbol of wholeness, and a setting in which creative transformation can take place.[4]

The idea behind a container is that human beings need a setting in which to hold the intensities of their lives. Typically, we do not have many of these. The people around us react to us, but they cannot hold us, nor we them. Circumstances often seem larger than we are.

Containers take many forms. Our bodies are containers: They hold ourselves. Intimate relationships are another kind of container, settings in which certain things can be said and done that cannot happen anywhere else. Our teams are containers, as are our organizations. Typically, our containers are incoherent—they hold inner contradictions and inconsistencies, and they are limited in what they can hold. When our "container" is full, we get "filled up"—unable to hear or absorb more.

Dialogue sets out to clarify and expand the container in which a conversation might take place. The premise I work with is "no container, no dialogue." More precisely, no consciously held container, no dialogue. As I will show, the container can evolve and deepen over time. Containers for conversation hold a particular kind of pressure. As they become more stable and conscious, they can hold more pressure. It seems to take a certain amount of pressure for human beings to think together. As people come together and bring their differences out, the pressure builds. Then the question arises, Is there a container to hold this pressure? If not, people will tend to try to avoid issues, blame one another, resist what is happening. It is possible to create containers that can hold the fire of creation. When this is the case, those within the container do not have the feeling that they will get "burned" or that things are "too hot." They may feel stretched, but included and safe.

The container concept provides people with a measure of psychological safety. But there is more to dialogue than psychological safety. Author Joseph Chilton Pearce, writing about childhood development, notes that the matrix of successful development for a child—initially the womb, later the enfoldment of the parents—has three elements: energy, possibility, and safety. All three of these are needed for growth to take place. Chilton Pearce's matrix is a similar concept to the container; and all three elements are needed.[5] In any setting, particularly one where you are about to have an important conversation, you might ask yourself: Is there energy, possibility, and safety here? If the answer is no, I believe you can predict before a single word is spoken that the results you obtain will be limited.

The concept of the container, and more important the experience of it, enabled the steelworkers to talk together in ways they had not done before. For example, a container was forged in the very first session I arranged to bring steelworkers and managers together. Here is what the union president had to say of it:

> The container was stretched to the max that day because it was being bent, popped, cracked, and when it was over that night, I was so tired I just went to my room and went to bed. The next morning when we all met, the container had strengthened itself. We had a bond in that room that we didn't really realize that we had.

The union president continued:

> The day that it was over, some of us rode back to the city together and we talked about that and we said, "Isn't that incredible? We sat down and no one got mad and left." No one from the management was screaming and no one from the union was screaming. We were men and we talked about it.

This container enabled conversations to happen that simply had not taken place before. But the goal was not to feel good together. It was a setting that enabled a search for truth.

Having a "container" in the steelworker dialogues meant that the people involved participated in creating and sustaining it continuously. This came through very clearly after several of the steelworkers had a chance to present some of their experience at the management conference mentioned above. It was a source of considerable amusement and puzzlement to them. They were surprised to find that they had developed an understanding of dialogue that others, like these managers, did not seem to have, and they pointed out something that resonated deeply with the consultants and corporate people in the room:

> The difference between all of the programs that we had—and they were numerous—and this one was that we didn't "buy into" this program, we were there at the ground floor and we helped to build what we call a "container" together.

For this steelworker and the others, there was a vital difference here: They understood through experience that they had a very direct responsibility for what was happening in the dialogue, that no one had imposed it on them, that it had developed through and from them.

THE ACOUSTICS OF DIALOGUE

I have been in some hotel conference rooms lately that have horrible acoustics. These are places that were supposedly designed to hold large group meetings. But I simply couldn't hear people unless they stood up and fairly shouted across the room. And there are some concert halls, in contrast, where you can hear the proverbial pin drop. Some settings are made for listening and speaking together, and others are not. Designing rooms or settings where human beings can talk together comfortably seems to be something of a lost art. But it was not always so.

In 1780, Benjamin Franklin and a group of the Founding Fathers commissioned the Congress Hall in Philadelphia as the place where the first United States Congress would meet.[6] The Congress Hall is a vast room with high ceilings. Its windows are placed at the very top to limit distractions from the outside. It is full of light. The seats are arranged in a semicircle, in such a way that every member of the group can see everyone else. What is perhaps most striking about this room is that it has extraordinary acoustics. One can hear what is said from anyplace in the room, even when it is spoken in a normal or even quiet tone of voice. This was a room made for conversations about governing the country. The Congress Hall was designed to put conversation at the center of governance.

Congress Hall is a physical container, one that clarifies and reflects the sound well, enabling people to hear what is being said. But Congress Hall is more than a physical setting. It is symbolic; it has a function that goes beyond the mere structure of the materials in the building. This symbolic container also serves as a reminder for the people representing their country of the meaning for which they are responsible.

Every conversation has its own acoustics. Each one takes place in an environment that has both physical, or external, dimensions as well as internal, or mental and emotional, dimensions. There is, in other words, an invisible architecture to the container. Most such structures are made for discussion, for thinking alone. We have very few designed for thinking together, for dialogue.

Inner Acoustics

Similarly, there are physical acoustics arising from the structures of our skulls and inner ear, and there are internal dimensions to our capacity to hear. What are the internal acoustics? What kinds of sounds can be heard within you? How delicate are they? How strong? Can you hear what is said without overly distorting or muffling it?

There is a great debate over whether human beings are capable of objectively seeing or hearing anything. Many cognitive scientists believe that we filter everything we see and hear. Some say we do this through the very structure of our nervous systems. Others posit that we carry maps or models within us, to which we refer as we learn new information.

However conceptualized, it does seem clear that human beings impose things on the sounds that they listen to. Unlike physical sounds, however, we distort or dampen our internal hearing not with hard, sound-absorbent carpets and tiles but with our readiness to listen. The shape of our internal container guides our ability to hear what is being said. The shape of a collective container equally determines what can be said and heard.

The oral defense for my doctoral dissertation at Oxford University was held in a container designed for discussion. This was a rite of passage, a ritual designed to mark a transition over a threshold. The goal was to keep things distinct between student and professor, to maintain order and hierarchy, to clarify meanings and make a decision.

The physical structure of the room for my defense clearly reflects the imbalance of power between doctoral candidate and examiners and greatly influenced the nature of the interactions we had. Two examiners and myself gathered in this small room. All three of us had dressed in *subfusc*, black academic caps and gowns. Three rectangular tables stood in the room, two next to each other for each of the professors, and one about eight feet away, facing them, for me. I was at the point of the triangle of their inquiries.

One of the professors had placed what seemed like fifty Post-it notes on the pages of my dissertation; I knew then that this was going to be a long day. The conversation started gradually, with the professors questioning me, one after the other, about why I wrote certain things in my thesis, why I left things out, and so on. I felt beginning to rise up in me a desire to explain in as powerful a way as I could why I was justified in doing what I had done.

It was a fencing match in which the professors made parries and then I deflected or countered them. Over time the ante was upped. Somehow we got to the point where they had begun discussing the implications of what I had said between themselves—questioning their own insights. I knew then that I had been successful. The ritualized nature of this exchange was reflected in the roles we played and in the transformation of the roles. After two hours of grilling, I had become a peer.

Afterward everything was different. The two professors deliberated for a while, gave me their verdict—I had passed—and invited me for a glass of wine in the college bar next door to celebrate and reflect on the process. They laughed and acknowledged that while they had to be deadly serious at the time, they also enjoyed my work (they did not say this during the defense), and just wanted to "push things a bit."

There is nothing wrong with this kind of exchange. In many ways, in fact, it preserves a ritualized dimension of life that mostly has been abandoned. But for many of the problems we now face, this approach cannot work.

By contrast, dialogue involves creating a very different kind of container, both physically and in terms of the ways people interact with each other. In a dialogue, for instance, we use a circle, not a series of lines or rows or a triangle. The circle is an ancient symbol for dialogue. It is an economical form, efficient in its ability to enable everyone to see and hear. It is a leveler: It implies that everyone is on the level. Interestingly, one of the derivations of the word for *truth* in English is *alathea,* which means "on the level." We talk about leveling with one another, meaning we are telling the truth. The circle allows us to do this. The circle is also, however, a lens—a focusing device. Things intensify in the circle. One cannot predict what will happen within it.

As simplistic as it may sound, try holding your next meeting in a circle, without tables. It will have a profound impact, I predict, on what you say and think and do. People can, of course, always resist or struggle against the structure. One manager, who was the coach and facilitator of the top group at a major United States corporation, tells the story of how he had convinced everyone to abandon their traditional table. One tall manager walked into the room, looked around, and asked, "Where am I gonna put my coffee?" He then looked over at the facilitator and said, "If I spill this on my suit, you are paying the cleaning bills!" He was not kidding. They then proceeded to have, they later reported, their best meeting in a long time.

PROTECTING THE BOUNDARIES
OF THE CONTAINER

Consciously managing boundaries in a group setting is an essential way to sustain and deepen the sense of safety that people feel. This is especially true if the stakes are high. In practical terms this means making a set of choices about whether there is to be an open, closed, or random and unregulated system. Shall people be free to come and go as they wish—an open system? Shall the conversation be closed, limited only to those who are invited and no others? Shall we leave it up to the individuals to decide this sort of thing—making it random?

Boundaries of this sort also relate to the ways people interact together. For instance, often in a group someone will (unwittingly or not) say things that upset or disturb others. Someone might say, "Well, George's comments really were off the mark to me. Let me tell you what I think." And he or she might proceed to make his or her point. George and the others have been put in a dilemma. He can ignore what was said and the implied slight in it, or he can object. Either option may prove difficult.

Let's say that George is given no chance to respond to what was said—in fact, he was made the object of someone else's argument, and depersonalized. Is this sort of thing undiscussable? Or do individuals feel free to raise the issue and inquire, asking for illustration, for the reasons behind the thoughts and feelings? Dialogue requires a willingness to raise these things for the purposes of testing them. Evoking an effective architecture means that someone will need to have the space to ask George, "Were you understood as you intended?"

Gradually growing a set of norms for how these kinds of interactions are handled is an important part of container building.

Fields of

Conversation

I t had been a full and exciting few days. The conference had brought
together people from all over to talk together and exchange ideas. And
they had talked, energetically and enthusiastically, though mostly after
the sessions. There had been many presentations, yet few opportunities
simply to talk together as a whole group. Finally, on the last morning,
the moment came. They were a large group—over seventy-five people. A
moderator opened the floor to conversation and sat back. The quietness
of the summer's day shone through the windows of the conference room,
casting a gentle light. People looked around. To the surprise of many, after all the intensity of the past days, no one spoke.

They sat for some moments, waiting. It gradually became

clear that there was, at least for then, nothing yet to say. The silence, not the speaking, filled the room and the people. This was a silence without tension, more a rhythmic listening, a breathing out. People seemed unusually patient, as if they were fishing on the shore, waiting for the sun to set. The bloom of the moment, its uncontrived elegance, and its fertile presence were both unanticipated and relaxing.

"I did not want to break the silence, but I found the words spilling out of me and into the room and knew that I had to speak," one man began.

The atmosphere of the exchange depicted above is one of four essential "fields of conversation" that can arise as people endeavor to have dialogue. For many, this experience represents a pinnacle, a goal to be achieved, even an end in and of itself. Yet one of the more important ideas about dialogue that we have discovered in recent years is the notion that the *process of movement* through different fields or spaces of conversation is much more important than trying to produce a particular outcome. It is the creative motion itself, more than any single feeling or insight, that I have come to associate with dialogue.

CONVERSATIONAL EVOLUTION AND IMPASSE

We can often become disappointed with the "progress" of our conversations. This is because you or your group may be getting stuck in a particular kind of conversation, finding yourselves unable to move.

For instance, people often wind up at an impasse, stuck in polarized positional battles. In fact, these positional wars—where one person advocates in favor of rent control and another in favor of free market forces to control real estate rental prices—quickly reach a standoff. Yet this kind of interaction may also be sought. People often believe this is the best and perhaps only way to get at truth. Failing to fight eventually seems repressive and false. No fight, no reality. A *New York Times* writer in a recent review of Deborah Tannen's book *The Argument Culture* worried aloud about this. In her book Tannen describes many of the conflicts in public discourse that devolve into nasty fights—media attacks on politicians, vicious legal battles, gender wars—that seem to fill the modern landscape. She excoriates Tannen's claim that these fights, and the combative spirit that lies behind them, are bad for us. "We like to fight," says the reviewer. Her fear seems to be that losing a fight means becoming a passive recipient of whatever cultural programming or political nonsense might come our way. This is so only if we imagine fighting should never happen or, on the other hand, that it is the end and aim of genuine discourse. Neither is true.

People may also become stuck in what one manager I knew some years ago called "terminal niceness." It was impossible, in his organization, to ever raise a challenge to the status quo. People were simply too polite to do this. Of course, the battles behind the scenes were intense, but ably covered up.

The notion that dialogue is *conversation in motion* can greatly liberate our concepts about what is required to have it. Yes, there are times of fighting and times of niceness, of politeness. But none of them is static. They evolve. The motion of dialogue is not a linear succession so much as it is an evolution. As the map I develop in this chapter shall show, the progression does not always seem to go in a straight line. What is more, dialogue does not necessarily stop when a group of people who have been talking together stands up and leaves. Often the conversation carries on in other ways and picks up later where it left off.

CONTAINERS HOLD POTENTIAL

This type of evolving conversation takes different forms depending on the quality and nature of the container. Containers for conversation hold different qualities of pressure, energy, and knowledge. These spaces evolve through particular inflection points or crises. I will define leadership here as the capacity to hold the container for gradually larger sets of ideas, pressures, and people as the different crisis points unfold. Leadership itself, understood in this light, provides a container in which tremendous change can occur.

Nelson Mandela, president of South Africa, is an example of a leader who is capable of bearing a great deal of pressure, and yet seems to remain free of bitterness. After spending some twenty-seven years in prison while his country was under the grip of apartheid, one would expect him to resent his captors. Yet Mandela, by all accounts, does not. In fact, Mandela seems to be a man who learned to transcend the pressures he faced.

A highly talented Bahamian architect named Jackson Burnside described his first meeting with Mandela recently as a remarkable encounter with humility. Burnside had held Mandela in very high esteem for years, and met him when Mandela came to the Bahamas for an official visit. The prime minister of the Bahamas and other political and community leaders were present. Yet Mandela made Burnside feel that he was the most significant person present: "Oh, I have been waiting for a long while to meet you. I have such great respect for what you do," Mandela said. Burnside was deeply moved by this. He said that even though Mandela towered over him both physically and as a historical figure, it was Mandela who prostrated himself. Mandela's humility and strength have provided a symbolic container for the changes that have taken place in South Africa, a reference point for noble acceptance and struggle.

There is always some kind of container present among any group of people. The question is, For what purpose does it exist? Some people say dialogue is about emotional intimacy in the end, and that the ultimate goal is to enable people to relate well together. Others say that without shared meaning there can be no dialogue. These advocates work hard to surface the different frames and assumptions that people carry. Still others worry about the internal contradictions that arise as people act, and wish these to be named and explored. But the container requires all three. If any one is left out, the overall ecology is unbalanced.

Dialogue is a process by which we can create containers that are capable of holding our experience in ever more rich and complex ways, making legitimate many approaches and styles. We can see this in the experience of a couple that continuously fights and has no space to understand the tensions they are feeling. We can imagine the change they might feel if they could walk into the arms of a very wise, understanding friend who could soothe and reassure them by letting them know that he sees the struggle each of them is going through. He could offer the kind of hope that motivates them to fight both for their own identity and for each other.

In this latter space, both people might relax and discover that they had thoughts and feelings they were unaware of and out of contact with because of the immediacy of the battle. They might come to see, in fact, that they had unresolved pain in their hearts that was being triggered by their interactions but was not initially produced by the other person. They might, in other words, start to move further "upstream" toward the source of their difficulties once they had a larger psychological and emotional place in which to relax and interact. They would have moved into a larger container.

Bohm used to say that if there is pollution in the river of our thought, then we have essentially two strategies we might pursue: removing the pollution from the river downstream, or changing something farther upstream. The evolution of the container spaces that I describe here are ways to tackle our thought and feeling farther upstream. It is a way of understanding how we might come into a greater measure of clarity, not just around our own inner ecology, but in the ecology of our team, our organizations, and—potentially, at least—society itself.

The intention here is to develop a greater capacity to reflect on and transform ourselves "upstream." In doing so, we are able to change and heal.

FIELDS AND CONTAINERS

The term *container,* as I have indicated, gives us a way of putting our arms around the more elusive notion of a "field of conversation." As I outlined on pages 254–55, fields are spaces in which there is a particular quality of energy and exchange. Containers are the relatively observable features of fields. Each field of conversation, as I outline in the next few pages, seems to have distinct characteristics, patterns, and pressures. Each one transforms into another only through crises, significant changes evoked by the people who are participating in the dialogue.[1] These crises are thresholds over which one must pass in order to experience dialogue.

FIELD I: INSTABILITY OF THE FIELD/POLITENESS IN THE CONTAINER

When a group of people first meets, whether the members know one another well or not, they generally do not have a container that can absorb or hold much intensity and pressure. In fact, most settings for conversation seem to be designed *not* to hold much space for what is new. The work setting, for instance, seems to be designed to require us to leave certain parts of ourselves at the door.

In these initial moments, people bring with them a set of inherited norms about how to interact. In a staff meeting, for instance, they may have a mental model about what is "supposed" to happen.

If it is a lecture, then they know to sit and listen. A board meeting has another set of formal protocols.

From an external standpoint, each of these settings can seem quite different. The initial intensity of a board meeting differs greatly from the initial chatter of a group of shop-floor workers in an automobile factory as they gather for their morning meeting. And yet they do not differ in one critical respect: These people have well-accepted and well-learned ways of interacting and being. They have accepted the social container in which they live. They are not, for the moment, reflecting on what lies below the surface—unstated expectations, tensions, differences. Some of these tensions and expectations are known to the people concerned. Some of them are not—they are part of the associations that they carry around with them. People, in other words, bring a set of taken-for-granted assumptions about the situation, rules about how to think and act within it.

These associations are profoundly influential. For instance, an experienced manager may see an entrepreneurial start-up business, its fast-paced energy, and its evangelical zeal as an opportunity. People with less experience living through such a start-up might see it as a "mess."

Many people, for instance, saw the extensive burning of the Yellowstone National Forest in 1988 as a sad and disastrous event, and they clamored for a change in the management of our forests. They worried enormously and felt it was a mark of failure that so much of the park burned. Yet many experienced forest managers saw this same event as a part of cycle of rain and drought that moves through the area every three hundred to four hundred years or so, as evidenced by the tree record. Typically, the Yellowstone forest has a means of self-regulation and most fires there burn very little. There are many tall trees and very little "fine fuel"—kindling for the fire close to the ground. While disastrous from a human standpoint, the ecology of the forest was likely working in Yellowstone that year exactly as it should have.

While people come to dialogue with a great many different expectations, at first this is not entirely obvious. Discussion about the differences seldom happens. For example, the health-care workers in Grand Junction came together with a widely varying set of hopes about what they were going to do in the dialogues they were attending. Some wanted to reflect on health, others wanted to fix the system, and still others wanted to make sure their competitors did not collude to drive down their market share. None of this came out until later. What we found, instead, was a pattern of politeness, cooperation, pleasantries. People did at first what they usually do when they gathered: told war stories, relaxed, complained about the changes in their industry.

In our initial research I described this space as one of "instability *of* the container"—at least insofar as the capacity to hold a more intense kind of conversation. My colleague Claus Otto Scharmer, who proposed the structure of the map on page 261, has suggested that we can think of this behavior as "rule following." The language that people use in these settings is one that remains consistent with the dominant social norms that they grew up with and are comfortable with. In some cases this is polite interaction. In others, like one high-tech company I know, people immediately start pointing out what is wrong and why nothing is going to work. They have set themselves enormously high goals—far outstripping anything ever done in their industry before. And they admit to feeling unable to do anything about this. But this is what people in this culture do when they first meet—they carry on a kind of aggressive banter about what is wrong and what needs fixing.

In this conversational field people do not surface what they "really" think and feel. Scharmer refers to this first space as being dominated by a norm where the (as yet unexamined) rules governing the whole are primary and more important than what any one individual wants.

To illustrate: I met recently with the senior management

team of a company that had two paradigms constantly in conflict. Some valued a random culture, others a closed one. The norms of the social whole were to have these dynamics play out but not to call attention to any of it. People would feel frustrated, but distanced themselves from any public engagement in the difficulties. Many felt frustrated but did not really know why—they knew only that certain people bothered them.

This is typical of this first field (Field I) for conversation: Though a range of taken-for-granted and socially generated norms are present, people do not either see them or know what to do about them, and operate as best they can, following the prevailing rules.

Scharmer points out that a key feature of Field I is that it lacks reflection. For example, in a session that I was facilitating, leaders from two divisions of a company were trying to find a unified approach to their strategy and were having trouble agreeing. Their culture was one in which the norm was to be polite and never differ publicly. But I knew that they had problems, because I had spoken with them all individually. They would raise privately what they feared to raise publicly.

At one point, people were trying to map some of the differences they faced, the different ways they saw the market, and their theories about what to do within it. I felt as if I were pulling teeth! They were reluctant to say directly that they did not trust the other division to look out for their interests. They felt they could trust no one, but to say such a thing would be heretical. One of the consultants they had hired to do some market analysis then spoke up: "You know, I really think you are digging for something that is not there. These people basically agree," he said as he looked around the room. "I think we are ready to move on." The face of the senior manager in charge of the strategy fell. One of the consultants he had hired had just given voice to the very things he was hoping would be challenged. It was a voice that reinforced the fear of reflection and sought a route to let people escape the pressure that was beginning to mount. In Kantor's four player system terms, Field I is usually characterized by "more-follow" sequences: some people move, others follow, no one opposes or bystands.

The emotional component that drives this sequence is often fear. People often feel no small measure of fear when they join a group of people, even one they know well. This fear seems to reinforce rule-following behavior.

A similar situation developed in the Grand Junction dialogues we conducted. People entered the project thinking mostly about themselves and how their interests might be damaged or helped by a conversation among the leadership of the health-care community of their town. One CEO, Mike, who arrived at the first session looking very reluctant to be a part of it, admitted this quite freely.

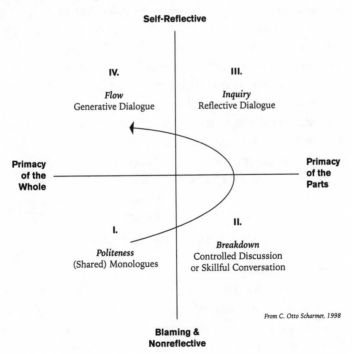

From C. Otto Scharmer, 1998

I said to him, "You do not look like you want to be here."

He replied, "I don't. I am here but I will not participate."

"Then why have you come?"

"Because I have to make sure that nothing happens here that will damage my hospital."

"Would you be willing to say at least that?"

"No."

The patterns of behavior that one sees in Field I have been chronicled in the writing of famed sociologist Erving Goffman. Goffman identified the enormously complex and varied ways in which people learn to maintain "face" to protect their image of themselves and to mutually protect others in the same way. This is perhaps one of the most fundamental rules that people follow in this rule-following space.[2] Field I is generally the space of "civility." Generally, this means a civility that represses, for the good of all, the free expression of the individual: We do not generally tell the boss that we think he is a jerk even if we think so; similarly, we generally laugh at others' jokes even when they are not funny.

If one's horizon is limited to this field, it can and will seem like a prison. Yet this will also prove to be true in *all* of the spaces. It can seem promising that one space may be more enlightened, more attractive, than another, though this is in practice not true. Each space is essential. As I said earlier, it is the sustaining of the movement *through* the spaces that is important here.

The Crisis of Emptiness:
"You Can't Make Dialogue Happen"

When people seek to engage in dialogue, this first phase of experience generally demonstrates that they cannot get to the level of shared meaning as readily as they might have hoped. Particularly for action-oriented people, it is quite frustrating to realize that we simply cannot *make* dialogue happen. This experience often leads to the first of a series of crises that seem necessary in developing a deeper space for dialogue.

The word *crisis* comes from an Indo-European root *krei*, which means "to discriminate, distinguish, or separate." We get the words *discern*, *criteria*, and, interestingly, *riddle* all from this root. A crisis is a turning point, distinguishing all that has come before from all that comes after. I think of a crisis in dialogue as a gateway to deeper silence and deeper listening. One cannot "outthink" a crisis; one has to go through it. We can try to avoid it, but then we do not let real change take place. Dialogue in this sense requires the emergence of a new kind of sensitivity and awareness, which is not something one can mandate. It emerges, in fact, as one realizes precisely that one cannot mandate it.

I have found that there is a series of crises in dialogues— not always experienced as such, but nonetheless critical turning points that require navigation and understanding. One of the reasons people get stuck and fail to experience what they imagine to be dialogue is that these crises are challenging. In particular, they challenge our identify. They ask us, each time, to reexamine who we think we are as we try to engage in serious conversation.

I call this crisis the crisis of *emptiness*—because one must quickly empty oneself of expectations if anything new is to happen. One must look for what has not yet happened, for what might be unexpected, different. The writer Scott Peck, in his theory of community development, uses a stage model, but he places *emptiness* toward the end. *Emptiness* to Peck is emptying out the falseness, making room for what is authentic, genuine. I refer here more to the initial dislocation that comes when we realize that our expectations are not going to be met, and that we cannot fully control the outcome we want to produce.

One of the things that triggers this crisis is when someone steps back and reflects on the total process of the conversation and how it feels. Generally speaking, making a comment of this sort about the process of a conversation while it is ongoing is seen as rude! It can break the happy somnolence of a group, and this triggers the breakdown described next. This move, where someone speaks the forbidden or unsayable, forces a change.

Of course some groups seek to appropriate "process" comments by making them part of the fabric of things. Meeting facilitation, for example, has become big business. The trouble with this is it can become a kind of crutch, a way of bypassing the crisis that requires people to face their essential inability to manipulate into existence a greater form of internal commitment and collective intelligence. While it is not always the case, reliance on facilitators can be a kind of work avoidance, a way of seeking to escape the crisis of emptiness, with a false hope that there is some method, some expert, some technology that can actually get us from here to there.

This first crisis is one in which people find their expectations being dashed. One of the cultural assumptions people have about the way knowledge is generated is that one person is likely to have information or knowledge that others need. This hierarchical view assigns responsibility and blame to an individual or group that people imagine are in control. In dialogue, people come to the realization that knowledge arises because of the shared experience of a collective. No one can make this emerge. In fact, efforts to do so simply get in the way. The crisis here is realizing that we all together are somehow responsible, and must discover what to do all together. This is a significant shift for many people who expect an expert to tell them what to do. Unfortunately, no expert can help here; the creation of new knowledge is a community activity and must be done by everyone. The team must decide its fate; the board must come to its own conclusions; no external help can do this for them.

FIELD II: INSTABILITY IN THE
FIELD/BREAKDOWN IN THE CONTAINER

As people move from initially conversing and deliberating together within the context of the accepted norms of the social whole, they shift to the point where they start to say what they think. This second field, or space for conversation, we call *breakdown*. It is at this point, Scharmer notes, that people "say what they think." Rule-revealing behavior becomes the norm here. The subsurface fragmentation comes up. But now there is a container that can begin to hold the intensity and pressure. People experience instability in the conversation, but it can be held. I originally called this space *instability in the container* because we now have both—instability of association *and* enough of a container to see it function.

In Field II, the social whole is no longer dominant. As Scharmer has shown, the parts become primary—in particular, the particle-like nature of the individual. The billiard-ball image of atoms colliding fits well in this space. People tend to collide and smash into one another. What this means in practice is that people begin to battle over whose meaning will have more power. In Kantor's four player system, Field II is characterized by move-oppose sequences; followers and bystanders tend to be silent and made to feel powerless. How people handle the energies and intensities of this space is a critical question for leadership, one I address in more detail in the next few pages. But it is clear that this can be either a time of creative change or of recycling old memories and viewpoints.

The challenge of this space is to change the meaning of the trauma that arises, both individually and collectively. In this space some of the pain that is present in and among the people can arise. This evokes what I refer to as the *crisis of suspension*—learning to find a way to cool down the exchange, as described in the superconductor example so that the entire group can move into a more fluid inquiry and reflection.

Unfortunately, many groups never get beyond this point. Things heat up, people try negotiating, compromise, or unilateral control, but they fail to move collectively into the space of reflection. Eventually, they recycle back into politeness, because it is the only other alternative that they know. People's appetite for dialogue is often limited because they have had experiences that never got beyond this point—and the promise of more of the same is unappealing.

People typically experience this dimension of the container's development as the time when trouble arises. They begin to interpret what is happening in terms of personal discomfort, are less concerned about censoring what they say, and tend to cling to their perspectives.

Recall the story of the first day we brought steelworkers and managers together. They were excited by their own progress and began to speak about forging "a single container" that could include everyone. This led people to relax and begin to reveal how they really thought and felt. One manager suggested that man-hours per ton be reduced. The steelworkers immediately reacted, seeing this as a betrayal. It meant cutting or losing jobs. Now they were not polite—they vented.

The resulting breakdown was a necessary step in the process of discovering just how difficult it would be to dissolve years of trouble, and it powered the process by which that could actually begin to happen. People learned that it was possible to come to the point of reflecting on the structures and forces that led to this breakdown, that they could suspend together their difficulties. This propelled them eventually out of this field of conversation and into the next.

The great quest in this phase is for a set of new rules or new ways of operating that can enable people to think, talk, and work together differently. But instead, the breakdown comes. The dominant emotion in this field tends to be anger. This seems to arise as people discover that not only can they not *make* dialogue happen, they also cannot get anyone to even agree with them!

Patrick de Maré spoke about dialogue as being fueled by the energy of anger and hatred. De Maré drew on Freud's theory outlined in *Civilization and Its Discontents*, in which he stated that human beings have a great deal of repressed hatred and violence in them, much of it the result of the formation of civilization. This repression, however necessary for human society, also has never had a chance to be processed or made conscious. It has just rolled around in the subconscious of humanity, spilling out at various times. Dialogue provides, de Maré believed, a way to enable the cultural healing and change that was required—for instance, after the trauma of war, dialogue can provide society a space for this intensity to come up and change the *meaning* of the anger and frustration. I agree with this. Field II is a necessary space for human beings to learn to move through. It provides the fuel for change.

When the steelworkers and managers found themselves caught in a series of reflexive reactions to one another, based on their long-standing collectively held memories, the temptation was to think that the idea of gathering as we did was a mistake. In fact, people came up to me at the breaks during this session and asked, "How do you think it is going?" their question really a statement of worry and concern. I reassured them: "How could we change a collective pattern like this if the pattern itself never came up?" The art of transformation of these patterns moved the group into the next field space. There they began to see the crisis as a vehicle for understanding what was happening among them. It changed in *meaning*. It was no longer a symbol of their failure together, but an opportunity for change and reflection.

Now, this does not necessarily mean that people have to have a difficult time, or that the experience needs to be violent.

In fact, as there is greater understanding of the inevitable frustrations that arise as a group of people struggle to learn to talk together, there can be a much greater ease and more fluid movement. Sometimes, though, this movement requires assistance by people who have experience with the cycles of dialogue.

In the Grand Junction dialogue, the underlying difficulties also eventually came out. During the first two-day session we held, I presented some of the dilemmas I believed faced the people in this system, for instance, their desire for more open relationships and collaboration across and between hospitals, and their fear that greater openness might erode their competitive positioning. The group spoke quite freely about these things, and how they had responded in the past to them—describing the paranoia that had sometimes loomed large in their minds. People began to remark that something had seemed to shift to enable them to say even that much.

Finally the CEO's lieutenant, who was required by his boss to remain silent, could not help himself. He nearly came out of his chair: "I have heard this in the past . . . that St. Mary's would like to see Community Hospital buried, would like to see it go away."

There was a moment of stunned silence. I could feel people begin looking for cover. Others then spoke up. "I would confirm that I have heard that also."

A doctor from St. Mary's Hospital said, "I have heard that too. But the only folks I have ever heard it from are Community Hospital folks. I haven't heard it from St. Mary's folks, HMO folks, or the community."

"Has anyone ever heard this before?" I asked. "Or is George crazy?"

People acknowledged that yes, there has been intense rivalry and people had heard rumors to this effect.

The CEO of the largest hospital, only recently arrived, began to inquire: "I have been here only a year and a half. But if there is anything I or my hospital have done that has produced this climate, I want to know about it and I want it to stop. Can you help me see what you see going on?"

People had begun to say what they thought. The result: The dialogue proved itself to be a setting where truth could be told and where genuine inquiry into the problems most troubling people could be discussed.

Another critical dimension of this field is that there is little or no real reflection yet on what is happening. People may advocate their positions but will likely not stop to inquire into what led them to think as they do. In this state, people are more concerned about expressing their point of view than challenging it. In its extreme, as Scharmer points out, this dimension collapses into blame. The underlying sentiment is "not only do we have different positions, but clearly yours is wrong and to blame for the difficulties we are facing." As it turns out, movement out of this field requires the very thing most lacking—self-reflection.

The Crisis of Suspension:
"I Am Not My Point of View"

For many people, the difficulty in engaging in dialogue revolves around the fact that the only thing they know is a seemingly endless recycling between the politeness and rule following of Field I, and the breakdowns in Field II. After a period of anxiety and frustration, they retreat into politeness and, sometimes, denial. This does not build confidence or hope that there is a way through the difficulties, and tends to build cynicism.

The recycling happens because people do not succeed in navigating the second crisis—the crisis of suspension. The crux of this crisis involves coming to the point of realizing that "I am not my point of view." I have a point of view, but that is not what I am. Field II is characterized by people taking positions and battling one another. The way through this is to suspend these positions and the assumptions that drive them, to come to the point of being willing to listen to other views. This is a move that truly changes the game people are playing.

The transition here is essential and perhaps one of the most difficult ones in the entire dialogue process. It is here that people may choose to loosen their grip on their positions and take in a wider horizon.

There is a crisis involved here because of the fact that people hold their assumptions as "necessary." Sometimes these become "absolute" necessities—people with fervent religious beliefs hold them as absolutely necessary, and therefore prevent any kind of real change toward mutual understanding. This is another shift of identity—one that says, "Though my positions may be right and well thought through, they are still not *who I am*. I can make space for other positions without jeopardizing my own inner stability." Coming to understand this is to navigate the crisis of identity inherent here.

The crisis of suspension also moves individuals into a zone of reflection that previously they had not been willing to occupy. Suspending my views opens the space not merely for more advocacy but also for inquiry.

Opposition as a Catalyst
for Field Change in a Group

An individual comment in a dialogue can precipitate a substantial change in direction for the conversation, especially if that comment comes from a space that the majority of the group is not in. In one dialogue, the vice president of the union compelled a new kind of inquiry by opposing the direction in which the conversation was going simply by reflecting on and suspending his *own* inner state and his reactions to it. The group really was not prepared to join him yet:

UNION VP: Everybody seems to be agreeing on just about everything, but those two sparks of mine haven't seemed to come together, and I don't know whether that's a positive or a negative thing. They just haven't come together.

UNION EXECUTIVE: Just don't leave it like that, what the hell are you talking about?

(Loud laughter)

COMPANY CEO: Let's suspend this!

UNION VP: I'm not too sure that—

MANAGER: Are you raising [trouble]? *(More laughter)*

UNION VP: I don't know whether or not we really churn when we have some positives and negatives that set each other off, or set us off. We've had so much getting along this morning, that it just hasn't—

UNION EXECUTIVE: More sickening than anything. *(Laughter)*

UNION VP: —just hasn't got me awake yet so . . . I can't really add very much. We're not getting there, yet how do we go about doing it?

This exchange prompted other people to begin to advocate solutions—to direct what they wanted to have happen. The group had moved out of politeness and into a Field II space.

FIELD III: INQUIRY IN THE FIELD
AND THE FLOWERING OF
REFLECTIVE DIALOGUE

It is at this part of the dialogue process that a recognizably different kind of conversation begins to take place. Here the energy changes. People finally stop speaking for others, or for "the group." There is a shift here from "third person data"—stories about other people and other places—to "first person data"—inquiries into how things look from where I stand. People do not simply stand on their position, they let the group know more about what it is about them that leads them to it. People are reflective in this phase—about what they are doing, about the impact they are having.

Perhaps most dominant in Field III is the spirit of *curiosity*. While many people privately will admit to themselves that they do not understand why things happen as they do, that in some respects they are as puzzled as the next person, they rarely if ever do this in public. As this phase of the container opens up, people become more willing to acknowledge such things. They do not have to have it all figured out or have all the answers. They discover that there is a larger meaning unfolding through the conversation—something that goes beyond what they might have imagined and constructed for themselves. It is at this phase that people start to be surprised—not by their negative reactions to others, but by the fact that they are thrown back on their heels, and by their realization that they are being forced to slow down and *think*.

We have termed this *reflective* dialogue, because it is here that people begin to notice and are willing to explore their assumptions. Scharmer described this state as *rule reflecting*. People are now willing to examine the rules that have governed how they have operated. They are prepared to begin to explore the nature of the structures that guide their behavior and action, and they do so increasingly publicly.

It is also at this point in the dialogue that new meaning can unfold, seemingly from many different directions at once. It is like a dam that once broken floods the low-lying plain of a subject, filling it to overflowing. People raise things from many perspectives. They do not feel compelled to have to agree. Ideas tend to flow freely, often grounded in the fact that people are speaking now for themselves.

Another critical feature here: People feel no obligation to require that others respond or agree with their perspective. Typical of Field II is the sense that if I say something, others must reply. People still treat one another as positions rather than as people in Field II, and their main aim is to find out if the other person is, in essence, for or against his or her point of view. In Field III this changes. While I may have a position, I am also a person with a history, a particular background, and none of this am I now seeking to hold back.

There are some striking examples that illustrate this space from the health-care dialogue in Grand Junction.

Here, for instance, is a comment that eventually became "famous" in our dialogue. Early on we spoke about the impact of the medical profession on doctors, as people tried to reflect on the most effective way to re-create the health-care system in the city. The conversation turned to the fact that there seemed to be differences between the ways men and women talk about health-care issues, about how the profession of medicine devalues or discounts feelings despite its claims to care.

One doctor then turned to another and asked, "When was the last time you cried in public?"

The group then explored for some time a range of different experiences people had had about how emotion and medicine danced together about what counted as acceptable expression and what did not. Not everyone was able to let their feelings flow. In fact, there was an elaborate system of what one person called the "modulation of emotion"—the ways professional appearance regulated feeling and its expression. This proved quite difficult to sustain. Recalls a nurse:

> I remember an instance where a man died, and the nurses started running around the room. And the wife came in, and she started telling her husband how much she loved him, and the nurses started crying with the wife. And the physician almost left. I did. I couldn't take it. And I went out to the desk, and everybody saw me crying. Nurses will do that. They'll come up and hug each other and be real supportive. But the physician, when he came out of the room, I could tell he was emotionally distraught, but he hauled off and kicked a trash can against the wall.

This man's violent reaction estranged him from the nurses, who could not let themselves express this kind of rageful feeling, only the grief.

The group eventually raised, after this conversation, in both a personal, and then remarkably impersonal fashion, the critical issues that surrounded the pressure to care for people continuously, and be provider of last resort for an entire community. These conversations evolved into a discovery of the immense reliance that people in the medical community have on technology.

This triggered a soul-searching inquiry by the doctors and board members responsible for major technology decisions into the sources of some of their decisions. This was not a group of alternative health practitioners, but people who had invested many years in maintaining medicine as it is traditionally taught, for instance, in United States medical schools. Here is what these doctors had to say:

> I think over the past fifty years there's been a development of an arrogance in medicine because of our toys, our antibiotics, our medicines, that what you're talking about . . . I think there's a much more important part, not only of individual practice, but hospital practice as well, and the whole culture of caring and medicine that has over the past fifty years of our toys and technology has been repressed.

> And then we realize that we're frustrated. And why we're frustrated is because we've had this artifice that's out there, and we've felt this power that was not real.

> [We] in this room are responsible for promoting what I'm talking about. We promoted that artificial position. And now it's awfully hard to say we're sorry.

This was a particularly poignant matter in this town, as it is in many small ones, where there tends to be redundant technology purchases because the people in different hospitals feel it unwise or uneconomic to leave to other organizations valuable revenue streams that arise from medical testing. But it became clear that the community tended to invest in technology to assuage this sense of limitation and guilt, and that rising health-care costs were at least in part attributable to a collectively held habit of belief in technological solutions that lead people to buy first and ask questions later.

When we started the dialogues, the CEOs of the various local hospitals rarely if ever set foot in one another's facilities. A few months into the process, these same CEOs began to meet to talk through major technology purchases and the implications for the community as a whole. Insight about a problem translated immediately into action. New action does not necessarily require an action plan; dialogue points the way toward a far more direct route to action—deep shifts in the shared meaning of a group of people. What I have found, in fact, is that the action plans produced in many teams and executive settings are elaborate ritualized dances that rarely culminate in the intended action. Insight that emerges as a result of a shared field of meaning and is jointly developed—what Patrick de Maré. Called "outsight"—simply and profoundly changes what people do.

This coversation space is also marked by a growing ability to speak across models—for people who generally have very different points of view to begin to talk and listen in ways that enable them to connect to people who are very different from them. It was when they were in this field in the dialogues that the steelworkers and managers began to feel understood by the other side. It is also at this point that people realize more fully just how little understanding there is among them.

The Crisis of Fragmentation:
"We Are Not Our Point of View"

As a group of people comes to the point of engaging in a rich flow and exchange of inquiry together, there is a point when pressure for another change builds. Up until that point, people generally are focused on their own point of view and their own personal contribution to the inquiry. They are, as noted above, in the "primacy of the part" end of Scharmer's continuum. As this experience develops, something new comes into place. People begin to see the extent of the fragmentation that has actually been present all along, though covered up. The impact our judgments of one another have on our effectiveness and our hearts becomes apparent. The possibility opens through this to see that what we together thought we were doing is not the full picture.

In one dialogue we held some years ago, this arose in a poignant way. One of the two Israeli men attending said he worried about the quiet reflection that the group had entered. He "learned through intensity" and felt that somehow this was missing. The other Israeli, a thoughtful academic, wrote a long note afterward describing his experience of the following moments. He said:

> [His] words struck something very deep, deep inside me. I then opened my mouth and begin to talk about intensity. As Jews and as Israelis, all of our lives are unbelievable intensity. The intensity and pain of the oppressed . . . the vivid memory of every persecution . . . the pain of every attack . . . the constant fear and expectation of more . . . and the intensity and pain of finding ourselves to be the oppressor and having to kill, torture, and whatever for our own survival . . . I simply expressed the pain.

> At that moment I realized [and spoke about], I think for the first time, the paradox of learning through intensity. We protect ourselves from intensity by creating intensity. Creating artificial experiences of intensity [i.e., entertaining, exciting, risky, and/or emotionally arousing] can shield us from our real, personal intensity. They can keep us from having to face the pain, anger, guilt, uncertainty, and doubt as well as the beauty that are deep inside of us. The real danger is creating moments of slowing down and silence, when the troublesome feelings and pain can

well up. So we keep things speeded up and learn to learn through intensity. And we learn to teach through intensity.

When this man spoke in our session, the room became very quiet. It was as if we were staring into a still pool, and in those few moments could hear a vast cultural pattern at work, one that operated like a reflex, automatically, without conscious awareness. People began to inquire into the ways that this pattern lived also in them, ways that they supported it. The inquiry began at a personal level with one man, but quickly went beyond that to explore cultural factors. In these moments we saw something of the collective ecology of a nation; we got at least a window into it, and a sense of a very new possibility: that a dialogue group could enable at the collective level the kinds of insights that are typically only possible for individuals—insights that can change the total nature of one's experience.

This fellow added in his journal:

When I spoke, I was speaking for myself—. . . as a Jew, as an Israeli. Afterwards, however, I really felt as if *the group had spoken through me*. I think I was giving voice to the shadow side of the holiness and peace that many of us were experiencing: the real pain and fear that we carry inside ourselves as members of families, groups, and organizations . . . the pain and fear that we are going to return to after the conference. It is very difficult to describe the experience in retrospect or to say what led me to believe that the group had spoken through me. Perhaps it was that I spoke so spontaneously and without forethought. Perhaps it was the reaction of the group. Perhaps it was the way in which people followed on what I had said.

The crisis of fragmentation is one in which a group of people loosen their preconceptions about who they think they are and what they think they are doing together, enough so that they may see a much wider set of possibilities. In this case the shift was from personal insight to at least the potential for cultural healing.

This crisis requires a letting-go of an isolated identity that many of have developed and used to survive in the world. It comes in part by grasping the extent of the loss that arises when we live in an isolated way. It also comes when we see the possibilities of developing other kinds of collective identities.

Rilke, in his essays on love, describes marriage as enabling two people to see further into the future than they otherwise might. Two people who come together can learn, in other words, to transcend the limits of their identities and come to the point of knowing a larger sense of destiny together than they might have experienced on their own. This is an example of the fruits of successfully overcoming the crisis of fragmentation. In it comes the realization that we are not our point of view, that the shared identity we have had is not what we thought, and that we can together see more than we might have on our own. This crisis, once navigated, enables people to move into a space where there is much more fluid creativity than ever before.

FIELD IV: CREATIVITY IN THE FIELD: GENERATIVE DIALOGUE

This fourth field and container space is the rarest of all the spaces. It is the one where people cross over into an awareness of the primacy of the whole, as Scharmer suggests. It is also a time when genuinely new possibilities come into being. As Scharmer also suggests, this is a space where people generate new rules for interaction, where they are personally included but also are fully aware of the impersonal elements of their participation. In this fourth space, people have an experience of *flow*—often a collective flow. Synchronicities arise more often here: One person will think of something and another will say it. People become more aware, in essence, of the primacy of the undivided whole that links us all, and so notice it more readily.

In this fourth space, traditionally held positions are sufficiently loosened that very new possibilities can come into existence. It is in this space where the two gay women I described in the beginning of this book found a way to connect with the woman who deeply disapproved of them, and they of her. The experience of an atmosphere large enough to accommodate radically different points of view without requiring any of them to change is a fundamental quality of this space. In it, many new possibilities and options can be seen that were hidden before.

A recent dialogue we held illustrates the qualities that arise in this space. It was one of the final dialogues in a year-long leadership program that my consulting company runs. People began sharing their feelings about the fact that the session was coming to an end—their relative readiness to take on the world and sustain a profound container for others, their own self-doubts about what they were ready to do. What emerged in the conversation was a quality of intelligence, depth, and flow that moved everyone. It was as if everyone were playing their part in creating a larger musical score, though no one had all the notes. Each one simply played his or her part:

Early on, one man began by reflecting on his own question of himself: "Have I used my time well?" Another man offered the metaphor of birth—that the process of learning together was more like a pregnancy. People responded with humor. Said one man;

> It's like you've got a child now. It's like, "oh shit I'm going to be a father!" So it's sort of like some grow-

ing up has got to happen for me. I use a lot of ex-
cuses . . . for not doing things in a more professional
way . . . So some maturity and sobering are starting
to sink into me.

A woman joked: "Have you thought about labor?" To which he
replied, "No, I have not, but I do want drugs!" Several people
began to reflect openly on their use of the time in the year-long
program, and the fact that they had found a great depth to their
commitment.

Into the stream of dialogue people reflected on the theme
of loss. Several people spoke about critical endings and how
they had handled them. This comment triggered a flow of other
reflections about the theme of loss, about ending. One man, for
instance, spoke about the time when his daughter, who was in
her late teens at the time, ran away from home:

And for me that was quite a shock, because she had
been within my home and within my field of protec-
tion, if you like. She was— And, so my fatherhood,
in *that way*, came to an end very rapidly, more rapidly
than I would have chosen, in a more *measured* way.
Had she gone off to University or whatever, then it
would have been what everybody had expected,
there would have been no problem, I would have *felt*
it in a different way.

But it came to an end very abruptly. And then, after she had been away for maybe three or four days, her
cat, which *also* lived within our home and was our—obviously we loved and was responsible for—the cat died.
And I remember burying the cat with tears streaming
down my face, partly because of the loss of the cat but
largely because I knew that that symbolized the fact that

my daughter would never come and live in my home again in the same way.

And it sort of shocked my wife and my son, who were there, that I was so upset about this. But for *me* it came very rapidly, and I had to deal with that loss. Of course, it wasn't the loss of my daughter—my daughter I subsequently met up with not that much later, and we had a great meeting, and I really felt rather jealous of what she'd been up to—she had some *excellent* experiences. And *particularly* when I found where she was living and what she was doing, I thought, "This is—I'd rather be doing that than what I'm doing." It was great, there was no issue there.

But what I had lost was my fatherhood, *that phase* of my fatherhood, if you like, now I'm a father of a daughter who is an adult, who doesn't live within that kind of sphere, although she comes down and lives with us often. So we've talked it through, and thought it through.

But it *was* a lot of feeling, and it was the ending of a particular *way* in which I held myself, I suppose, a kind of containment, but a way in which my presence extended, it is now different. And it was very painful, and very good to feel it. By *feeling it so much,* it was really clean. And there was nothing left as a result.

People responded to this not by reacting to other's experiences, but by connecting what was happening in the conversation with what was happening in themselves. The wider theme that emerged here was about the release of structures that limit the flow of meaning. From one perspective these appear as loss. From another, they are ways life makes space for something new. Perhaps most striking here was the unplanned collective artistry that coordinated around this theme, where the people acted as servants of the emerging flow of meaning as well as participants within it. While there were personal stories, the dialogue was not about the personal stories but about the deeper meaning that came through all of them. This is the magic of dialogue.

One other important feature of this fourth conversational space is the discovery many people make that they simply do not have words to describe the experience that emerges. To genuinely move into uncharted territory is at times to be struck dumb. We do not know what to say. This can be quite disconcerting if we are used to controlling our experiences through our words. To get a feel for this, try deliberately not speaking for a while in settings where you are generally talkative. Present experience is often fused with our memories of how things have been. People often use talk to continue to bring for the world with which they are familiar. Ceasing this can, for the moment, change the pattern.

Learning to access the part of ourselves that do not yet have a voice can also be quite freeing, as we realize that we must evoke something from within ourselves. We move from reporting our memory to speaking our hearts. And we shift to a mode where it can be legitimate to speak our thoughts, to notice and value our insights, and not to discount them because they seem underdeveloped or "small" in comparison to more articulate positions voiced by others.

In this fourth space of dialogue people become quite understanding of one another's inability to be articulate, because they experience their own limits. They also become more aware of their participation in the wider group—and discover that what they say impacts everyone. This can be a space of immense discovery—one where we find, for instance, that the language system we use tends to blind us to certain experiences.

Western languages, for instance, tend to be noun based. They tend to objectify the universe, to try to measure it, to capture it. This can leave us trapped in categories. The indigenous peoples of North America have a very different language structure—one that is verb based, in motion. According to Native American scholar and linguist James Youngblood Henderson, these languages focus not on what is seen but what is heard. And what is heard is in motion. For instance, there is no word in Micmac, one of the Algonquian languages, for tree. Instead, people speak of different trees according to the sound that the wind makes when it blows through the leaves. The word for *forest* in Micmac translates as "shimmering leaves." Language, they say, is a container for the forces or spirits of nature.

Unlike Western European languages, native languages like the Algonquin teach people not to forget the "glue" of life that binds everything together. Henderson was struck by the way Westerners become caught in their categories:

> Take the words *income tax*—they created that word that you call the tax code and devoted their life to it. I said once to someone, why did they live in New Hampshire? And they told me how these categories had dominated their universe, they only lived in a place where they don't pay [state] taxes.

> I don't want my son and daughters to do that—to live in imagination. We go walking in the forest and say, this is this, and this is that. See this footprint here, that insect walking over it, that's called time. That's the closest we get to time. If insects can walk over a footprint, you know it's been there overnight. . . . It's as good as my watch if you know what you're looking at. But Mic Maq and Cheyenne are so totally related to this world that you call nature, we don't have a word for it, it's just too abstract.[3]

The point of Native communication is to create an experiental interchange, one that is completely grounded in experience. An English-speaker must deliberately distinguish between a statement that is a report and one that is a person's own experience. In Algonquian languages the distinction is made automatically. The phrase "There is a war in Indonesia" would become "There is a war in Indonesia, he said to me" as if it were a report.[4]

The worldview behind the Algonquian language system is that people must find their experiences for themselves, from the inside. Says Henderson:

> We have a theory of the universe that's been given to us that covers a lot of stuff about relationships but not about *things:* how to maintain families, and how to maintain love between brothers, sisters, and cousins and nephews, and how to live in an environment that looks hostile but is very giving. . . .

Their language is intimately connected to the earth. To understand them, he says, you have to "be" nature, to be the world. This is the experience that can emerge from the fourth space of dialogue—a connection with oneself and the world around that allows a fundamental new sense to emerge.

Intriguingly, this fourth space is also one where words take on a power that they do not seem to have in other spaces. This fourth conversation space brings about a level of alignment and connection among people such that, as Bohm put it some years ago, "People are no longer primarily in opposition, nor can they be said to be interacting; rather, they are participating in this pool of common meaning which is capable of constant development and change." When someone speaks from this experience, their words have a thunder behind them that is greater than if they were simply speaking on their own or for themselves.

The Crisis of Entry (or Reentry)

There is a fourth crisis, a fourth boundary to navigate in the dialogue process. However powerful and flowing a conversation becomes—either within yourself or in a group, you do not live in this experience permanently; you must leave it. The return is a return to a world you departed, but from a different place. You return to the world of "politeness," of "civility"—knowing now that very different kinds of conversations are possible. And yet you find that many people around you either have no interest or no experience (or both) in this. They look at you as if you had been away a little too long, and have lost perspective on the "real world"—which for them may consist of only one or two of the conversational spaces you now know exist. People typically are well aware of Field I and II, and might imagine but have little experience with Fields III and IV.

Returning to the world you have left produces a crisis, because it is hard to give up the hard-won sense of power and potential that you have experienced. And it may feel as if you are the only one who can understand what you know. The crisis here involves *learning to let the meaning of this familiar old world change.* Your relationship to it changes. Initially, the world does not change at all, and you do discover you have no need for it to change. In this sense you can move back to the third space more readily than you might have before you took your journey: You can reflect on your own moves and their impacts. You can begin to understand when people are speaking across frames and clashing, and suspend these clashes as opposed to seeking, as you might have before, to "fix" them.

Joseph Campbell, in his description of the hero's journey, notes that the challenges of returning are among the most formidable the hero faces. This is because there is an inconsistency between the world that permits great insights and freedom of expression and the "ordinary world" that seems to deny the value and legitimacy of such experiences. Many of the ancient myths picture the return as a kind of responsibility, a requirement to bring new insight into the life of the community. This can weigh heavily on the individual traveler. Indeed, it is quite possible to become addicted to this fourth space, to imagine that this is indeed the pinnacle of experience, that everything else is subservient to it.

But as I have said throughout, the intention in dialogue is *motion,* movement. I have found people who imagine—and I know I initially believed—that achieving a sense of deep conversation and even communion with a group of people, out of which can come profound new insight and action, was somehow the point. But by equating this space to dialogue, it becomes too precious, too inaccessible, a new-age fantasy that in a way denies the real possibility for transformation, which is a continuous cycle of change.

Leadership emerges when an individual or a group understand the shape of the world, and so are not deceived or overly intoxicated by any particular arrangement of its features. The attempt to retreat into an experience of edenic fantasy, of intimacy, without going through the challenge of reentering the world of the mundane eventually becomes quite toxic, quite limiting, and life denying.

FOUR DIFFERENT QUALITIES
FOR SILENCE AND TIME

Looking through the lens of the four conversational spaces I discussed can illuminate a variety of experiences that are central to the emergence of dialogue. People's experience of silence in conversation varies greatly from one field space to the next. In first space, silence is socially awkward, even strange. People do not sit together long in silence without someone becoming quite uncomfortable, thinking it odd that no words are being spoken. The expectation is for action, for direction. Its absence can be very disconcerting.

The second space treats silence differently. There is tension. People may disagree and attribute another's silence to judgment about oneself, or perhaps even to calculation—"He is sitting quietly to think of his next move!" (Or "I have him on the ropes.") Silence here is conflictual and may seem even dangerous. In the third space, silence is pensive, thoughtful. People are reflecting, waiting, looking inward, listening for new possibilities. Finally, in the fourth space, the silence is whole and, at times, sacred. The wisdom of the wider group takes precedence over the chatter of the individual.

The uses of silence are displayed in the ways time is understood as well. Our sense of being and our sense of time are very intimately linked. One of the reactions to the proposal of using dialogue for anything that requires action is that it simply takes too much time. But through dialogue you can discover that there is plenty of time. It enables you to experience time differently.

Kronos and Kairos

The sense of time also changes through the evolving fields of dialogue. Most of us live in what I would call sequential time: measured, linear, one moment after another. This kind of time we could call *kronos*, after the Roman god of time. *Kronos* still controls us; most people have his emblem strapped to their wrist! The relentless pressure arrow of *kronos* time is the one most of us try to manage. We often have the sense that it is scarce, that we must ration it.

But there is another kind of time: the time of the seasons, of the moment. This kind of time, which is called *kairos*, is the sense of time you have when you walk outside in late August or early September and say, "Fall is in the air." How did you know? *Kairos* is the sense of time you get when you go to the beach, and can tell whether the tide is coming in or going out. Again, how did you know? Your own inherent awareness of cycles and rhythms tells you. *Kairos* time reveals the movements of natural rhythms; it is the sense of "appropriate time," the "right" time for something. Where *kronos* follows the external schedule, *kairos* follows an internal one. The cycle of gestation and birth for a child is pure *kairos*.

The process of dialogue helps us to rediscover and appreciate *kairos*. We have had many dialogues where two hours go by and people are shocked: "Where did the time go?" they ask. "It seemed like we had barely begun." They lost the sense of *kronos* and were following the present-moment rhythms of the conversation. When *kronos* reasserts itself, it often feels like an imposition: People in dialogues often complain: "Why are we following an arbitrary schedule? Something important is happening here!"

We must learn to appreciate and accept both kinds of time. Both are necessary in the world as we know it. But usually *kairos* is dominated by *kronos*. The process of thinking together with a group in dialogue seems to enable people to shift their experience of time. They embrace *kairos*. They gain perspective, they rest, and they develop a keener sense of when to act and when to reflect.

In the first space *kronos*, the aforementioned god of linear time, is dominant. Things have clear beginnings and endings. People want to know the sequence. As people move into the second space, they often find time to be "running out"—their differences take up more space than they had imagined. And people become quite irritated by the seemingly limited time that they have to speak. There is not enough *for them*. *Kronos* still is dominant here, but under pressure. In this second space people generally refer to other times and places as ways to reference what is happening now. People are generally not fully present yet. In these first two spaces, thought—in the sense of memory—is still largely, unreflectively, dominant.

In the third space, a change begins to take place. Here we see the emergence of *kairos* time, the time described earlier as "the right season." People become more fully present in this space, in the present moment. *Kronos and kairos* seem to have an uneasy coexistence here. People become quite reflective and aware of the conversation as taking place in time, but also lose track of it and begin listening more for the sense of meaning that is unfolding.

In the fourth space, *kairos* dominates. Hours go by and it seems only minutes have elapsed. It is very difficult to interrupt dialogues that are in this space when the pressure of *kronos* arises.

Convening

Dialogue

L eaders of dialogue are convenors. The word *convene* means "to assemble with others; to come together." The four phases of dialogue, or four fields for conversation, give us a template and way of thinking about convening leadership. Leadership in each field differs. The requirements differ for holding the container, for engaging the crises, for navigating the pressures within each field.

For dialogue to happen, the principles outlined here must in some way be followed, so that the energies that produce the container—listening, respect, voice, and suspension—are actively encouraged and practiced. But again I emphasize that this cannot simply happen at an individual level. People all together must suspend their assumptions and let the container itself evolve. As they do so, as they in essence let the space between them and within them change, something very new can begin to happen. As I have said before, this cannot be done simply by the application of intellectual principles that are not backed by the living experience of the people themselves. Dialogue is not a technique in this sense, even though the principles that lie behind it can be articulated.

What follows is the outline for a guide to these spaces, and the leadership required within each of them.

LEADERSHIP FOR FIELD I

When a group of people are in this phase of leadership, they typically cover up differences or are simply unaware of them. They are caught by the structures and rules of the social whole and often feel unable to change or challenge them. Leadership here, when it seeks to evoke a more dialogic exchange, must somehow challenge the status quo and incite change. Several elements are critical here:

Clarify Your Intentions

Perhaps first and foremost for beginning any kind of dialogue effort is the realization that how you see the situation is critical. Do you have a set of prejudgments about these people that makes you think they "need help"? Is this something you would be willing to tell them and risk having disconfirmed? If not, your intention to fix them will likely be at odds with an effort to evoke a shared inquiry that has any kind of commitment from them.

Entry is Everything

The way you approach a situation will determine a great deal about how it will unfold. I have found that the first few moments of any exchange contain the seeds of the totality of the interaction you shall have. The importance of these initial conditions, of the way you choose to interact with people, sets much in motion. In this sense, any move you make is an intervention into the system you are entering.

Join Each Person Differently

Each person within a dialogue is different; each one speaks a different language. Each one prefers a different "system paradigm." Each one has a different story and way to make meaning. Listening carefully to each person and speaking uniquely to him or her matters enormously when creating the initial setting for a dialogue.

Create the Container

As discussed in many different ways, the container for the conversation must be created if there is to be a significant change. The four core practices and principles for dialogue are valuable here. They set a basic context from which to operate. It is not necessary to be explicit about having all four qualities active in the group, but they must be in some way present for there to be a full dialogue process. These dimensions help:

▪ **EVOKE THE IDEAL**: The promise of dialogue is that a small group of people might do something that impacts the world. Evoking this potential, supporting its articulation, and asking people to reflect on it can make an important difference to progress going forward. What I mean here is asking people to listen for the potential of this group, at this time, to create potent results.

▪ **SUPPORT DREAMING OUT LOUD**: The pressure of politeness tends to suppress people's willingness to dream out loud. We are far more expert at cynical judgment than at visionary thinking. And cynicism is often well founded: "Vision statements" and empty promises about the future are just as deadening and just as much a part of the culture of politeness as the taboos on openness. Dreaming about how things might actually be different, given honesty about how things now are, requires the critical ingredient of *support*. This means an unwavering sense of reinforcement that does not judge what is said or done. A good test of a leader is his or her ability to actually do this, and not collapse into sophisticated (though sometimes unspoken) put-downs of the people around him or her.

▪ **DEEPEN THE LISTENING**: People must come to the point of realizing that they listen in their minds and hearts, not through their ears. Opening a space for conversation that fundamentally changes the core meanings and, therefore, outcomes in a group requires that people discover that their listening matters.

▪ **MAKE IT SAFE FOR OPPOSERS**: In this work it must somehow be legitimate for people to oppose what is happening and not feel obliged simply to agree. Bringing opposition out makes it more likely there will be real dialogue and inquiry.

▪ **DARE PEOPLE TO SUSPEND**: The power of opposers requires an equal competence at suspension, if only by a leader at first. The power of someone who is able to make room for perspectives not his own, even maddeningly different ones, can open an enormous space of possibility.

Leadership in this space means helping people to manage, or experience, the crisis of emptiness. Having the understanding that you cannot make dialogue happen, that it must emerge, and having the resilience to stay steady while people react when they find their best efforts at dialogue meet with more polite exchange, can propel people forward.

LEADERSHIP FOR FIELD II

In this space, people discover that the interpersonal disturbances they were hoping would not arise are in fact present and actively limiting effective exchange. Conflicts flare up. Leadership in this space involves learning a great deal about the structures of the system, providing an atmosphere of safety and reassurance—that conflict, too, can be held here, and taking action that is revealing of the quality of reflective inquiry and coherence that one would like to see in others. Some elements that we have found helpful here:

Map the Structures

The key step now is enabling people to come to the point where they can find a safe place to identify the forces that are at work.[1] Why do they work this way?

For example, a program officer of a major foundation once invited me to help teach a group of senior leaders for a year-long program they were organizing. In our planning sessions he had told me that they had failed to do any work on "productive engagement" the previous year, and this had proved a real hindrance to the group; race, political, and personal conflicts swirled around but often went unresolved. "Was this something you thought of ahead of time and tried to implement?" I asked.

"Yes, but the vice president rejected it. But this year we want it." By "we" he meant the grudging acceptance of the VP.

As we talked, it became clear that three different forces were at work here: One was the program officers' own model for how to manage these tensions—which was to bring them out and talk about them. Another was the VP's approach—which was not to talk about them at all. A third force was the group's, a mix of the views of the two leaders. Serving any one stakeholder attitude well would disappoint or threaten the others. What is more, the very issue that he wanted me to address in the group was repeating itself in the foundation's leadership between the VP and this fellow. For his program to have any real impact, the inner contradictions between these forces would have to be addressed. They were as real as the tangible pressures of wind and wave beating on the outside of the building.

At the core in most of these Field II situations is a set of structural dilemmas: If people raise difficult issues, they are chastised, and if they fail to raise them, they betray their integrity, the people, the process—or all three. Naming these things makes it possible to inquire into them.

Facilitate Cross-Model Conversation

Helping people to see that their differences are as much a function of the different languages that they speak—for instance, the different action moves they prefer, or perhaps the different preferences for governance and power that guide their behavior—can greatly ease people's ability to get along. What people in this space attribute to nasty motives by the other guy (ones they not only do not understand but do not *want* to understand) can be shown by a skillful leader to be two very different ways or models, of seeing reality. Facilitating among these different perspectives means developing the ability to suspend them for oneself, and to provide a safe setting for all of them.

Educate

Often people do not have a clear understanding of the alternatives open to them. They imagine, when faced with a tough conversation, that their options are either to repress what they feel or fight. The third option is to engage in the ways I am suggesting here. Learning about this, particularly now, in this second phase, is an essential step. People tend to be somewhat more ready, since it is quite clear that what they have been doing is not working. It is important to explore with people the possibility of how a wider horizon of inquiry exists if they choose to enter into it. A leader here would be wise, for instance, to seek to work at all three levels: creating new capacities for action, developing people's predictive intuition, and informing them about the invisible architecture that guides behavior and thought.

LEADERSHIP FOR FIELD III

Embody Reflective Inquiry

For this phase the key is to embody the kind of reflective inquiry that you aspire to see in others. Instead of finding problems with others and seeking to correct them, you can reflect publicly on your reactions and what took place within you, inviting others to do the same. You can also look for ways to deepen and broaden the inquiry.

Listen for Emerging Themes

It becomes possible in this third field to pay attention to themes that come from a group's overall interests and ideas and yet are not being articulated by any single person. Listening for the group's underlying questions as well as its unspoken voices activates energy and greater depth of exchange.

Model Leading from Behind

Leadership here is participatory; you do what is required not as an expert but as an increasingly equal member of a larger process of inquiry.

Predict and Deal with Retrenchment

Typical of this phase is the temptation to imagine that as people discover they are learning to talk and think differently, they are in some ways "special" or "different." This amounts to the formation of an idol within the group, and is a sign of the rigidity of thought that can limit the free flow of dialogue. Noting this and exploring it can help keep a dialogue alive and fluid.

LEADERSHIP FOR FIELD IV

Embody Service

The question for this phase of a dialogue is What is the highest end to which this conversation and/or group of people might serve? What can be done here that cannot be done in other settings? Leadership in Field IV is servant leadership; it is intended to provide for the needs of others in the team or group, or as a group seek to discover what it can best provide for others.

Reflect on the Whole Process

Another key element of leadership here is to make conscious what it has meant to participate in the complete cycle of the dialogue.

Encouraging people to think broadly and deeply at this phase greatly increases the chance that they will learn to sustain what they have learned.

Seek Paths to Resolution

Dialogues that produce insight also reveal possibilities for action. Leadership in Field IV is alert to the possibilities for action that can emerge from the conversations people have shared.

Allow the Leadership Role to Move

It becomes very apparent in this fourth field that leadership is in constant motion. Whoever is able to articulate what is happening has, for that moment, a position of leadership. No preestablished individual can be made the one and only leader. In this phase, leadership is a function of a special kind of meritocracy—the ability to listen for and articulate what is already moving in everyone.

See the Whole as Primary

This fourth phase of dialogue is characterized by the realization that there are forces at work that are larger than any single individual. Leadership at this point requires us to ask, what are the questions emerging out of the whole of this process? What is waiting to be said or done that goes beyond what any one person might have said, but is true for all?

The Ecology

of Thought

There have been some remarkable shifts over the last few hundred years in people's understanding of interdependencies of the earth's ecology. To the early white settlers in South Africa, or the first loggers in the Brazilian rain forests, the environment was an unfettered resource to exploit. Today many people realize that the earth is a set of interlinked living systems, and that unilateral actions in one part may stimulate devastating unintended effects in others. For instance, unlimited mining can produce corrosive pollution and destruction of local rivers and water supplies. Rain-forest destruction harms the earth's atmosphere. A decision made in China to manufacture hundreds of thousands of new cars each year will, over time, almost certainly increase the pollutants in the air that North Americans breathe. Increased emission of greenhouse gases into the earth's atmosphere will also very likely raise the temperature of the earth's surface.

Yet our growing preoccupation with the external ecology obscures a much more subtle, and I believe equally important living system—what I call the *internal ecology* of human beings.[1]

DEFINING THE INNER ECOLOGY

The inner ecology is the system of interlinked patterns of feeling and thought running through all people. In other words, it includes our individual and collective memories, our individual and collective associations, and the pathologies of thought outlined in Chapter 2. These memories comprise our culture—the assumptions, the habits of thoughts, and ways of working out problems people need to function well together. But the ecology also extends beyond this. It encompasses our creative capacities, our ability to go beyond our thought, to our perception, awareness, and understanding of the living principles also named above.

These twin aspects of our inner ecology—memory and awareness—are woven through the entire fabric of our experience. The framework of this book outlines three levels of this ecology: the behaviors we exhibit, our predictive intuition about the traps and difficulties in conversations, and the invisible architecture or "fields" out of which our conversations arise.

This chapter articulates the emerging theory somewhat more fully. It does this by exploring some emerging ideas about this internal ecology, showing how the ideas I have been exploring in this book form the outlines of a more general theory of it—and provide a framework for its central generative processes.

The idea of the inner ecology implies that, despite what

we often believe, our thoughts and ways of living are often not only our own. We share patterns and habits of interaction, of thinking, and of feeling. What may seem like individual problems really are not; they may well belong to us all.

Most of us imagine that our thoughts are separate from our feelings, our bodies and our perceptions. Our thoughts are "in here," within our skull, while other phenomena exist externally, signaled to us through senses that are as narrow and specific as a telegraph wire. But according to recent physiological and cognitive findings, our thoughts are actually intimately connected with our feelings, bodies, and perceptions of the outside world.[2]

When we think of something that we like, for example, we feel good. Our thought doesn't "make" us feel good; the thought and the feeling are interwoven in a coordinated neurophysiological system: the *thought* and *feeling* arise together. This system includes the endorphins that are released in our brains, the neural pathways formed by the memory, and the mental associations we make, many of which stem from the social context of our families, our associates, our friends, and our history. It is impossible to separate these elements to say which "caused" us to feel good. They are powerful because they act together. Our language tends to confuse these matters: for instance, we speak of "thoughts" and "feelings" as if they were separate and clearly distinct. But they are more accurately described as part of a single interconnected and tightly interrelated system.

Put differently, perturbations we receive through our senses stimulate our nervous system, which is itself a product of a vast process of evolution. Nature is as much within us as it is outside of us. These perturbations are not simply conveyed to us as representations of the external world, they are directly shaped by our nervous system as well. A great deal of information about the so-called external world actually arises from *within* our own nervous system.[3]

Some years ago anthropologist Gregory Bateson introduced a related notion—that of an "ecology of mind."[4] Bateson attempted to show that every living system has a "mind"—which emerges as a function of an evolving pattern of communication and meaning. This "pattern which connects" gives it form, shape and direction. Bateson sought an explanation for the underlying pattern of relationships that linked living things, and found it in his notion of *mind,* which includes not only mental processes, but also living relationships, where information (and, more importantly, difference) is registered and which causes energy to be released.[5]

Using the idea of the inner ecology idea as a lens, we can come to understand the network of problems that seem to plague conversation and limit dialogue. Many of these, I will propose, are part of an interlinked living network, one that has a profound influence on us, and yet one that also seems hidden from view. After all, we do not, as I have already suggested, usually think about how we think. Our experience just comes to us.

During this exploration we need however to keep one caveat in mind. To identify our inner worlds with an idea that has emerged from the study of the external environment is potentially hazardous, at least to the degree that we unwittingly imagine that the external world is "just like" the internal world. I do not think it is. There are dimensions of our internal world that do not exist in the external in the same way, but which are nevertheless quite important. For instance, our internal world is characterized by *interpretation,* that is, our ability to make sense of what we see and hear and experience. Modern empirically based science is reluctant to see interpretation as externally valid data, that is something that can unambiguously be directly and empirically observed by a neutral party. But the idea of an inner ecology can suggest to us ways in which our inner worlds are part of a wider living system, one that has important impacts on how we think and what we do.

IMPLICATIONS OF THIS APPROACH

The idea that we have an internal ecology stimulates a number of lines of implication and exploration. First, as I have been suggesting, our thoughts and feelings are part of a large system—both within ourselves and in connection with other people. Some people are surrounded by predictable patterns of behavior and action—patterns that are reflective of the local ecology of their thought. Picture the cloud of dust that followed the cartoon character Pig Pen everywhere he went. He carried his own ecology!

A second important implication flows from the first: our thoughts and feelings have a magnetic influence on our worlds. Despite the fact that our nervous system has a certain inherited structure, it is also plastic. We can have a definite influence on our own experience. Thoughts and feelings, in this sense, *have tangible impacts.* They do not simply float above us; they draw to us certain ideas and experiences, and repel others. They have impact on us because they influence the form and figure of our awareness.

One way people have conceptualized this influence is to speak about how human beings perceive their worlds through "interpretive frames." They argue that we have mental models that filter our experience and guide our actions—in any meeting you go to, different people will be running different videos in their heads about what is happening and what should happen.[6] But thoughts are more than lenses or frames or video projections. They are magnetic: they attract ideas that are similar and repel ones that are different. I recall one senior manager in a large organization who seemed to be surrounded by people who doubted his competence. The story people told was that he was in line for a very senior job and yet somehow got passed over. "You see," they added knowingly, "now he is just not all that effective." The story had a certain captivating quality to it; it organized my thoughts even though I had never met him. It was now very difficult for me to meet this person and see him any other way. When I finally did meet him, I discovered that he, too, had accepted this story. The ecology of his world, including his own thoughts about himself, other people's interactions with him—indeed, his entire demeanor—reflected this pattern. The world that surrounded this fellow seemed somehow dampened, without energy. Other people carry a sense of themselves as successful, or flexible, or kind, or angry, or fat, or unloved—this too affects the ecology of thought around them. Our inner ecology, in other words, is continuously organizing the material of our awareness.

GROUP PATTERNS

Groups also carry their own ecology. A group planning a change initiative within an organization will establish a certain presence for itself. That presence is composed of their own thinking, along with the thinking of others around them. If the group and the organization begin to repel each other, then there may be a problem with the ecology of thought in that system. Systems can encompass both sides of a divide, but if you are a member of a change or pilot group, there is little you can do directly to change the thought on the other side. You can only start on your own side, unilaterally, by "trying on" some new thoughts that may help you develop new capabilities.

The idea that there is an interlinking network of thought among humanity was captured by David Bohm in his proposal that we have a "system of thought" that connects us all. Bohm proposed that human thought consists of interconnected elements comprising not only the ideas in the mind, but the patterns of interaction among people, including bodily interactions and even social arrangements. He compared this system to a set of "reflexes." These reflexes are a conditioned set of responses to a variety of circumstances. Memory operates as a kind of reflex response to given circumstances. Bohm notes:

> If somebody asks you your name, you have an immediate answer. It's a reflex. With a more difficult question, there's a way the mind searches in the memory for answers; there's a searching reflex set up. . . . I'm proposing that this whole system works by a set of reflexes—that thought is a very subtle set of reflexes which is potentially unlimited; you can add more and more and you can modify your reflexes.[7]

The great majority of our interactions are informed, Bohm suggests, by the layers of memory in this system of thought.[8]

PATHOLOGIES OF THOUGHT

Another dimension of the inner ecology I have described in this book as the ways thought produces problems for us. These problems appear everywhere, but are rarely dealt with as problems in thought itself. In this sense, the ecology of thought contains habits common to us all that can be quite limiting. For example, as I showed earlier, we may become mired in certainty, and lose our capacity to be aware and suspend our assumptions. Or we may become dazzled by an idol, an image, and lose our ability to speak our own voice. We may lose track of the underlying coherence of our world, seeing our experience as composed of separate and unrelated parts, and impose violence through our judgments of ourselves or others. Or we may lose our sense of participation in our experience, feeling ourselves to be separate and "cold" observers only.

Each of these difficulties in thought is embedded in the way the current ecology operates. And each one of them arises because of the ways we are dependent upon and are to some degree hypnotized by our memory. Each of the pathologies of thought I have articulated emerges from memory. For instance, we come to experience our worlds through fragmented images and interpretations of life, images that live in memory. We make idols, interpretations, that we fail to see as interpretations. It is only when we see the world through our memory that we objectify it: we cannot do this when we live in the present moment and perceive more directly. When we come into the present moment, the idols dissolve, and we have a more direct sense of the unfolding nature of our voice and presence. We know who we are and what we need to say for ourselves.

Part of the challenge of transforming the ecology is to transform our memory—or at least the way we experience it.

BEYOND MEMORY TO PERCEPTION

To do this requires we go beyond memory. This entails developing our perception or awareness. Such capacities lie beyond thought and are somehow insights that enable us to perceive and change our thought. From this creative capacity come the acts that in essence lay down new tracks, transforming memory and experience. We do this all the time, in art, in business, and in life—developing new products, breaking with traditional ways of shaping colors on a canvas, producing new and exciting ways of governing ourselves. And we often fail to do this, particularly when we most need to.

As I outlined in the section on new capacities for behavior (Chapters 4–7), there are four principles that can more generally describe the nature of creative awareness. To cultivate your capacity to speak your voice, you must develop a sense of the unfolding nature of things; to develop your capacity to listen, you must cultivate an appreciation for how you participate in creating your own experience; to develop your capacity to suspend assumptions and certainty, you must develop your awareness, and to develop your capacity for respect, you must cultivate your sense of the underlying coherence of Life.

THE WAY WE TALK IMPACTS WAY WE THINK

While doing something about the inner ecology of human beings may sound like a daunting if not impossible task, I believe we have at our disposal a very simple and yet profound way to influence this ground. For it turns out that this inner ecology is reflected in the way we talk. And so, to change the way we talk is to begin to change the way we think. We can influence and regenerate the inner ecology of human beings by transforming the quality of our conversations.

The way we talk emerges out of our inner ecology. It is not fanciful to say, therefore, that our words shape our world. In the words we choose and the ways we put them together (and the ways we listen to other's words), we literally define the sense of what is possible and not possible. At the same time, our world shapes our words. The way we talk is not simply a function of our own will, our minds and hearts, and decisions. We speak the way we do about the things we speak about because we are a part of a much larger system, an ecology that links the thoughts of all human beings. Change in one part of that ecology can have impacts on the whole of the ecology, precisely because it is a living system. As odd as it may sound, President Clinton's now infamous personal and political difficulties had a very direct impact on the minds of virtually everyone—certainly in the United States. Clinton's actions forced people to confront some of their own attitudes about sex, its appropriate bounds, and the challenging forces that move within every human being. Clinton's resilience, while discounted by some as unconscionable slipperiness, also revealed a way to stand and survive even a nearly totally overwhelming onslaught and attack and not completely lose dignity or power. Clinton forced public reflection on issues that have generally stayed below ground, shifting the political discourse and illuminating many assumptions about privacy, leadership, and moral balance.

Just as food and water flow through the microorganisms, plants, and animals of an ecological niche, thought flows from our surroundings through us and back to our surroundings, changing us as we give voice to it and changing our surroundings as those words emerge from us.

WORDS COUNT

People have always had a sense that their words are important. I am suggesting that there is a reason for this that goes beyond what we might imagine. Words count. You cannot take back your words. This is because they have energy; they are living carriers of the ecology and atmosphere in which you live. We all know times when one right word well spoken uplifted and changed everything, changed the underlying meanings of a situation. And we also know times when a few words poisoned everything, where it took years to recover.

In our conversations we are either engaged in thinking alone, and so cling to our positions, or we are doing something new, which is to bring out our hidden potential, our capacity for appreciating the unfolding order of things, our sense of profound participation in life, and with one another our capacity to see the underlying coherence of our world. Which we choose is a function of what we come to understand about ourselves.

By changing the way we talk, we change the way we think, not just as individuals, but all together. If we could restore our inner ecology in the ways we think, we might have an enormous impact on our worlds. In this lies some of the immense potential of dialogue.

TRANSFORMING THE INNER ECOLOGY: INTEGRATING THE GOOD, THE TRUE, AND THE BEAUTIFUL

Transforming the ecology of thought is done as we pay attention to the way we bring our words to life. The vehicle by which we can shift and restore the inner ecology lies in how we accommodate and integrate the three great value spheres of human experience, or what the Greeks spoke of as the Good, the True, and the Beautiful.

When the ancient Greeks wrote and spoke of these, they were reinforcing a set of ideas that were held as different aspects of a coherent way of understanding what it meant to be human. As Ken Wilbur has argued, today these elements have become far more highly differentiated. Science has been the star performer here: The pursuit of objective truth has completely reordered the world the Greeks once knew and produced enormous advances. It has produced innumerable (and often wonderful) technological breakthroughs. But differentiation has become fragmentation. Where once these three were aspects of a single approach to life, today they have "grown up," left home, gone independent, to the point where they almost refuse to recognize one another any longer. The Good, the True, and the Beautiful do not talk well together. So we now have a deep pattern of cultural fragmentation among these three core value systems. Each of these three tends to exclude or neutralize the others, as they have developed and differentiated themselves.

RECALLING THE QUESTIONS:
THE PURSUIT OF THE GOOD

That there are divisions among these three dimensions of experience is hard to refute. For instance, the scientific and material perspective, in its pursuit of technical and objective "truth," provides us with what seems like irresistible logic to pursue any and all new technological possibilities. "If we don't, someone else will," we are told. To speak of restraint is to seem utterly backward and out of touch. To ask Will it be beautiful? or Will it serve the common good? may seem important but almost futile questions, the victory of the objective domain so firm that to ask to slow things down to entertain alternative or broader views seems oddly out of touch with reality, distant secondary questions, or best left to other experts to sort out later.

Scientific materialism has tended to crowd out other perspectives to the point that it *denied they had any relevance*. Here is Wilbur's (passionate) take:

> Put bluntly, the I [subjective experience, the Beautiful] and the WE [intersubjective experience, the Good] were colonized by the IT. The Good and the Beautiful were overtaken by a growth in monological truth that, otherwise admirable, became grandiose in its conceit and cancerous in its relations to others.... The subjective and interior domains—the I and the WE—were flattened into objective, exterior, empirical processes,

311

either atomistic or systems. Consciousness itself, and the mind and heart and soul of humanity, could not be seen with a microscope, a telescope, a cloud chamber, a photographic plate, and so all were pronounced epiphenomenal at best, illusory at worst.[9]

If you cannot have concrete, objective, and certain knowledge, for instance, about ethics or aesthetics, then they cannot be taken as seriously as those domains where you can have this kind of empirical precision.

Some years ago in a groundbreaking book called *Soft Energy Paths,* environmentalist Amory Lovins challenged our unintegrated momentum. He questioned many of the then-prevailing assumptions about energy conservation and resource utilization. Critical of the relentless and unthinking use of non-renewable energy sources, he noted that we pursue these technologies doggedly. We say, Technology is the answer! But, he noted, we forgot to ask, What was the question?

What was the question? The core question for the modern scientific and management model is What is efficient and effective? This is clearly a valid concern. And yet, of itself, it is also utterly inadequate. The Greeks had a different question, one that sought to integrate the Good, the True, and the Beautiful. They asked, What is the good life? And Do we have the courage to pursue it?

To the Greeks, this question required people to think not only about humanly created structures and norms but those "according to nature," which included the whole living cosmos. Man looked to both the wider cosmos, the heavens and the earth, for direction. The assumption was that the good life entailed harmonizing one's interior experience with the natural order of things, which included aspects of each of all three domains. The "Good" itself was symbolized by Plato as the Sun, the source of everything. He believed the challenge for any individual, particularly those who aspire to leadership, was to discover this animating source within all things, in nature and in the affairs of men.[10]

Today we have rejected this line of thinking, in part because of the successes of modern science. There is no direction forthcoming from the heavens, modern science has informed us. Human beings must invent their own meaning if they are to have any. We have come down to earth, so to speak, and in so doing lost much of this original vision. So today we have transformed the question What is the good life? into the question What is the most efficient life? In this sense the quest for the good has become degraded, "flattened," and is now merely a quest for power, for what is effective, divorced from any larger sense of meaning or purpose or aesthetic.

THE THREE LANGUAGES AND THE GOOD, THE TRUE, AND THE BEAUTIFUL

Intriguingly, you can immediately connect this to your conversations and everyday situations by listening to the "languages" people speak in the sense of power, meaning, and affect. These three languages have a very close correlation to the value spheres of the Good, the True, and the Beautiful. We can hear the traces of these value spheres in the immediate and concrete way people speak every day. And you will find that they, too, have become quite distinct from each other, and impoverished because of their lack of interconnection. So, for instance, recall that the language of "power" focuses on efficiency and action. People who speak it constantly want to know, What are you going to *do*? But without realizing it, this language is often spoken from the narrow perspective of the system immediately at hand.

What are you going to do, not, Will what you plan to do be *any good* in a wider sense?

Separated from the Beautiful and the True, the Good becomes tyrannical and oppressive. Separated from affect and meaning, power becomes one-sided, domineering, narrow.

The Good, strictly by itself, is barren. Without the True or the Beautiful to balance it, the pursuit of the Good produces moral rigidity or even tyranny. Today we see deep cultural antagonisms in America, for instance, between advocates of some form of moral absolutism and those who preach "situationalism" or moral relativism. These are debates about what system of ethics *"we"* should use. The conversation between these camps often devolves into positional arguments and is lacking in serious inquiry. This was the prevailing undercurrent for much of the thirteen months of anguish over President Clinton's relationship difficulties. How "we" define our moral and ethical standards requires we take seriously the highly personal objective experiences of each individual concerned, how each person feels. And we must produce some means of having serious and relatively objective inquiry into experience, including experience that is annoyingly different from our own.

Fostering better dialogue between people who have deep differences on this score requires the three levels of dialogue I have argued for in this book: a powerful invisible architecture, or container, in which to have the conversation, one that legitimates each perspective without implying the other is right; enough predictive intuition to see how the face-to-face dynamics and traps that arise between the people would tend to get in the way of a good conversation; and the active presence of the four behaviors of dialogue: listening, respecting, suspending, and speaking one's voice.

THE BEAUTIFUL

A similar story could be told about fragmentation in the realm of the Beautiful. In beauty resides the aesthetic and sensuous dimensions of life. It is the domain of subjective perception, of what I think and feel, and of artistic expression. For Plato, love of beauty was a central component in coming to know oneself. Love of physical beauty, of the sensuous, Plato suggested, could lead one to an appreciation of invisible beauty, and ultimately to a love of wisdom and beauty itself. One of Plato's most famous and sensuous dialogues, the *Symposium*, takes place at an all-night drinking party, where its participants give long speeches on the subject of love while becoming quite drunk. To the Greeks, beauty was still closely tied to true understanding: You could not have one without the other.

Yet how many managers and leaders today consider whether the policy they are about to pursue is in fact beautiful? Do they "love" the policies and ideas they pursue? The questions seem largely irrelevant today, since we have come to separate beauty from power, affect or sensuality from ethical action. The emerging worldview on which dialogue is based suggests otherwise: Far from an irrelevant, "soft" concern, the beauty or aesthetic of any subject is an essential component of its successful deployment and sustainability. We can see a similar pattern here, too, with respect to the language of affect or feeling: In many settings it is discounted because we do not think in a fashion that respects equally and integrates all three languages.

At the same time, we can also see that fragmentation plays out here too. An unrestrained pursuit of the Beautiful without regard to either the collective implications of the Good or the objective constraints of the True creates a kind of false sense of superiority in the arts—as keepers of the vision and soul of humanity, while at the same time an ineffective stepcousin.

THE TRUE

Truth today has also been separated from the other two domains—from beauty and from pursuit of a collective good. We understand truth as science, an inquiry into hard facts and observable data. But today's objective conceptions of truth have usurped older and richer meanings, and unnecessarily crowded out its richer implications.

Drawing upon the Greeks' understanding, truth can be understood not merely as objective scientific truth but as the *spirit* of truth. I once heard truth compared to a deer at the edge of the woods, coming to drink. The truth is coy. If you make a loud noise, it tends to flee. If there is a still place, without disturbance, the most essential truths of the moment can come forward. This story refers to the subtle dimensions of truth that we might contemplate. Truth can refer to internal dimensions, not merely external material ones. Put another way, an inquiry into what is true in any given situation can include rigorous exploration of the interior dimensions of experience as much as it can the objective, exterior dimensions.

The ancient Greeks did not necessarily have the right answers. But I think we could say that they had some of the right *questions*. Today the questions that animate us have changed dramatically. In other words, we might reinvigorate our lives by learning to ask new questions. Asking large questions seeds the ground with new possibilities. While at first glance this may seem to be unstrategic work somehow not central to achieving the ambitions we set out for ourselves, I suggest that inviting the senior leaders in any setting to reflect on the deeper questions that animate them, and that animate their organization, is some of the most important work they can do. This is because it forces them to think about their choices, many of which are often made unconsciously, out of habit, or out of fear. Choices sown with these energies inevitably collapse. Think of inquiry of this sort as the ultimate act of efficiency: dealing with problems far upstream, before they surface and require expensive rework and change.

These two aspects of our inner worlds: the levels of depth—invisible architecture, predictive intuition, and behavior—and the dimensions of breath of the Good, the True, and the Beautiful make up the wide range of possibilities present in human experience. Together they comprise our inner ecology, one in need of restoration, something that may be possible through dialogue.

PART V

WIDENING

THE CIRCLE

Dialogue   and

the   New   Economy

"The most important work in the new economy is

creating conversations."

—Alan Webber, editor, *Fast Company* magazine

The late 1990s have brought a dramatic collision of new economic, social, and political forces, compelling many to believe we are in a time of both great peril and profound promise. Success requires a new set of rules and strategies, both to navigate in the new economy and to ride the turbulent societal tides.[1] These conditions produce a context particularly ripe for dialogue.

In their book *The Caterpillar Doesn't Know*, Kenneth Hey and Peter Moore trace the progression of this collision of forces. They argue that in the years since World War II, for instance, American society has shifted from an era where the priority was on creating "communities of wealth," through the dislocation and instability of the 1980s to our current time of reassessment, where the focus is gradually changing to creating "communities of meaning."

Communities of wealth were built upon the value systems and priorities of the postwar generation—the growth of the consumer society, a reliance on traditional and hierarchical control structures, and a relatively stable bipolar global political balance. Communities of meaning represent a shift toward the personal, toward independence, and toward self-development in work. Hey and Moore argue that organizations that pay attention to this trend will succeed; those that do not will fail. Whether you believe this to be true or not, it is evident that people are beginning to place more and more explicit attention on personal growth as it might unfold in the workplace. Where once these needs were met outside work, today they are assumed, especially by young people, to be a central feature of their work. Their central question: How much of myself must I leave at the door when I come to my job?

That human society is in a transition is difficult to refute. Many familiar landmarks seem to be passing away. The collapse of communism and the revolutions of 1989 on the global scene marked perhaps some of the most significant political changes in the past seventy-five years. Despite the promise of economic prosperity and the "victory" of capitalism, the global economy continues to experience serious shocks ranging from shrinking real wages to the most recent domino effect of Asian economic instability.

But these problems have been evident for some time. In the late eighties and early nineties American organizations began a series of extensive downsizing and restructuring exercises, leading to the elimination of some 2.5 million jobs.[2] There has been an almost frenzied pursuit of the "lean" organization. But we can downsize for only so long before there's nothing left. In his book *The Future of Capitalism,* MIT economist Lester Thurow argues that these changes may well mark a kind of transition to economic free agency and independence, where firms are no longer the central supplier of employment.

The interaction of a set of major forces undergird this transition and are producing a period of "punctuated equilibrium"—a term Thurow borrows from evolutionary biology. Punctuated equilibrium is a change process marked by long periods of stability that are suddenly and dramatically altered. This is one of the reasons given to explain the disappearance of the dinosaurs: a sudden cataclysmic event, such as a comet striking the earth, producing massive extinction. Thurow argues that we are now in such a time with respect to global social and economic forces, These forces interact like the vast plates on which the continents of the earth float, destabilizing the institutions of the past, forcing a major rethinking of organizational status quo, and compelling us to create a new set of strategies for success.

Thurow identifies five "geologic" forces that are producing a moment of profound change: the end of communism, the technological transition and its concomitant commitment to developing brainpower industries based on intellectual capital, a dramatic aging of the population in the United States, a truly global economy, and a multipolar political world in which there is no single dominant player or unifying ideology other than market capitalism itself. He argues that the United States is entering a period of new isolationism, where it can no longer easily be the world's policeman, and may find it hard to justify military action on foreign soil for causes it cannot understand. With the threat of communism gone, the pressure to take care of domestic issues rises considerably. This is the platform on which Clinton ran, and for which he was elected. Bush proposed that he be the foreign policy president. He lost.

Reflected in and perhaps fueling these shifts is what Hey and Moore call the quest for "communities of meaning." In times of fundamental change, human beings are forced to reconsider basic values. Today this quest is being fostered, in some parts of society at least, by a unique set of historical forces—enough prosperity to think about change, enough uncertainty to fuel it, and loss of credibility of major institutions, and, most critically, a global economy that seems increasingly to value higher skills.

People are making new lifestyle choices—and emerging with a very different set of values and ambitions. "Personal downsizing"—people who are simplifying their lives by selling large houses, quitting their corporate jobs, working from home—has become increasingly popular. Transferable individual skills and key relationships have become sources of competitive advantage and, in today's wired world, are producing very different rules for success. All of this has led to an immense surge in personal transformation and growth efforts, which are, argue Hey and Moore, beginning to have an impact on corporate leadership and organizational structures.

There is, however, a problem with all this. Most think of "transformation" as something focused on individuals. But I believe this is no longer adequate. I believe that what is required now is something new—we cannot focus simply on personal transformation but, rather, on collective change.

Dialogue's promise stems directly from one very important dimension of these changes—the emergence of the networked economy and the centrality of communication within it. In his new book, *New Rules for the New Economy,* the executive editor of *Wired* magazine, Kevin Kelly, identifies three features of this new world—globalization; favoring of intangibles like information, ideas, and relationships; and intense interlinking, all three of which, he says, are rooted in "ubiquitous electronic networks." According to Kelly, the emergence of the network economy has spawned counterintuitive laws that it behooves the wise to follow: Power lies in embracing decentralized control; generosity produces wealth (read: give away your intellectual property if you want to get wealthy);

support the network, not my node within it; and freely abandon the successful known for the emergent unknown.

Now, many of these sound like idealistic prescriptions for a world one might hope to see, not necessarily one that is actually emerging. Microsoft's aggressive pursuit of the software world no doubt did not feel like generosity to their competitors. But Kelly validly underscores the vitally important shifts toward networks. Whether human beings will accept and follow new principles as a result remains to be seen. One thing is clear though. As Kelly puts it: All of these changes presume the ability to communicate: "The new economy is about communication, deep and wide. . . . Communication is the foundation of society, of our culture, of our humanity, of our own individual identity, of all economic systems. . . . This is why networks are such a big deal."[3]

It is naïve to assume that the desire for communication or even insights about a network economy is sufficient to produce it. We must develop the capabilities in ourselves, our organizations, and in our networks. We need the capability of forming a network with "dialogue inside."

Widening the circle, growing the capability for dialogue in a variety of domains will enable us to make progress in solving many of the problems that arise in the new economy. What follows are descriptions of domains where dialogue can make a specific, practical contribution.

COORDINATION IN NETWORKS

There is a class of problems for which dialogue is the best— perhaps the only—real solution: those in which traditional competitive market conditions, and top-down, hierarchical structures no longer work.[4]

We can see many such examples in the business world as enemies are becoming partners and allies. When Steve Jobs introduced Bill Gates as the new ally of Apple at the 1997 MacWorld conference, it became clear that computing had entered a new era. Microsoft had long been seen by Macintosh devotees as the enemy—the firm that stole the Apple operating system and forced the company into being a niche player in the business they essentially invented. And in many ways it was true. Microsoft had taken from Apple the momentum it had sparked. Now came Steve Jobs, their folk hero, the catalyst behind the personal computer, inviting Mac fans to grow up and appreciate the $150 million in investment capital that Microsoft contributed to Apple to help sustain it through tough times. It was certainly the case that Microsoft had Apple over a barrel. By capturing ninety percent or more of the operating system market, Microsoft had effectively won the competition for dominance. Further, many of Apple's core software applications were produced by Microsoft, and Apple needed Microsoft to upgrade it to keep Apple users happy. Jobs realized he had no choice in the matter but to accept Microsoft's help. Jobs had, in his words, grown up. He had learned to see the world in a less hierarchical, either/or fashion. Jobs followers were less sanguine; he got booed. Old habits die hard.

There are many other such examples that defy conventional models of market control, and for which dialogue can offer necessary connective tissue. Shell Oil in the United States has formed alliances and created over fifteen different new companies, thrusting some fifty percent of its employees into positions where they no longer work for Shell but still have considerable business with and substantial ties to the company. These people can remain coordinated with one another through dialogue, despite separate operating companies and lines of responsibility.

The CEO of a major hospital is trying to bring together a group of independently minded doctors to work more closely in alignment with the administration, to contain costs, and to provide wide service to the community. He has no formal authority over any of them. These doctors all have other options they can pursue. How can he create a fair exchange and prevent further divisiveness?

In each case, and many others like them, alliances and networks take precedence of the command and control forms of governance. But it remains to be seen whether human beings can learn to operate successfully in these circumstances.

OVERCOMING PROFOUND DIFFERENCES

Another setting for dialogue involves situations where people have massive differences not only of perspective, but also of worldview and identity. It can be a major task even to define what the central problems are in these cases. The Chechens have mistrusted the Russians for centuries, and the Russians in turn fear the domino effect of granting Chechnya independence. Greek and Turkish Cypriots share an island but are miles apart in terms of their willingness to cooperate. But these "cultural" differences are not limited to national interchange. Engineers typically mistrust executives. Medical doctors are often at odds with administrative and business groups within hospitals. Such cultural or "worldview" differences lead people to describe their "problems" in different ways, to hear certain facts as salient and others as propaganda, to call one side freedom fighters and the other terrorists, one generous and the other self-absorbed.

Such differences must be resolved for there to be sustainable change. As Edgar Schein has pointed out, to the extent that we need to coordinate our actions and establish a common understanding of what we are trying to accomplish, some form of dialogue *must be used* if we are to make any progress at all.[5]

Traditional kinds of control do not work under these conditions. You cannot *make* people think together. Solutions or control imposed from the outside will likely be resisted. These problems require an approach that enables people to see how new kinds of insight and collaboration can emerge despite the deep differences in their views. As I have implied, even the most intractable differences carry the energy and seeds of transformation if they can be nourished properly.

The failure to reach a common meaning can have a devastating impact on an organization. One of the worst outcomes of such a failure is inaction. The "baby Bell" phone company NYNEX, before it merged with Bell Atlantic, kept a running battle for some years at its most senior levels over how to balance its mix of investments in the future. Should they strengthen their existing network? or should they try to capture high value-added business? The "technologists" pushed for new investment. The "traditionalists" feared that without investment in their network infrastructure, they would lose their business base and perish before they could capitalize on the high-margin "digital gold rush." "Everyone agreed" at one level that they must do both: but neither camp understood the reasoning and assumptions of the other. As a result, they could never decide on which new things to invest in and which to ignore. The company lost much valuable time because of their indecision.

A failure to think together also crippled another major global technology company, Omega (a pseudonym). Here polarization not only prevented action, it limited the chance even to consider new possibilities for product breakthroughs. In this corporation's context, one leader's authoritarian hand prevented the possibility of greater collective intelligence.

Omega found itself in an internal conflict over whether to invest in digital technology for its products or to stay with analogue, where it had a huge lead. At the time, the new digital technology looked expensive and uncertain. A small cadre of people advocated going the digital route. A larger group, including their highly autocratic leader, believed that analogue was the answer. "Digital drools, analog rules" people began to say. The problem was that there was no informed conversation anywhere in the organization about what to do. Each camp carried very deeply held and largely negative assumptions about the other. This polarization was reflected throughout the business, where there would be both digital and analog development groups in every major region, and very little coordination across groups. Neither believed the other understood the challenges ahead. Hierarchical authority and a misguided belief about their own market supremacy prevented them from acting in time—in *either* direction. Now they are desperately trying to catch up, as much of the industry has passed them by.

If we cannot talk together, we cannot work together. Schein's claims for dialogue—that it is a necessary prerequisite for group action—stem from his view that it is one of the only ways to determine whether organizational communication is valid.[6] These are problems of coordination and joint-problem solving that must be handled with an approach that gets past differences in a productive manner. But such interactions must not only create "agreements" as a conflict resolution approach might, it must also use the conflict to help fuel the discovery of new insights and sustainable learning. Dialogue, properly understood, can be useful precisely in these situations where people either have not wanted to "come to the table" or where they must create the social glue in order to build a new table.

OVERCOMING THE LIMITS OF TRADITIONAL MODELS OF COMMUNICATION

Understanding the nature of dialogue can help us transform our assumptions about what constitutes a good conversation. These include confusions and inner contradictions in values like "openness," beliefs about how we must structure and manage conversations, and the role of the facilitator.

Many organizations today promote something like "openness." They call it tolerance, "open and honest communication," "engagement," or even "dialogue." And there is some evidence that these efforts, which are typically implemented through large-scale trainings, do produce some results.[7] But if one looks carefully at what actually happens in organizations that espouse such values, one finds that creating that openness is not as easy as it sounds.[8] Ironically, in practice, "open communication" often means "speaking candidly" in the sense of blaming others instead of examining one's own part in creating the situation one dislikes.

Chris Argyris has written for many years about these problems.[9] He attributes behavior like this to inconsistencies between what people actually do and what they believe they are doing, as well as to a socially generated value set that rewards covering up difficulties in the name of smooth face-to-face relationships. This amounts to what Czech president and writer Václav Havel once called "living a lie."[10] For instance, one firm I know had a senior executive team that spent many millions creating a culture change program that promoted "open communications." But when it came time to express difference, people demurred. After all, they said, if you spoke out, you would not seem to fit in. Fitting into a culture where people were "open" came to mean you did not disturb the waters when real differences arose. The people colluded to suppress truth—in the name of openness.

Dialogue, practiced well, has a far more radical edge that encourages us to learn to tell the truth about our own and others' inconsistencies in a way that begins to enable us to transform them. It encourages openness that causes us to reflect on our own responsibility, and to build a culture where this is seen as a strength rather than as a weakness.

Dialogue also challenges the fundamental belief that we must manage carefully the political implications of what we say in organizations. This assumption stems from the culture of thinking alone. It has led to the view that organizations are machines, mechanistic devices that must be managed as such. Inevitably, this belief shows up in the way we conduct meetings: They must have structure, an agenda, a clear purpose and predetermined outcome for every step of the process, and someone to "drive" the process, as we would any mechanical device.

Thinking together requires that we challenge this way of doing things. In dialogue, for instance, it is important to make space for what is not programmed or planned for. Dialogue flourishes when we do *not* have a clear-cut agenda for a meeting, especially as a group begins to interact. This can allow a freer exchange so that people can begin to learn to talk together. While it can appear chaotic at times as people learn this new form of interaction, this can allow the conversation to become more conscious and focused. Dialogue is not a random "free-for-all." If you and one or two close colleagues were to talk about something that really matters to you, you would likely stay focused because of your commitment to the topic. You might think broadly and widely but not carelessly. So it is with dialogue, in a larger group. People find themselves listening more intently, thinking more clearly, and yet working much more spaciously and creatively than they ordinarily do.

The fashion today to manage conversations is to hire a facilitator. This has become so commonplace that many organizational teams today have people permanently assigned to assist them. Yet this has the feeling of a Band-Aid solution. I think there can be real value in it when the facilitator has the requisite skills. But they must also move out of an overly controlling, overly structured approach if they wish to evoke dialogue rather than discussion. When we are trying to move into dialogue, conventional, structured approaches to facilitation can be debilitating. A dialogue is a conversation among peers. In this sense, everyone is responsible equally. While a facilitator can get things moving, he or she must move out of a position of control so that the awareness of the process is shared by everyone. The key question to ask is: Are we operating in a way that increases our own awareness and reduces our dependence on any external controls? Dialogue can help us to overturn these dependencies and teach us to think more freely.

DISCOVERING THE POWER
OF "IGNORANCE" MANAGEMENT

Knowledge management in business and organizational settings generally has to do with finding, extracting, and sharing knowledge that lives in the people in an organization or network. Often this is thought of as storing knowledge in a digital database and making it widely and easily accessible. Knowledge understood in this sense is basically a recording of memories, of things we know. But rising expectations about "knowledge management" may be misplaced.

Increasing our effectiveness requires we discover what we do not know, our ignorance, not our knowledge. There are several kinds of "ignorance." One is "blindness." We cannot, for instance, see the ground we are standing on. As Bill O'Brien, former CEO of Hanover Insurance, puts it: "An eye cannot see itself." Your colleagues are often much more aware of your strengths and limits than you are. A second kind of ignorance is "unawareness"—you have tacit knowledge you know, but you cannot say what it is.

Knowledge management systems are generally not very good at getting at either kind of ignorance. But it is in precisely these domains that we have the most to offer one another: Only through a conscious reflective process like dialogue can we surface this ignorance and make use of it.

There is a third kind of ignorance, one that stems not from unwitting limits or difficult-to-access understanding, but from the fact that human beings deliberately withhold information from one another.

In one of the world's largest knowledge management efforts, the World Bank is spending over $50 million to build a global knowledge management system. Its proponents believe that capturing information about a development project in Lima, Peru, and then comparing it with one in Mexico City or the Philippines will greatly increase efficiencies, reduce errors, and save time by fostering cross-organizational exchange of information. Yet the biggest problems in the bank have to do with people, not information. There are deep divisions among and within the different functions and layers of the organization, a factor that stops people from sharing information freely. The bank's critics also see it imposing its beliefs on its constituents, greatly reducing its effectiveness. Indeed, the bank's own criticisms of its projects suggest that only sixty-six percent succeed by its own criteria, tracing the cause to both these factors. The bank's knowledge management system contains memories of successes and failures. But it cannot of itself enable people to overcome the barriers between them.

Finally, one cannot get insight or wisdom out of a database. Nor do they emerge out of the tacit practices of people in a given craft or profession. Much has also been made of the link between the informal or tacit knowledge of a firm and knowledge management, based on the premise that around the water cooler, where the know-how in the heads and hands of the repairmen is shared, genuine learning takes place. If harnessed, some propose, this could enable organizations to innovate and extend this "local" knowledge much more widely.[11] This kind of knowledge certainly is valuable. But there is a vast difference between this "operational" knowledge and the consciously generated insights drawn forth when people think together in entirely new ways. This is not simply a matter of extracting tacit understandings but of creating something new. Insight, I suggest, comes from the field of meaning that is created when a group of people—or even an individual—gains access to it. It is this field of shared meaning that dialogue can enable us to create.

Dialogue holds the potential to enable us to perceive and use our ignorance because it helps us to reflect in ways we would not on our own. And it holds the potential of helping us gain insight as we see past existing knowledge to new possibilities.

DEVELOPING THE RESILIENCE TO CHANGE

Functioning with the intensities of our world requires resilience. Dialogue can help by stretching our minds to inquire into point of view we might not naturally accept, and so holding more possibilities and options open. We are moving from a time when people were expected—at least if one worked in a large corporation—to know what problem was likely to arise next and have a ready answer for it. Now we are entering an age where we cannot know what is coming. Much of your knowledge is likely to be obsolete within a year. The explosion of global capitalism and digital communication through vehicles like the Internet is changing the face of our economic and social structures at a pace that is dizzying and virtually impossible to absorb. How are we to understand all this, let alone keep up?

These are not individual problems. To the extent that we insist on dealing with them alone, I suspect that as individuals we shall feel more and more pressured and isolated. Many of us in the

United States are in the habit of valuing the self-sufficiency of the "rugged individual." It is true that the individual does count and I am responsible for myself. But the issues human beings now face go beyond solutions that any of us can conjure up. We need to make a collective shift as well as an individual one. This means learning to think with others and not merely on our own.

Recently in Antarctica, studies of the survival habits of emperor penguins have brought some intriguing findings to light. It had long been a mystery how these animals could survive the intense winds and frigid temperatures of this strange continent. Temperatures of fifty degrees below zero Fahrenheit and winds of one hundred miles an hour or more are not uncommon there. It turns out they survive by forming circles, with their bodies nestled together, to retain heat. And then they slowly rotate the circle, so that no one bird is exposed to the wind too long.

They form circles. This is an apt metaphor for the power of dialogue. How are we to deal with the cold and challenging winds of change? I will suggest we might do the same, by engaging in dialogue in our organizations and communities, to generate the resilience we need.

The new economy we face in the twenty-first century consists of a very different set of forces from any known before. Shifting bases of power and an enormous emphasis on knowledge make the way human beings talk and think together of paramount importance. Human beings create, and share, knowledge through conversation. It behooves us to heighten our abilities on this score.

Cultivating

Organizational and

System Dialogue

THE PROBLEM WITH
PROGRAMMATIC CHANGE EFFORTS

In an article entitled "Why Change Programs Don't Produce Change," Harvard Business School professor Michael Beer and his colleagues document the cynicism most people in large companies feel about the programmatic change efforts that periodically seem to sweep through their cubicles like a noxious gas. Of the culture-change programs they surveyed, they found no evidence of actual change at the level that was promised by corporate consultants. Indeed, even where

modest gains *were* noted, they weren't in the direction anticipated.[1]

Top-level management often drives these transformation
efforts. These leaders employ platoons of advisers, business
school professors and consultants who, armed with the latest
models and theories, often *do* surface many of the important issues facing the firm. Yet, if we measure success by assessments
of such factors as productivity, attitude change, or financial performance—especially if the issues they are designed to tackle
are complex and nonroutine—many of these efforts fail.[2]
Indeed, evidence suggests that as a rule, only relatively routine
changes can be brought about within an expert-driven and "rational" framework of this sort. Success is most likely in those
organizations where restructuring is limited to well-delineated
parts of a business, and where (contrary to the rhetoric) little
or nothing is left to the individuals to define for themselves.[3]
But for those who require that human beings learn to think differently as well as to act differently, corporate change efforts are
notoriously ineffective.

One of the reasons for this is that these programs are riddled
with two kinds of inner contradictions. The first, pointed out by
Chris Argyris, is a structural contradiction in which one set of
causal forces pulses one way and another pushes in a different direction. This is also what David Kantor calls a structural trap.

For example, fundamental change depends on people taking responsibility—what Argyris calls internal commitment—
for the issues they face. By contrast, however, change efforts
almost invariably prescribe both the change *and* the logic everyone is to follow to achieve it. People do what is defined by others, the "others" usually being their bosses. In this sense, the
change programs usually have embedded in them the very problem they claim they want to change: It is a contradiction in
terms to use a top-down, control-oriented approach to try to

manufacture learning and empowerment instead of creating conditions where they naturally emerge.[4]

The second contradiction is embodied in our habit of taking terms like *empowerment* or *learning organizations* and making idols out of them.[5] In such a case, empowerment becomes a "thing" to achieve, not a path to follow. "Creating a learning organization" becomes a standard to impose, not a process to germinate. In both cases, hundreds of companies have adopted these ideas and tried to turn them into programmed efforts at change. While the organizations' *rhetoric* may be about internal commitment and learning, the reality is that people are often "volunteered" to participate and given little choice. In some companies, peer pressure may make the concept of a learning organization fashionable. However, this often backfires, for even as the idea becomes attractive to some, it becomes a source of dismay to others who mistrust fads.

From the perspective of the ecology of thought, this set of outcomes is predictable. A damaged ecology of thought typically turns living processes into objectified "things," discouraging reflection on contradictions and incoherence. People justify such an approach by announcing that "we do not have the time," or "we have to get results right away," or "we need action not talk," thereby deflecting efforts to suspend the certainties and assumptions that sustain these problems.

A DIALOGIC APPROACH TO CHANGE

A dialogic approach to change in organizations and large systems must take these problems and contradictions into account if it is to be effective. In everyday experience this comes down to individuals and teams developing disciplines and practices to notice the degree to which they are basing their thought and action on a sense of how things are supposed to be. They need to come again (and again) into what writer Jon Kabat-Zinn calls the "bloom" of the present moment. It is the difference between "memory-based" and "presence-based" management.

This approach suggests that only when we are *present* can we set aside our habitual reactions, and the buzz of our minds, with its ceaseless efforts to sort everything out and create smart answers. We can learn to do this too in teams: At meetings, for example, instead of jumping immediately into the agenda—which is based on everyone's memories of what has already been done and projections of what should now be accomplished—a group can be still and listen to what is "true right now." Some of what emerges may well *be* the agenda already proposed. But some of it may be completely new, completely unexpected, requiring that we think *now*, not just report what we have already thought at some other time. This means, in the terms I set above, stepping "above the line" of reflection, out of reaction and breakdown and into a space of inquiry. In this way a dialogic approach to change focuses primarily on developing practices and capabilities on a large scale, where habitual and stuck patterns of interaction and thought are continuously challenged and reflected upon.

One of the things that first attracted me to dialogue was not simply its promise to enable "openness" between people, which was clearly something for which there was (and remains) a deep hunger, but the possibility that a group of people could, by becoming aware of the "sea" in which they swam, fundamentally alter it. Dialogue has confirmed my belief that while we *have* an ecology of thought, it is *not what we are.*

This becomes especially obvious when we discover we can come to see some of our own blindness and habits of thought in action. Think of a time, for instance, when you accepted your parents' image of what you should do with your life—and then realized that you had inherited something that was not really yours.

As Humberto Maturana puts it, you cannot see the place on which you stand; it is too close, too connected to you. Once you see it, you realize you have moved, and your field is enlarged. For this reason, seeing out limits clearly—perhaps for the first time— is actually evidence of progress, not falling back, though the experience can at first be depressing or disturbing. There is a part of us that is able to discern these things, even as there is also a part that blindly accepts our perceptions or habits of thought.

It is now possible to discern the outline of a large-scale dialogic approach that can transform the ecology within which a system exists by gradually developing this capacity for awareness and perception. Just as there are four ways of building new capabilities in individuals and teams, there are also four practices that can enable whole organizations to become dialogic. In these practices the infrastructure and operating systems, the formal and informal processes, support:

■ *Suspending* taken-for-granted ways of operating in order to develop the capacity to "see the system" and reflect on the structures and forces that produce incoherence.

■ *Respecting* the ecology of relationships that develop in and around the organization—with suppliers, customers, regulators, investors, competitors, and employees.

■ *Listening* in order to stay present and fully participative.

■ Finding, enhancing and strengthening the organization's central *voice* or story.

One word of caution: We are still in very early days with respect to both the application of these ideas and a more comprehensive articulation of how they might work. But I predict that in the coming years, a wave of people will discover how a genuine foundation of living attention and awareness can be sustained in ever-larger systems.[6]

SUSPENSION AND STRATEGIC DIALOGUE: MAKING SPACE FOR NEW PERSPECTIVES

First, to invite people to stay present and remain in a living inquiry with one another and all that concerns their enterprise suggests an organic, not programmatic approach—one that takes seriously the already existing fabric of interactions within a company. This form of inquiry moves improvisationally, without enormous planning in advance. In this approach, people must suspend their control and see what unexpected outcomes might emerge.[7]

Don Laurie, for instance, a consultant to senior managers of several large companies, has worked extensively with strategy theorist Gary Hamel to bring about breakthrough discoveries based in unleashing imagination of people in companies. Because of his experience, he explicitly doubts the ability of senior teams to direct such an effort. Instead, he and others who follow this approach often will invite some one hundred to three hundred people from a cross-section of the organization to attack the strategic challenges facing the company and then inform the senior management—and often a wide group of others in the company—of the results of their investigation. Typically senior managers react at first quite defensively to the suggestion that everyone in the change process, and perhaps everyone in the company, hear about the results of this large group's investigations without their having a chance to vet it. "You mean we are not going to see the results first?" more than one manager has asked, incredulous. Within KPMG in Holland, explicitly removing some of the control from the top and devolving it lower down unleashed enormous energy and led to insights about the business and its potential that have significantly reshaped it. Most people acknowledge that unless they had suspended their more traditional approach to strategy making and looked at the problem from many angles and in many different ways, they would never have accomplished the results they did or generated the level of extraordinary commitment and enthusiasm that came from the ranks of the organization for the change effort.[8]

RESPECTING THE SYSTEM ECOLOGY: ALLIANCES AND THE CREATION OF THE NETWORK COMMUNITY AT SHELL

An organization-wide dialogic change effort needs to take seriously the impact it is having on its wider ecology—the network of relationships in which it exists, the physical and social environment in which it operates, and the boundaries that it must respect. Shell Oil in the United States undertook a remarkable transformative journey that significantly shifted the governance structure of the organization and produced dozens of alliances and joint ventures, atomizing the once-solid and traditional structure of the organization. In the midst of these changes, Shell has begun to explore a means of enhancing the network of interactions among the people that does not impose but, rather, inspires respectful connection.

When people are searching for their sovereignty, it is essential to acknowledge it in them by extending respect. This must be operationalized and made concrete so that it goes beyond mere lip service. Shell's efforts at growing a "network community" illustrate this kind of dialogic movement.

In 1993, Shell Oil Company made just $21 million in net income on sales of $18 billion, the lowest in its history. At that time, the company was organized in a traditional command-and-control, top-down fashion. All the decisions flowed through the upper levels of the organization. Strong "silos" isolated leaders from one another. People identified strongly with their function.

This crisis of performance coincided with the arrival of CEO Phil Carroll. Trained initially as a physicist, Carroll's approach, as he himself once put it, was "hopelessly inept," but he was committed to learning. Carroll legitimated an organizationwide inquiry into how a truly transformed organization might look. This approach was founded not so much on a programmatic effort as a consistent search to unleash energy and install competencies at all levels of the organization. It has not been a "tidy" and systematic process; speaking to the people there today, one would hear as many stories of nightmares and struggle as victory and results. While the price of oil has helped to improve the company's overall performance, it does not entirely account for Shell's turnaround figures: In 1997, the company earned some $2.3 billion in net income on $28 billion in revenue.

At the core of Shell's efforts is a change in the governance structure of the company. In 1994, the initial shifts involved creating a leadership council that emphasized independent business units with individual boards. Shell formed "independent operating companies" out of the former divisions. The role of the leadership council was "to provide forums for the senior leaders to discuss areas of mutual interest and nurture the transformation across the company." This took some hard swallowing by several of the top leadership groups at first because, for the first time, they began to realize that they were *not* going to be making all the critical operating decisions—the heads of the new operating companies would be doing that.

The managers of these new businesses did not stand still. They created alliances and joint ventures with many other companies, including competitors. For instance, the Oil Products Company formed a multibillion-dollar joint venture with Texaco to merge all of their "downstream" facilities, including all the retail businesses. Now one company, Star, owns all the Texaco and Shell retail stations. The newly formed Shell Services company, which was responsible for information technology when forced to stand on its own two feet, made an alliance with the new Global Services company of Royal Dutch Shell and split off completely from Shell U.S. In all, some 40 new ventures were formed with other companies, including Mobil, Amoco, and Texaco. Of the twenty-two thousand employees that once had the word *Shell* on their badges, now some ten thousand do, the rest having become part of the large "family" of companies within this wider system. In the space of about five years, Shell has gone from owning ninety-five percent of its assets to wholly owning only sixty percent of them.

Change of this sort does not come casually, though the oil industry has—despite its capital intensive structure—always been a risk taker, largely deserving its wildcat image. Nevertheless, companies that support differentiation of this sort, devolving power and freedom to lower levels of the organization, inevitably face the challenge of managing the need for integration. Shell is no exception. As the transformation and formation of alliances proceeded, employees were thrown into confusion: "Who am I now?" many asked. "Whom do I work for?" "To what do I now belong?" Many feared there would be a loss of shareholder value as the atomization of Shell proceeded.

Out of these concerns a group of people within the company began to develop a new concept for organizing in what they came to call a "networked community" of companies. The group of Shell Companies and its related ventures formed "strategic initiative teams" to address the problem of organization, given this new operating reality. It was not organized by "control through ownership" but, rather, "influence through relationship," as they later called it. Through a powerful process, these teams produced a set of now-accepted recommendations that included CEO executive sponsorship. They formed a group of network leaders from across the global community of entities: They created a "network learning and support center" to foster capability development; they encouraged the free movement of people across and within the community; they created an information technology infrastructure to enable people to reflect together; they instituted an "after-action review" process, adopted from the United States Army, to enable systematic reflection; and they initiated "communities of practice"—groups of chemical engineers across the different companies, for instance, that would come together to learn and share information.

But it was the *process* that team organizers used to bring together this highly diverse and potentially fragmented group of people to produce these recommendations that illustrates the power of a dialogic approach. The initiative began with forming three different teams that included the top leadership of Shell and many others involved in the wide reach of Shell business entities. They focused on such questions as What does it mean to be part of Shell? and What leadership structures should the new Shell have in order to build the right framework for accountability? Many people had an influence on this process, both from within and outside Shell. But the structure of the four major sessions that these teams launched over an eight-month period combined the resources of two experts on networking, Jeffrey Stamps and Jessica Lipnack, coauthors of the book *The Age of the Network,* and several internal Shell facilitators, including William McQuillen, Jim Tebbe, and Linda Pierce, who have had considerable training and understanding in dialogue.

McQuillen, Tebbe, and Pierce used a dialogic process to guide the inquiry of these teams. This meant that they sought to take steps to "increase awareness of the whole," as they put it. They sought ways to have initiative embody in living experience the very structures and ecology that its convenors said they wanted. In this sense, a dialogic approach meant that they worked directly on the ways people interacted in this setting, and sought to let these patterns of interaction themselves be the soil out of which the recommendations would grow.

For instance, they used the concept of "node" meetings to compel the teams that formed around their particular questions to interact with each other—a notion that met initially with significant resistance. People wanted to dig in and solve "their part" of the problem. The facilitators sought ways to notice and interrupt these habits of thought.

They also sought to produce a common space where shared meaning could emerge. This meant not paying homage to the seniority of the CEO, for instance, but creating shared ownership of the results. As one manager said:

> We were counting off in one-two-three's and Phil [Carroll] took a number just like everyone else. He happened to be a "three" and I happened to be a "three." The stripes were off and he just sat there, thinking about ecosystems and what it means to be in the Shell family. He had a voice just like anyone else. This taught me a lot about leadership. It taught me that he would learn and be there, through action.[9]

They did this by deciding not to have prescribed agenda for the sessions, remaining flexible in how things evolved, inquiring within the group about next steps in the process, and monitoring the "container." Dialogic facilitation also means knowing when to relinquish control. As one of the participants remarked about the close of the first major session:

> The network seized control. We now owned the process; the parts took ownership of the whole. Prior to that it was thirty-eight people—and then we became one.[10]

Group meetings like these are notorious for burying critical differences under the guise of "momentum" and the need to "develop a single voice." In this process, at least some of the key differences were deliberately brought into the light. For example, one of the subtexts for this process emerged as competitiveness between the strategic initiative teams. At one point, one of the most senior leaders of the company raised serious doubts about the "value of the networking stuff." The facilitators took this issue, which had come up in one of the teams, and made it a subject for the whole group to reflect upon. They made themselves available as coaches but not as authorities, making room for significant differences of opinion.

Building a culture of respect for differences right into the process, they made this effort distinct. This group developed an embodied sense of how a network might work well by experiencing for themselves—and overcoming—some of the traditional barriers and limits that arise. It was, in fact, the story of their process, and the energy evident in their efforts, that proved highly compelling to the senior management group when they finally got to see the recommendations of this group. Many in the transition team had believed that the senior group wanted simply to see their recommendations. Instead, members of the senior group were themselves struck by their own hunger for the energy of the process and the potential it held for bringing about genuine changes within Shell and its community of companies.[11]

LISTENING AND PRODUCT DEVELOPMENT AT FORD

A dialogic approach to organizational change means cultivating an organizational capacity and infrastructure for listening. Yet it is also true that "organizations don't listen, people do." So how can we create a better understanding of organizational "listening"?

As I outlined above, listening is not neutral. Like individuals, organizational or institutional "listening" is a construction, a function of the structures and ecology of thought embedded in the corporate culture. Listening in organizations is, as a result, often highly specialized and selective.

A given profession, for instance, will teach its practitioners to develop a fine-grained capacity to listen for particular kinds of problems and solutions. Institutions reflect the structures of how its professionals listen. An emergency room "listens" for the symptoms of people in relatively high degrees of crisis. Everyone from the triage nurse who first examines a patient to the attending physicians listen for keys to diagnose what is happening, and immediately categorize patients according to the life-threatening nature of their illness. A sales organization might listen for high-potential clients and sort them according to region, volume, qualifications of the buyer, or many other factors, depending on the product.

Different listening ecologies can result in conflict and lack of coordination within an organization. For example, the service department in one high-tech organization I am aware of is under extraordinary pressure to resolve customer difficulties quickly. Failure in this company's product can severely hinder its customers' business transactions. Problems are easy to define and often dramatic. However, the service department is severely under capacity; it cannot take care of every problem at the same level of priority. The customer service mode of listening is to grade each request according to its technical challenges. Since almost every customer purchases a service contract with this company, representatives are obligated to pay attention to every call. Therefore, highly complex problems go to the most experienced people and more routine problems go to the "front line," more junior technicians.

This kind of listening drives salespeople mad at this organization. The salespeople's way of sorting customer problems is to pay attention to the largest customers first. The bigger the customer's total billing, the more likely he is to buy if he is well taken care of. The service department's failure to respond quickly could (and has) sometimes meant the difference between a further sale and a competitor winning the client's business.

Noticing and resolving problems like these was the ambition of Fred Simon, program manager for the Lincoln Continental development project at Ford Motor Company. His goal was to create a new product development process—in his case, the creation of a new car—in such a way that the usual conflicts and tensions that arose between engineering teams and between management and engineers were minimized. Fred and his team developed a method and infrastructure for listening—in particular, for the kind of interpersonal listening that could enable people to conduct difficult conversations more effectively, remaining open to the possibility that they could accommodate and learn from their differences.

When Fred was younger, he had been part of the team responsible for building the Ford Taurus, a car that is widely reputed to have saved Ford at a time when its profitability was falling and its future was in jeopardy. Now Fred was responsible for deploying a $1 billion investment in producing a new car against stiff competition from Japan and Chrysler. Fred's goal: to create the same conditions that were present with the Taurus. As he recalls:

> My first thought was If only I can get these people together—most of whom didn't actually work for me in the sense that their careers depended on it. They worked for me on this car program, but they really were part of chimney organizations around the company, and their next promotion and their next assignment depended on those chimneys, not on me.

So I thought, If I can get these people to think of each other as *people* and to care about each other as individuals instead of as job descriptions, I can move in the direction I was trying to move in creating that kind of team.

When I met Fred, he was considering whether to agree to support a project in conjunction with the MIT Center for Organizational Learning. My task was to set up and initiate the project. At the time, Fred told me that he was not really all that interested in our ideas and that he was quite sure he did not want a group of academics "messing around" with his project. He did say he was interested in knowing if we knew how to help people come together though.

We initially worked with Fred's senior managers so that we would not, as he put it, "disturb the people doing real work."

We started with the question How do we want to work together as a leadership team? There were, I think, ten of us. We wrote down on a flip chart all of the things we'd like to see in our working relationship.

After it was all up on the wall, Bill asked the question: "Well, if we all agree that's how we want to work together, why don't we work together that way now?"

I bet it was quiet for a minute, which in a meeting like that seems like forever. And finally, the manufacturing manager, Al Gibb, said in frustration: "Well, I'm willing to work that way, but *she'll* never work that way."

So we knew where we had to start. We started with the tools of conversation, and we began to trust each other a little bit more and work together a little bit better. Meanwhile, the rest of the people could see a change. There was a subtle change, but they could see a change. And they were asking questions about it.

We spent about eight months with this group, deepening their ability to think and talk together as a team. They had a range of differences that revolved around functional lines. The finance people were notorious naysayers on new car projects. The engineers typically viewed the accountants as having no understanding about what it took to produce a car; the finance people, on the other hand, saw the engineers as profligate spenders. None of these attributions were discussable. At the end of eight months, however, all of it was being discussed.

The team, using systems thinking tools, mapped the biggest problem they had—late parts. When a new car is being designed, many engineers are responsible for creating drawings of the parts from which a prototype car can be built. This prototype is then tested and evaluated, a second prototype is built: Out of this process, lessons are gleaned to manufacture a new car. With so many parts, many engineers need to coordinate precisely in a defined schedule to produce the car on time. But there are often delays, particularly with United States car manufacturers. Fred's team was determined to find and reduce these delays. In this process the management team discovered a significant delay between the time an engineer knew a part was going to be late and the time he told anyone the part was going to be late. As Fred noted,

> That time delay, once we identified it, could be anything from a week to eight or nine months. We started exploring why that delay took place.
>
> It didn't take a rocket scientist to figure out what was going on. The delay took place because no engi-

neer in his right mind would trust us to tell us; once he identified a problem he just looked for a solution. The last thing he needed was to tell us he had a problem before he had a solution, because all I would say was what are you going to do about it? He would get the problem back anyway. Only now he's going to get "help," right? Because I'm going to call him and I'm going to say, How are you doing on that problem? Why haven't you solved it yet?

So he wasn't going to tell us—he'd have to be crazy to tell us. So we knew the leverage point for us, at that stage in the program, was to create enough trust in the system that he'd be willing to tell us he had a problem—so we can get things corrected up front. And everyone can work on them. Because if he waits eight months, fixes the problem, it affects somebody else's part, whereas they could all be working together for that eight- or nine-month period.

The late parts were produced by a fear of criticism and resulting lack of communication between engineers and management. The top team introduced a series of learning laboratories where, in three days, they taught engineering teams who were interested everything they had learned in eight months. Eventually, some two hundred engineers were exposed to a new set of organizational learning tools.

Springing from this new climate, Fred and his team broke many production records. One remarkable record had to do with addressing the parts-on-time issue. As Fred saw it:

We averaged 50% of the parts released on time. If you have 50% of the parts released on time, that means in your first prototypes you can test only 50%

of the designs. The other 50% are cobbled parts, and you're not really testing them.

With the new interaction skills in place, the teams were able to release 98% of their parts early.

This team set many other records as well, including sending back $65 million in funds set aside to fix problems once they showed up in the manufacturing process.

Many factors contributed to these successes. But a central one that Fred and many others often commented on was the freedom of communication and the capacity to reflect directly on previously undiscussable issues. For perhaps the first time, managers were prepared to listen to engineers in a way that led engineers to feel safe to raise problems early. Engineers many levels below Fred could (and did) call him and ask to halt major parts of the process, violating the unwritten rule of respecting the layers of bureaucracy and hierarchy in large organizations that require people to talk first to their immediate boss.

Many of the engineers that worked for Fred remarked that the most significant change, and the catalyst for the powerful results they were to produce, was a function of the changes in the leadership. Management had genuinely changed and everyone could see it. As Fred put it:

We had done enough programs by then to see that this technique of working with teams was far and away more powerful than anything else that was being done.

Enabling a climate of connection proved immensely powerful. One implication was that teams within the organization learned to interact in very different ways. For instance, when the first prototype of the car was built, the engineers discovered a disturbing problem: The batteries quickly went dead. The numerous electrical components in the car drew more current than the alternator could support. These components were designed by different teams within the car development process: The climate control division handling heating and air-conditioning; the electronics division designed the clock, radio, and instrument panel; body engineering handled the lights. They designed their components independently. No one wanted to give up the functionality they were tasked with just to satisfy the other groups. Each engineering team was rewarded and managed by their functional bosses, not Fred, who was the program manager.

Before the culture changed at Ford, conflicts like these typically would simmer until the team responsible for overall electrical distribution, for example, would go to senior management and ask them to decide what to do. At that point it was usually too late to keep all the functionality that each independent group wanted. After the introduction of a dialogic approach, however, the engineers on the electrical distribution team brought the problem to senior management's attention early. Based on the training they had received in the learning laboratories, they realized that the problem was a "tragedy of the commons"—a systemic trap where no solution can be found within the system itself—and that every individual's action made the larger problem worse. What was required was a larger perspective. Fred understood this, and listened, but not to punish the individuals—which is what could easily have been feared as the result of bringing up a problem that engineers were paid to "fix." Working together, they solved the electrical distribution problem and preserved most of the functionality each group wanted to bring to the car.

Through the learning laboratories, the Lincoln Continental Group produced an infrastructure for listening. Teams learned a set of basic tools and skills for conversation, and through a climate of permission, where engineering teams began to talk openly together about problems they were facing. The direct impact of these moves on business results was unmistakable.

ENCOURAGING THE VOICES:
IKEA AND VOLVO

One of the largest barriers to learning of any kind is the fear of failure, of making errors and losing face. The support required from leaders of people embarking on change processes of this sort cannot be overemphasized. Support must come in the form of leaders *embodying* the very changes that are being asked of others. This means leaders must learn to sustain a stance of unwavering support and appreciation, so that the voice of the organization might actually emerge. Göran Carstedt has run both Volvo France and Volvo Sweden, as well as serving as president of IKEA North America and then IKEA Europe. He believes very deeply in supporting and protecting the abilities of people to express what they know but have often felt inhibited in saying. Carstedt's gift seems to stem from an ability to inspire others to express their genuine voice.

Carstedt has produced a string of significant operational successes over the past fifteen years by deliberately bringing an attitude of respect and support to the managers for whom he was responsible and asking them to show *him* what to do. His approach is to bring out people's own voices and let them see that they have the power to make a difference:

> If you believe in people and their latent capacities, then the more authority you "give away" to them, the more you get back in initiatives and ideas even you did not foresee. We believe in radical decentralization, in pushing authority down to the level where those dealing directly with customers have the freedom to exercise it.[12]

His story illustrates the kind of capability that a leader must have, but also the climate that can emerge when the voice of an organization can speak compellingly to both customers and employees.

When Carstedt was first made president of IKEA Europe, he was faced with a business that had leaders from many different countries. Everyone, including the chairpersons of the company, expected him to centralize the IKEA headquarters and "build a monument," as Carstedt put it, to centralization. Instead, he went to each of the country presidents and asked them what they thought needed to be done. He introduced an internal board system and gave significant responsibility to the local leaders: "If anything is going to happen, it is going to happen here, where you are," he told them.

Carstedt was faced with a similar challenge when he first came to the United States. IKEA is a Swedish company, and had for some years struggled to find a way to penetrate the American market. The national product "voice" of IKEA, many in Sweden felt, would be lost if they abandoned their tradition and tried to meet the United States market on its own terms. At the same time, they knew that what had worked well in Europe was unlikely to work in the U.S. His goal was to create an "alloy" of all the necessary elements: Swedish culture, IKEA product philosophy, and local U.S. market needs. The net result was a new voice for IKEA in the United States that proved quite successful.

Carstedt repeated this approach in Volvo France. When Carstedt took over leadership of the company in 1982, Volvo was a virtually unknown brand, selling only ten thousand cars per year, and holding only about 1.7 percent share of the market. Many did not believe the Volvo could sell in France; it was too stodgy, "safety conscious," old style. Carstedt was determined, and he believed that the only way to double the sales of Volvo France—an expectation that had been put forward four years earlier but never realized—was to gain the commitment and investment of the dealers.

He held nine regional meetings with the 150 French dealers. At each of them he used U-shaped tables and took a facilitator's role. He told the teams:

> I want to know from *you* what you think should be done and what Volvo can do to help you sell more cars. Tell me what we are doing wrong, what you want from us, and I'll see it is done if I possibly can.[13]

Carstedt took on a role of supporter and challenger but not an imposer of ideas. He discouraged the saluting that often comes with hierarchy, and he listened. Soon the dealers invested their own funds in upgrading their showrooms. And he validated and supported Volvo's company voice in France with advertisements that said things like: "Performance is measured in seconds—and also in years," emphasizing both Volvo's speed and longevity, important to the French market. He also emphasized safety, which resonated with the French consumers in ways that went beyond what anyone had initially predicted. Another advertisement showed a little girl in the backseat with the caption, "You need to protect the future, especially if the future is behind you." Carstedt took the entire network of French dealers to Sweden to show them the progressive and powerful work taking place in Volvo factories. He wanted to make them aware of their company heritage, to connect them with Volvo's past and to enable them to represent the car well to their customers.

Each of these moves—supporting dealers, emphasizing with pride the Volvo heritage and giving the message that "there is a lot to be done and, you can do it"—produced remarkable results. Sales doubled to twenty-two thousand cars by 1986, and profitability returned.

OUTLINES OF AN APPROACH

These organizations represent a few of many who are beginning to attempt dialogic efforts at change. Several features make up a dialogic change process; here is a summary of a few that have assisted these and other organizations.

Map and Transform the Structural Traps

An absolutely critical dimension for making large systems change efforts work is mapping the structural traps that arise at critical interfaces. The unwitting contradictions and dilemmas that arise in these settings undermine the vast majority of efforts to make change. For dialogue to work, you must create a container strong enough to surface and explore these traps. Failing to do so will only cause you to reinforce the very difficulties you might wish to transform.

Engaging the Embedded Ecology

In many of the examples above, people have made a sincere effort to engage the underlying ecology of thought rather than simply impose a new logic for change from the outside. This means creating ways to reflect on what is happening, not only for teams but for the overall system. Ford's efforts at using systemic mapping of the self-produced limits in the new product development process are one such example. KPMG deliberately changed the structures behind their usual approach to strategy formulation. Shell developed a living environment for learning in which people could experience firsthand the challenges of being in a network to put them into position to design ways to overcome them.

Actively Reflect and Inquire

In each case described above, people deliberately attempted to create ways for people to reflect on what had happened to them and why, often while it was happening. This, too, is unusual: The action-based focus in most organizations prevents people from realizing that their reactive behavior may only be compounding the problems they face.

Design Infrastructure
to Operationalize New Behaviors

At an institutional level, the challenge is to find ways to build infrastructures that support and sustain the four practices for dialogue. *Listening* at Ford required a series of "learning laboratories." *Suspension* at KPMG required the creation of a new floor and organization within the organization. *Respecting* the system ecologies at Shell required cross-divisional teams designing a variety of processes for facilitating collaboration and communication across the network. Bringing out the organizational *voice* at IKEA meant holding open forums for conversation in the countries where the business was based, relatively agenda free, to enable people to listen themselves while management supported their speaking out.

Dialogue

and Democracy

W e have explored the way dialogue might work, both as individual and group experiences. But in some ways the greatest promise of dialogue may be ways to establish it at social, national, and even international levels. This promise has certainly been adopted by growing numbers of politicians, business leaders, and educators. Even the Pope, in his 1995 Easter message, urged people to relinquish their selfishness, their desire for power, and the use of force to accomplish their ends, proposing instead "dialogue as the only way to promote equitable solutions for a society, marked by respect and reciprocal acceptance."[1]

While these are often noble sentiments, the challenges of

actually producing this sought-after openness, neutrality, and high-mindedness are not easily achieved. While people might innately carry these abilities, they often will not be able to sustain them particularly under pressure. Nevertheless, in some quarters people have now produced large-scale shifts of meaning around critical sets of organization-wide and even national issues.

The exemplary cases below reveal what might be more widely possible: genuine social change and even in some cases collective healing, enabled by processes of productive engagement and dialogue. Patrick De Maré, one of the pioneers of group level dialogue, felt that human beings needed large group settings in order to help them change. As a psychiatrist, he looked at the trauma of war and its impact on a society and asked the question Are there collective methods that could enable real healing and reconciliation to take place? He was particularly interested in ways to take aggression and hatred and turn them into something productive. Put in the language of the architecture of dialogue, is there a way to enable large groups of people to shift from Field II behaviors into Field III?

The same question could be asked by any leader of a larger organization: What must we do to keep the flame alive; to keep the conversational ecology flourishing? Bureaucratic rigidity is notorious at stifling the best of visions. Changes in this ecology can allow dramatic changes; dialogue, in turn, can allow this to happen.

This chapter explores examples of two kinds: efforts to produce dialogue that have worked and those that have not.

CONVERSATIONAL VIOLENCE: FOOD LION AND THE MEDIA ON TRIAL

In February 1997, Ted Koppel, the anchor of ABC's *Nightline*, invited representatives of two warring camps to reflect together about their difficulties. ABC News had been successfully sued by the Food Lion company for misrepresenting young producers and reporters as qualified meat processors when in fact they worked for ABC. These reporters had taken hidden cameras into the Food Lion processing kitchens and purported to show poor handling of meat. The ABC reporters had lied about their experience in order to get the jobs. In response, Food Lion had initiated and ultimately won a $5.5 million lawsuit against ABC for damages for fraud, trespassing, and breach of loyalty to Food Lion.

ABC News's actions had upset people in Salisbury, North Carolina, home and headquarters to Food Lion. After the ABC broadcast, shown on *PrimeTime Live* Food Lion's stock had plummeted fifteen percent. Eighty stores had closed that following year.

The results of the trial—and the ruling against ABC—upset many more people than ABC's transgressions had. The implication most feared by journalists was that a society that went strictly "by the book" might be prevented from uncovering wrongs that were in fact deeply damaging to people. In their view, their ability to act as guardians of democracy was at stake. Food Lion executives argued that the media, yet again, had gone too far, and that some sort of check on them was now required. The *Nightline* episode, called "Hidden Cameras and Hard Choices," was intended to bring out these differences and provide a forum where people could contemplate the issues.

Koppel made an effort to set up a neutral and objective setting for the conversation. He assembled a panel of media people, including Diane Sawyer, the anchorwoman who first reported the show, Roone Arledge, the executive producer of ABC, and Don Hewitt, the producer of CBS's *60 Minutes*. He also invited senior representatives from Food Lion and their lawyers. Behind both groups sat members of the jury from the trial.

Koppel is notable in the media industry for his efforts at convening forums for reflection on major issues. Part of his competence includes his ability to set a container, primarily by inviting a diverse set of voices and establishing his own personal credibility and objectivity. This includes naming, quite openly, some of the factors that might intrude on or limit his neutrality. The ability to do this is a particularly useful skill for any facilitator in Field II spaces, where breakdowns are likely to occur or are invited. Koppel's introduction was exemplary:

> If you ask am I objective tonight, the answer is no, of course not. But if you ask whether I can treat the issue of hidden cameras and undercover journalism objectively, I'd like to think the answer is yes, but you'll have to be the judge of that.
>
> We have come here to North Carolina precisely because it is not New York or Washington or one of those other cities presumed to be in the media's back pocket.

Koppel also invoked an ideal: He tried to get the group to aim higher than rehashing the issues of the case:

> Clearly we are here because of the Food Lion case and I fully expect that some of the issues raised by that case will be discussed tonight. But we are all of us here determined to move beyond the case and to talk about the hard choices raised by hidden cameras and by journalists posing as something they are not.

Despite these efforts, the conversation that ensued amounted to a barrage of positional advocacy, with Koppel acting as traffic cop. Both the Food Lion people and the ABC News people took strong advocacy positions and for much of the broadcast remained stuck in them. The Food Lion representatives said none of the things reported on the original show were true, and that ABC had illegally obtained the information. ABC insisted that what they found, including people getting food out of Dumpsters, was accurate; no one had disputed this. They claimed that the company had lied and covered up its wrongdoings.

People found themselves embroiled in the very conflict about which they were trying to reflect upon. The Food Lion representatives began by complaining about the way ABC had spoken publicly about the case. They, along with former senator Alan Simpson, who was also on the show, claimed that the forty-three hours of outtakes showed reporters staging the events about which ABC claimed to be reporting. *Staging* here became to be an ambiguous word—did it mean setting up journalists as meat processors so that they could film inside? Siding with disgruntled union workers who knew about the film crew and looked for wrongdoing? The intense pace of the conversation prevented inquiry into this.

Diane Sawyer, the journalist who initially reported the case, leapt several times to her own defense on this point. Despite Koppel's warning that they not retry the case, and her promise not to do so, she simply could not help herself:

DIANE SAWYER: May I make an appeal, Ted?

TED KOPPEL: I know you're going to, you've been making it surreptitiously throughout the whole program. Go ahead, get it off your chest, Diane, and if the rest of this program ends up being about the Food Lion case, on your head be it. Go ahead.

DIANE SAWYER: No, I don't want it to be and it shouldn't be and we will disagree on this and I certainly respect that you [speaking to the Food Lion representative] disagree on this. I just want to say, because you've said it a couple of ways and I would appreciate at some point if

we could, William Jeffers, who's the lawyer who was
with us in Greensboro to address, indeed, what the judge
did say in court. I contest what you say the outtakes
show. We say something very different. I feel, given what
you have said, it is very important to say to our audience
we did not stage anything. What you saw on the broadcast was the way it happened.[2]

The hook Food Lion lawyers put out—that ABC staged
things—was impossible for her to resist. This back-and-forth vol-
ley is a good example of discussion—of people thinking alone, the
ping-pong nature of conversation dominating—not dialogue.

Yet it is in precisely moments like this—where the temptation to react is so very strong, and where one's integrity and credibility is on the line—that the choice to *defend* or *suspend* can be
made. The road less traveled is to suspend—to change this well-
worn, well-rutted habit and dare to take a new stance that shifts
the energy of the conversation. It is the habit of defending, and the
"felts" that surge at times like this that actually run the conversation. Defending per se is not bad. Doing so unconsciously or re-
flexively, however, can stymie communication. The urge to
advocate comes so quickly that by the time we notice it, it is too
late. And yet it is possible, I believe, to come to the point of understanding one's own reactions and have the wherewithal and
muscles to suspend them. Doing so can change everything.

Defense and "verbal brawling," as writer Mark Gerzon calls
unproductive discussion, was clearly not the intention of Koppel,
or, I suspect, of some of the other participants. Often, though,
when people express an intention to find a way to raise the conversation to a new level, they fail. Why? And what might be done?

In this situation, the conversation remained stuck at what I
have called Field II, or breakdown, and Koppel managed this space
in a unilateral way. People advocated their views. They did not in-

quire into others' perspectives in order to make their own reasoning vulnerable, but instead did so simply to make their point. For instance, Don Hewitt tried to defend the use of hidden cameras. He said, "Can I ask a question?" and then went on:

> Twenty-five years ago, using a hidden camera, Mike Wallace exposed a phony cancer clinic that was bilking patients that should never have been licensed to operate in the first place and was shut down after California authorities saw what Mike did.... Anybody have a problem with that?[3]

"Anybody have a problem with that?" is a good example of a statement disguised as a question. Hewitt may indeed have genuinely *also* wanted to know what other people thought. But his opening salvo was a clear defense of the use of hidden cameras. This incoherence—between what he is saying and what he claims to be saying—that he wants to ask a question—is the kind of thing that fuels the fire of advocacy wars. People react to this, sometimes without even understanding it, and simply push back.

The heat of the exchange was, of course, in part produced by the climate in which it took place: an hour-long television show, two parties embroiled in a legal battle and emotionally attached to their positions, and the possibility of ABC appealing its case, making all their statements available to use in court. One might argue that because of this, the likelihood of the vested interests moving beyond where they were was low.

But I would suggest that even with high stakes like these, more could be done. In this case people did not have any guidelines or even simple tools with which to reflect. They did not suspend their views. They did not say, "Now, I could be wrong here, and I want to learn, from your perspective, what I am missing." They did not notice the difference between times when they were in a ping-pong discussion and when they were moving toward reflective dialogue—that is navigating the "crisis of suspension." That alone might have at least slowed them down enough to notice what they were doing, and made possible a different tone.

The participants did not really inquire. The assumption people used in practice was that because everyone seemed eager to defend their views, the only way through was for each to advocate their own view harder. Yet as a strategy, "advocate harder" is self-defeating, since it simply triggers others to do the same.

Many television journalists imagine that quick retorts and sharp exchanges make for good TV. At the end of the show Koppel commented that while the discussion had lasted an hour, half an hour might have been better. This would be so only if the purpose were to limit the kind of exchange they had had. If this was true, it was only because there was so little movement or momentum to the dialogue, so little space for reflection. The third field, or inquiry space, can be as infectious and powerful as breakdown and debate. Once people come into this space, it is hard for them to get out of it too. It takes work, the willingness to suspend, and the tools and competencies to do it.

My colleagues Diana Smith, Robert Putnam, and Phil MacArthur, top-notch dialogue consultants, have a model that is particularly relevant for groups that get stuck in the Field II conversations.[4] They suggest a continuum in which we can *facilitate, name,* or *engage* a group and its issues. Koppel tried to facilitate as the traffic cop, bringing out inconsistencies in people's statements, limiting their pontificating, pointing to the higher ground and larger issues. Facilitating in this sense means trying to make sure the basic ground rules are followed, that no one person dominates, that the critical issues get an airing.

But armed with the ideas here, Koppel might have tried something else. When the conversation itself became a replay of the issues, instead of just trying to warn people off this, he might have called attention to it and named it: The way we are talking right now—each one advocating, no one inquiring, everyone defending a position—repeats the exchange we have had. Do people see this? Can we make an effort to do something else?

If that does not produce a shift toward more fluid listening, then you can move to the last level, engagement. This ups the ante considerably. There are several possible ways to go here. Koppel might have said, "Advocating this way is unlikely to move us to the point of reflecting on *why* we have these views. So let me ask: Why do each of us feel pressured to defend ourselves? What stops us from slowing down and inquiring? Alternatively, he might have tried this: What might we learn that is new from each other? Can we begin to ask What are we missing that we do not want to hear? Finally, he might simply have invited a greater measure of disclosure: Let me invite you to tell us not your positions but your first-person experience right now as you have this conversation this evening. What are your dilemmas? What do you fear? What do you fear you might give away or lose if you fail to defend well? Let's leave some space and respect the possibility that there is no right answer. I would caution against anyone fixing anyone else's views for the moment.

The Food Lion case shows how the expressed interest in reflection can be easily sidetracked by a range of forces that stem, ultimately, from pathologies in the ecology of thought. These people believed their own points of view. They were also quite certain of their perspectives, advocating them strongly. Each one had a partial, abstract take on what happened that they tended to believe was the whole story. And they inflicted a kind of conversational violence on one another in the interest of "getting at the truth," that mirrored the combative tactics on both sides.

Unless people like Ted Koppel and others who are in leadership positions and clearly have a wish to deepen reflection and improve the quality of thinking around them can learn how to begin to shift the atmosphere in which these kinds of exchanges take place, reflective and generative dialogues are unlikely to occur.

BUILDING A CONTAINER
FOR DIALOGIC RELATIONSHIPS:
THE HAGUE INITIATIVE

"An eye for an eye and we all go blind."

—Gandhi

Dialogue is often proposed as a helpful process for resolving international conflicts.[5] In recent years there have been several examples of successful unconstrained and off-the-record high-level exchanges between key players in some of the most pressing conflicts of our time.[6]

The Peace Palace in The Hague is one of the world's most powerful symbols of neutrality. Inaugurated in 1913, it was funded by the American philanthropist Andrew Carnegie. Many nations have participated by contributing art and materials. For example, since 1995 the Peace Palace has been the location for a series of meetings between Chechens and Russians, brought together in a dialogue about Chechnya's desire for independence. Conducted quietly over the past several years, the efforts of a few people have had some promising results and shown it is possible to hold a forum where political enemies and rivals can learn to think together.

In 1991, Bruce Allyn, a negotiator and Russia specialist who works for Monitor Company, and *Getting to Yes* author Bill

Ury began a project on ethnic conflict resolution in the former Soviet Union that formed a remarkable container for dialogue. Sponsored by the Carnegie Corporation of New York, Allyn and Ury, along with a group of international colleagues, formed an initiative to consult with the Russians and leaders of breakaway republics of the former Soviet Union. The embers of ethnic identity in these regions had not gone out; now with the controls of the Soviet Union gone, the reassertion of nationalist aspirations was inevitable.

Initially, their work consisted of a series of informal exchanges with leaders of both the autonomous Republic of Tatarstan and officials of the Russian Federation. This close work in Tatarstan, which helped to consolidate many lessons in international experience and provided technical advice on negotiating with the Russians, proved to be a model for help in the even more volatile Chechnya.

Allyn and Ury found that the structure of each conflict was similar: each republic sought greater or full independence. They saw their lack of independent nation-state status, such as was received by Georgia and Ukraine and, as a double standard and hypocrisy. Many of the ethnic republics were created as part of Stalin's repressive campaign against ethnic minorities in Russia—the trend toward ethnic cleansing. By dividing them and co-opting their leadership and independence, Stalin had hoped to assimilate them and remove any threat to his authority. In several of these republics, armed violence erupted in the mid 1990s, notably in the Armenian enclave of Nagorno-Karabakh region and in Chechnya.

The Russian government tried in 1992 to forge a formal federation of these states within the remaining territory of Russia. Two republics, which had particularly complex political and ethnic situations—Tatarstan and the north Caucasus, which includes Chechnya—did not sign at that time. They were incorporated into Russia by conquest, have a non-Russian majority population, a history of their own governing structures, and are dominantly Islamic, not Russian Orthodox.

Eventually, Moscow signed a treaty with Tatarstan in 1994 that granted Tatarstan significant autonomy. The president of Tatarstan, in consultation with a range of international experts in The Hague Initiative, got Russia to accept Tatarstan's Constitution, even though it contained many contradictions with Russia's Constitution. The principle of the "creative use of ambiguity" enabled the Tatars to avoid the violence that plagued many other states.

The Hague Initiative set up a container in which it was possible for the successful experience of Tatarstan to be openly considered and reflected upon by all the parties involved in the conflict between Chechens and Russians. President Shaimiev of Tatarstan at one of the Hague sessions said:

> We included in the treaty the recognition of both constitutions, though they are in fact not fully compatible. But at this stage, it as a required fruitful compromise. . . . It was a two-way street. . . . Simultaneously, in order to overcome the most pressing conflicts, we signed twelve intergovernmental agreements in the framework of the treaty on specific issues of property ownership, taxation, defense, customs, and other questions.[7]

To avoid bloodshed, new approaches often are required. The Tatars compared their situation to that of Quebec in Canada, which for fifteen years has not respected the Canadian Constitution.

In a session held in March 1996, top officials from Russia and Chechnya as well as international experts developed a ten-point plan for ending the war in Chechnya. As Allyn describes it:

A key element of The Hague Initiative proposal, which was adopted unanimously by the participants, was the readiness to defer the question of the political status of Chechnya to a later date. . . . The "deferred decision" approach was officially endorsed by Russian and Chechen leaders four months later . . . when both sides agreed to postpone the question of the status of Chechnya for a five-year period. The Hague Initiative proposal also called for direct negotiations between President Yeltsin and Chechen President Dudayev, which was also later endorsed by the Russian President. . . .[8]

The agreement demilitarized Chechnya and called for free and fair elections.

The principles behind The Hague Initiative reflect the ideas about dialogue described in this book:

All meetings of The Hague Initiative have a facilitated process designed to achieve three goals. First, the moderator seeks to facilitate a candid dialogue to understand more deeply the *interests* underlying the official positions of the conflicting sides. As the dialogue proceeds, facilitators write down key points in two languages for all to see and reflect upon. Secondly, the moderator leads the group in joint brainstorming regarding possible creative *options* to meet the basic interests of all sides. Third, the process is designed to evoke an appreciation of the psychological and emotional wounds created by the conflict and the need for healing and *reconciliation*.

All meetings follow strict guidelines: all comments are off the record and cannot be quoted without permission; no members of the press are allowed in the closed sessions; all participants are acting in an unofficial capacity and cannot make official proposals for acceptance or rejection; an edited transcript of the meetings can be published only after each participant has reviewed the text and deleted any of his or her comments inappropriate for publication.[9]

In these comments we can see evidence of each of the four practices for dialogue: an effort to create a safe container that is jointly owned and shared by all participants in a climate of mutual respect; conditions that sustain listening and participation—namely a "leveling" of the ground that requires that no one act in an official role, making this a virtual, not "real" meeting; the production of a common text that anyone can edit; a focus on interests, not positions, both of which support suspension and reflection; and the creative brainstorming of options in a climate where no one can be quoted without permission, to encourage the speaking of one's voice.

The attempt in these gatherings is to develop an approach in which new levels of shared meaning can emerge. But the story goes beyond this. Allyn and Ury have sustained relationships with nearly all the key players in these sessions for many years. Their network of association is itself a container for these talks—one that they have deliberately nurtured for years, going back to the pre-glasnost days of Gorbachev. There is, in other words, a long and deliberate history of efforts to cultivate settings in which the principles described in their model can be made to work. This, too, I suspect, is typical of and essential for genuine dialogue for difficult national-level problems: finding the players who have sought—for decades, in some cases—a way to bridge differences, and who have the resilience to hold all the tensions and include them in their thinking.

A RETURN TO CIVILITY:
UNITED STATES CONGRESSIONAL RETREAT

In late 1996, David Skaggs, a five-term Democratic congressman from Colorado, decided he had had enough. Appalled by the quality of hostile debate and conflict, and disturbed by what he calls "the metaphysics of mistrust" among his fellow legislators in the United States House of Representatives, he turned to several of his colleagues—including another Democrat, Tom Sawyer of Ohio, and two Republicans, Amo Houghton of New York and Ray LaHood of Illinois—to find a solution. Together they approached others, and within a few weeks forty-three Democrats and forty-three Republicans had signed a letter and sent it to the House leadership, requesting that they support a congressional retreat to reflect on the quality of civility and discourse in the House.[10]

The 104th Congress had bred an extraordinary amount of vitriol. They had shut down the federal government over the 1995 budget battles with President Clinton. And they just finished a review of Speaker Gingrich's ethics and censured him. The bad feeling on both sides of the House were tangible. And yet it was an almost impossible thought—conceiving of a way to change the culture of this institution. There had, until Skaggs and his associates took the initiative, never been an effort to reform the way members interacted in a reflective "offsite" environment. Many people were desperate for a way out of the conflicts but could see little possibility for it. The sheer intimidation factor of the long history of the institution, the high turnover rates, and by chance of timing a relatively less senior congressional class made the likelihood of change all the more difficult.

This did not stop Skaggs from seeking an alternative. As he puts it, "Legislatures don't function without trust among the membership. Trust doesn't happen without people getting to know each other. And that doesn't happen without time to-gether. What was missing in the House was the time to know each other." His intention was clear: "to get to know each other morally and emotionally, uncomplicated by the usual desire to win." And so the idea for the retreat was born. He had his doubts, too, about people's willingness to participate: "The challenge was to get more than a handful to be open to the idea. It was a pretty dramatic notion that we might do this. It had never happened before—to take a weekend and sit with the other side, with people who are professionally heavily self-defended." But the susceptibility was there, to be felt, because there was a real hunger and desire to change things.

Mark Gerzon, author of the book *A House Divided*, was asked to facilitate the event. Gerzon's first letter to the Bipartisan Congressional Retreat Planning Committee (BCRPC) consisted primarily of questions. He did not propose any actions; instead, he initiated an inquiry with the members. They were impressed. His approach throughout was to invite the members to assume responsibility for the event, to "lead from behind" as much as possible. Many concerns emerged about how the retreat was to be structured, and Gerzon consulted many people to gain their views.

In March 1997, 215 members of the House attended an unprecedented three-day retreat held in Hershey, Pennsylvania. The members took several extraordinary steps to build the set-ting—what I would call the container—for this gathering. They excluded the media from attending but found a way to speak to them after the fact. They also limited the number of staff al-lowed into either the planning or the retreat itself. And they in-cluded spouses as full participants in the meetings; some 180 spouses and 100 children attended as well. Perhaps one of the most impactful moves they made happened on the journey to Hershey. The organizers arranged a train ride from Washington and invited everyone to bring their families along. This was, according to Skaggs, very helpful, though "an unnatural experience. Seeing your adversaries with their kids on their shoulders was a powerful humanizing force. People took in a lot of data before they actually arrived." To insure that they took the right level of responsibility, the organizers had also decided to have members facilitate the event themselves, to insure privacy and confidentiality, though this evolved to having outside facilitators playing supporting roles.

Some members debated whether in fact the quality of discourse had declined. Pew Charitable Trust funded a research study on the number of times members broke the formal rules of decorum in the house. Professor Kathleen Hall Jamieson of the University of Pennsylvania found that breaches of basic civility had been extreme in 1946 and 1994, years following shifts in control of the House.

The event began with a video capturing the history and majesty of the traditions of the House. Historian David McCollough gave a keynote that, by all accounts, inspired the participants, reminding them of who they were and what they were doing. McCollough and these initial events evoked the "ideal" and made conscious the possibilities, an essential move, I have suggested, for taking people from Field I, politeness, into the other phases of dialogue.

The event had four working sessions. In the first, members divided into twelve groups of about thirty people, each facilitated by a pair of Democratic and Republican members. They each took time to state one personal goal they had for the retreat. Many had predicted that the members would have found such an initial session tedious. But by many accounts, these first gatherings proved valuable; no one was ready to leave at the close of the session.

The second session, Saturday morning, invited members

in an open format to reflect on the question How has the quality of discourse in the House of Representatives affected you personally? Next, in small groups, they reflected on the obstacles to raising the quality of discourse, mapping these with Post-it notes. No Post-it note identifying a barrier could be put up unless it was signed by a Democrat and Republican. The members reviewed all the opinions stated by the members, prioritized the ones they felt they could eliminate or reduce. That Saturday evening they had dinner and dancing.

The sense of connection among the people grew throughout the weekend. By Sunday morning it became evident that something significant was happening. Many of the usual attitudes had, at least for the moment, subsided. The group held an "open mike" session in which many people spoke. After a few heartfelt laughs, this final session, members were asked to begin by saying, "If I were in charge of the House, I would . . ." The group identified sixty possible action steps for making changes in the House, including the notion that the leadership hold regular bipartisan meetings to work out the differences among them.

Many people attending the event found something significant had happened. The "spirit of Hershey" became known in the House as a reference point for a different kind of conversation. Despite these efforts, and a considerable amount of enthusiasm at the time, follow-through by the leadership has not been what was promised; and the spirit of discourse at times violates the experience at Hershey.

This unusual gathering speaks of the hunger that people feel for genuine conversation, and of the enormous structural barriers to having it. Gerzon and his associates had an understanding of the need to "create a container" for this event, and to do so in a way that enabled people to own their experience. In large part, they succeeded. Some of the planning committee, returning from Hershey by train, reflected that they could not have planned the event to work as well as it did; they felt no small measure of grace at work! Said Skaggs later, "Something was going on there that got people's attention at a different level."

The Hershey retreat exceeded the planners' and many of the participants' expectations. At the same time, the follow-up from this event was disappointing. The agreed-upon bipartisan leadership meetings never happened. Because these were considered the critical first step, little else followed. But the spirit of Hershey continues: The organizers have another retreat planned.

Sessions like these are important first steps in a larger change process. Such efforts are always filled with apparent retrenchment; two steps forward, one step back. Profound institutional change is certainly not a linear process. That said, there is something inherently problematic about "retreats" of this sort that can undermine the very changes people seek to make. By having to leave their familiar setting and find a relatively unstructured neutral meeting place, they at once make space for themselves and bypass the problems that produced the difficulties in the first place. If this is understood, and the gathering such as the one in Hershey is taken as a first step toward bringing more self-reflection and change in the House itself, then something significant will have happened. If not, then the risk is that they reinforce the very norms they intended to alter.

The model I have explored in this book is that fundamental change requires that we pay attention to the underlying ecology and structures of behavior that produce our difficulties in the first place. These "structural traps" can be temporarily bypassed, liberating energy and good feeling. But then, very quickly, back at work, the familiar structures reassert themselves, and it is as if nothing much has changed. Gatherings like the one at Hershey can grant people perspective. But back at work they face the challenge of deliberately inquiring into the structures that have given rise to the need for such an event in the first place.

Exploring the limiting structures that prevent genuine dialogue, for instance, in the House, is an enormously challenging task. But it is also not an impossible task. Despite the built-in bias toward debate and polarization that the party system provides, Hershey showed people that they can learn to differ more effectively, without the venom that sometimes seems to insinuate itself. The inquiry might proceed to another series of questions: What are the structures that are likely to continue to limit effective dialogue in the House? What are the highest leverage moves that individuals or the House as a whole could make to impact these structures? What traps need to be addressed? What dilemmas are people in? Who can see the traps most clearly?

PRISON DIALOGUES:

THE TRANSFORMATION OF MEMORY

In 1994, Peter Garrett was approached by David Parsons, a probation officer who worked at Whitemoor Prison, one of six maximum-security prisons in England, with a project. Garrett, who had spent some nine years in close conversation with physicist David Bohm, was developing plans to bring dialogue into practical settings. The probation officer had heard of Garrett's work in dialogue in England and in Europe and wanted to know if it would be feasible to hold dialogues in the prison system. He wanted to know if it would be possible to help the prisoners find a way of articulating their feelings other than through violence, and to cultivate new attitudes toward themselves and society.

As Garrett thought about it, he realized that the opportunity was more significant than might have been visible at first glance. Prisons hold people who have broken one of the rules of society. They give us a place to store those elements of society who are unsavory and unacceptable. We lock out of sight what we do not want to accept as a part of ourselves. But the more important question to ask is Does this in fact enable us to deal with those elements of ourselves effectively?

We are taught when we are very young to lock away behaviors and attitudes that do not fit. This civilizing process is quite necessary, but it has a cost. As Robert Bly once put it:

> When we were one or two years old we had what we might visualize as a 360-degree personality. Energy radiated out from all parts of our body and all parts of our psyche. A child running is a living globe of energy. We had a ball of energy, all right; but one day we noticed that our parents didn't like certain parts of that ball. They said things like "Can't you be still. Or it isn't very nice to try and kill your brother."[11]

The question is What do we do with this energy? Bly's answer: We put it in a bag that we carry around with us:

> Behind us we have an invisible bag, and the part of us our parents don't like, we put in the bag. By the time we go to school, our bag is quite large. Then our teachers have their say: "Good children don't get angry over such little things." So we take out anger and put it in the bag. By the time my brother and I were twelve in Madison, Minnesota, we were known as the "nice Bly boys." Already our bags were a mile long.[12]

The rejected parts of ourselves do not develop. What remains in the bag regresses or devolves, Bly says, toward barbarism, making it increasingly awkward to live with. We spend our first twenty years putting things into our bag, trying to be acceptable, but splitting ourselves in half. We spend the rest of our lives trying to get these rejected parts of ourselves, our shadows, reintegrated into ourselves.

The problem here arises, too, because what remains in our bag also gets projected around us onto the environment. The worst parts of ourselves—our anger, our craziness—when we are not in touch with them and they are locked away have the nasty tendency to leak out when we are not looking. And they can color our entire perception of the world. Many writers pointed out in the late 1980s that Americans' perceptions of the heinous Russian empire, for all its actual faults, told us as much about ourselves as it did about them. We reject what is a part of ourselves, what we do not want to integrate. The irony is that the rejected parts are destructive precisely because they are not acknowledged.

It is not merely individuals that have "bags." Bly suggests that whole towns have them and seem to require that everyone puts the same things into them. And as Garrett considered the prison dialogues and the possibilities of them, his focus was on the societal "bag"—that which we as a society lock away and put out of sight. What gradually emerged was the idea of a project that would involve holding dialogues in prisons, and then in halfway houses, so that people could begin to understand something about the much larger bag, the larger shadow, as Carl Jung calls it, that society itself carries around. Holding dialogues in prisons might be a setting in which it is possible, Garrett believed, not only to assist groups of prisoners but also to help them and others gain insight into the collective shadow, the collective bag. Dialogue can provide human beings with access and insight not only into individual or group patterns but social ones that are carried by all the individuals. The dialogue can be a container in which these social pressures and thoughts can be suspended, seen, and potentially reintegrated.

Perhaps most significant, Garrett felt that exploring dialogue in prisons would provide insight into the core "civilizing" process of society precisely by exploring how it had broken down. His idea is that these civilizing processes seek to bring people under control, to live in an orderly and acceptable fashion, but in so doing damage the "infrastructure of thought" in which we all live. As a result, everyone learns to repress and reject vital parts of themselves. Some people are less successful at this than others, and we lock them up. But the wider question remains, What is the impact of the civilizing process on human society? Does the way it creates stability have unintended side effects that create more difficulties than we might have realized?

For the past four years Garrett has run dialogues in prisons. Each Tuesday morning, inmates convicted of murder, armed robbery, drug smuggling, and other violent crimes meet, along with prison officers, staff, and the prison chaplain. There is no hierarchy to speaking or to the selection of topics; anyone can raise any issue. A second group that meets in the afternoon is made up of sex offenders, men convicted of rape, child abuse, or child murder, or serial killing. Both groups meet once a week for about an hour and a half. People are free to come and go to these sessions as they please. It is entirely voluntary.

The British prison system uses a "dispersal" method, meaning that the worst offenders—murderers, serial murderers, serial rapists, pedophiles—are kept for several years in one of six prisons, and then moved suddenly to another of the six. The purpose is to prevent the prisoners from forming relationships that could lead to a security threat either to them or to the prison system itself. From the vantage point of the prisoner, this means that he could be given an hour's notice, and then told he was to leave one prison and move to another, never to return.

The things these inmates discuss in the dialogues range from the impact of their crimes on their lives and on their victims' lives to the nature of life in prison. The prison dialogues afford these inmates a chance to talk through and think about the pain in their lives. There are few places where this is possible in prison life, but the harsh realities are to some degree transformed by this process.

Research conducted on the prison dialogues by the Institute of Criminology in Cambridge, England, validates these observations. Says one report:

> The Dialogue Group, where staff occasionally joined prisoners in their "thinking out loud" was often mentioned as a place where staff prisoner encounters were at their best. . . . Relationships in the Dialogue Group were at their best because they were honest, and yet could be critical. "It's one of the most honest places in the prison." . . . Prisoners felt that this was a place where staff could be seen and known as they really were, and vice versa.

The report later continued:

> The conversations we witnessed [participated in] were unusually mature, open, and constructive. They were sometimes extraordinarily moving. It was as if the prisoners (and sometimes staff, when they took part) stopped being in prison, and became, once again, themselves. The impact of this "space" on the individuals who participated, their relationships

with each other, and on life in the prison was, we felt, wholly positive.[13]

It is apparent that the dialogues are providing a powerful place for reflection for the prisoners as well as for prison management and staff. Perhaps most intriguing, though, are some of Garrett's own insights from having spent five years working with some of the most serious criminals in the United Kingdom. His message is that dialogue produces changes in everyone, often in quite unexpected ways:

I have been surprised to discover that in confrontational and dangerous situations, people really want engagement not withdrawal. This was something counter-intuitive to me at first. . . . There is a particular kind of engagement in confrontational situations, which involves a healthy mix of support and challenge, along with authentic enquiry about one's own and the other's experience, that transforms such situations into something creative or all involved.[14]

Dialogue provides the kind of engagement that enables profound change and learning of this kind to take place.

Taking Wholeness

Seriously

"And what is good, Phaedrus? And what is not good?

Need we ask anyone to tell us these things?"

—Plato, *Symposium*

As the reader of this book already knows, the practice of dialogue is deeply grounded in, among others, the concepts articulated by David Bohm and Chris Argyris. When these two men first met in 1989, Chris Argyris introduced himself by saying, "You know, I think we have something very important in common. We both take wholeness seriously."

One of the core premises of this book is that the awareness and understanding that we need to resolve difficult conflicts, to align disparate cultures, and to integrate the dissociated forces prevalent in our wider society are already present within us. As Socrates suggests, we do not need anyone, in fact, to tell us these things. This, of course, does not stop our dominant culture from trying to convince us otherwise. If there is any one thing that dialogue has to offer above all else, it is a process and method by which the awareness and understanding that you already possess may surface in you and be acted upon. This is what it means to take wholeness seriously.

In this book we have explored the ways a dialogue might unfold over time, in stages, and the implications for leadership that follows. We have examined some of the reasons dialogue might not occur as readily as we would like—the obstacles, structural traps, barriers, and rigidities in thought that seem to permeate so much of human experience, making both dialogue and fundamental change so difficult. And we have looked at some of specific ways dialogue has been applied, to bring about practical change.

What remains is to reflect on the frontiers that dialogue opens before us. The three domains spoken of in ancient Greece—the Good, the True, and the Beautiful—serve as guideposts to these frontiers.

The Good, you will recall, related to the domain of morals and collective action; the True, to the pursuit of objective truth, and the Beautiful, the realm of morals and aesthetics. Together they formed the horizon for integrating the interior and exterior dimensions of human life.

In this chapter I explore the possibility that dialogue, as I have unfolded it, could serve as a potent vehicle for integration—of the supposedly "soft" and imprecise interior dimensions of human experience, like morals, artistic expression, meaning, and introspection with the supposedly "harder" and more objective exterior dimensions, like empirical research.

A PATH TOWARD WHOLENESS

Any leader today might ask this question: In what ways am I helping to bring the good, the true, and the beautiful into the policies and actions for which I am responsible? One potential for genuine dialogue is to enable human beings to overcome fragmentation among these three languages and discover a means for common inquiry and understanding. In this sense, dialogue is a journey to find a new language for wholeness, one that lets us work on our most pressing practical problems in such a way that we include all three elements, finding a way for all three languages to be relevant. We have genuine dialogue when all three dimensions are present; when one or more are absent, we lack it.

So it makes sense to look at some features and dimensions of our emerging world through this lens. In the remainder of this chapter we explore three particular issues: the impact of the Internet and the seductions and limits of "digital dialogue"; the changing context of power in corporations and society, and finally, the reshaping of language that a commitment to dialogue might require of each of us.

INTEGRATING THE BEAUTIFUL:

THE HEART IS AN ANALOG DEVICE

The subject of "digital dialogue" is one that holds much promise for these ideas, and also much peril. Much is being made of the potential of a "wired" world for transforming commerce, liberating knowledge, and fashioning many new avenues of human interaction.[1] Yet in most of the talk about this tangible symbol of the revolution of connectedness blooming among us, there is little mention of the kinds of changes in how human beings talk and think together such that they might make better use of these powerful tools.

Human beings have done considerable work creating the operating systems, networks, and browsers required to make using the Internet possible. We attend to this external ecology but tend to overlook the internal one. What is the operating system for human communication? What is required for it to work well and at depth? In what ways is it dysfunctional? I have outlined in this book three levels the human operating system must attend to: the new behaviors, structures of interaction, and invisible architecture for shared thinking. Yet we do not find much work being done on these in any systematic way. The focus is largely on making the tools work. The underlying assumption here is that the presence of the new tools will force changes in these kinds of levels of human function, to the degree that this is desirable.

But I have a more cautionary sense about it. Everyone can have their own talk show on the Internet. But who would listen? One friend of mine points out that the Internet is a narcissist's dream: You can publish your own books, even invite voyeurs into your home from anyplace on the planet. While it is tempting to imagine that high band width conveyance of information also increases its quality, ultimately what lies in human minds and hearts determines the depth of our exchanges. The Internet can be seen as the attempt of our literate and isolated culture to somehow return to community. People seem to imagine that if we were all digitally connected, then we would all be in touch, and the great malaise of the age—the isolation, pace, disconnection that many of us feel—would be allayed.

But so far the digital revolution is giving us *connection but not contact*. This is the case precisely because we are not yet paying enough attention to the levels of experience required to bring about genuine dialogue. There is nothing stopping the Internet from being a medium that actually profoundly enhances these levels if we turned our attention toward enabling this to happen.

While we are now able to send more and more information to one another, we are not necessarily any more capable of sharing understanding, insight, or wisdom, or our hearts. Perhaps most important is the realization that the human heart is an "analogue" device: continuous, fluid, wavelike. It cannot be broken down into information packets and beamed somewhere only to be reconstituted exactly as it was before. The ambition we have to create a precise digital replica of human thought and expression reflects a commitment to systematizing the exterior world. But it again tends to miss the interior. The overall intention of the scientific mind-set has been, as Ken Wilbur put it, to "colonize" the domains of the We and the I. One sees this same energy at work in the expansiveness and near imperialism of the digital revolution. *Everything* is going digital. This is not in itself "bad"; more, it symbolizes the predominant tendencies we have to try to explain and objectify all aspects of human life. This is the objective True at work, out of touch with the subjective Beautiful. What would the voice of the Beautiful be in this context? Perhaps simply to remind us that one simple touch of a human hand could far exceed all the impact of all the digital libraries in the land. Connection without contact.

In this book we've seen how the operating system for human communication—the foundations, in thought, of our conversations—are fundamentally damaged. That damaged condition will not change simply by virtue of extending the media through which it is working. For instance, it lets people amplify their individual voices, though it does not necessarily invite an equal emphasis on reflection about the quality of those voices. It enables more suspension of perspectives but may not support the principle of awareness so much as reinforce people's prejudices and certainties. It all depends on how it is used, and to what extent we educate ourselves to activate the three levels of dialogue spoken about in this book.

When the United States House of Representatives placed all the volumes of depositions, transcripts, and reports on the Internet, making it possible for individual citizens to "make up their own mind" about President Clinton's difficulties and acts, we saw an unprecedented application of the Internet's ability to give us all access. But I still ask What did we learn? Did this massive dump of data actually shift the way individual human beings feel and relate to this scandal? To the parts of themselves that tend to condemn what is outside of them, because it corresponds to painful realities that are *inside* them?

I know many people who see on-line communication as a great benefit. They can access it anytime, they can say whatever they want without the fear of being silenced through interruption (or simply through the group's body language). Many people find that in general the quality of their dialogue on-line is much better than it is face-to-face. That comment itself is revealing. The on-line connection filters out much of the noise that we get face-to-face. In one sense this certainly *is* beneficial. We can throw out rough drafts of what we have to say. We can reflect without the pressure to respond. It is quieter and in this sense enables us to access and present to others the better parts of ourselves. It is almost meditative: We are in a conversation, in a very real sense, with ourselves.

Yet the parts of ourselves that need transformation do not go away simply because we can filter them out of our email communications. These are often the parts that we hide from ourselves, and leak out only under pressure when we interact with others. These are the very dimensions of our interactions that contain much power, and that require the most work.

The Power of On-Line Inquiry

No one really can say what the impact of the digital revolution will be. Looked at through the lens of dialogue, however, certain possibilities do emerge. For instance, dialogue activates reflection and the capacity for *suspension*. The capacity to be aware of what is happening as it happens is a central component of a dialogic way of being. As I intimated above, this carries power and gives us the freedom to create, because we can learn to release our enslavement to memories from the past. Learning to reflect, however, particularly in large groups, requires discipline and work. The on-line media do provide a kind of practice field for this more challenging face-to-face work, and could be used in this way. What is more, the Internet also compels a new form of *listening*. When we see or hear different people speaking through email, or even video exchange, we must choose to process what is being said. We have the potential for hearing many more voices than we might ordinarily.

There are several powerful examples of this now. Buckman Laboratories, a chemical company based in Memphis, has created a knowledge network that provides virtually real time linkages to a large percentage of its twelve hundred people. Buckman makes more than one thousand different specialty chemicals in eight factories around the world; they are located in some eighty countries. Its "K'Netix" system has been studied by many different organizations around the world. Here is how it works: A salesman in Indonesia once made a request for a pitch control program for a local pulp mill. Several hours later, someone from Memphis responded with the Buckman chemical to use and a reference to a master's thesis on pitch control of tropical hardwoods, written by an Indonesian. Soon after, another manager logged on from Canada, and described his approach in British Columbia. Then came examples from Sweden, New Zealand, Spain, and France, advice from the R&D department in Memphis, chemical specifications from Mexico and South Africa. The initial request generated eleven replies from six countries, and helped to secure a $6 million order.[2]

The Global MBA program at Duke University is another example where on-line discourse and inquiry is having a potent effect. The MBA class takes all its sessions on-line. They are a global group, with representatives from Asia, Europe, and North America. They meet five times face-to-face but conduct most of their inquiries through bulletin boards and on-line conversations. Class members have a great deal of intensive time together, and then stay in touch through the Net. The overall experience, people report, is reflective discourse. The feedback loop of intensive face-to-face work and on-line work becomes quite generative for the students and faculty. They can reflect and learn together in a way that is not possible when only one avenue or the other is available. The Net may well develop our ability to reflect. This is essential if it is to support dialogue and not merely discussion.

It is quite possible to envision different kinds of infrastructure, tools, practices that might be available on-line—for instance, that could stimulate the four core practices for dialogue and enhance new capacity. One could also imagine learning about how the technology is likely to be received in any particular community, such that one could have better predictive intuition about how to use it. America Online, for instance, is a largely open-system approach as well as being a powerful virtual marketplace. It is equally predictable that closed-system people would not be comfortable with AOL, wanting more closed-system norms to prevail: more regulated space and access, for instance. Different people require different containers to thrive.

REFRAMING THE GOOD:

THE POWER OF THE CIRCLE

In his book *The Gift*, Lewis Hyde tells the story of early interaction between the Native Americans and the Pilgrims. The Indians brought a fine peace pipe to this first meeting and gave it to the British visitors. They were thrilled, and immediately began to think of sending the pipe back to sit in the British Museum. The early settlers were surprised to find then that when the Indians came for another visit, an expression of goodwill would be for the British to bring out the peace pipe, smoke it with them, and *give it back*. The phrase "Indian giver" comes from this early misunderstanding. For a while the settlers were thinking that a gift, once given, is possessed, the Indians followed another model: that the "gift must move."[3]

There are, in this story, two different understandings of property, but also two different visions of collective association and ethics, and the power that comes from them. There are, in other words, two different conceptions of the Good. One gave rise to the capitalist market economy. Goods are for possession, for keeping. The other, prevalent in most tribal and indigenous societies, sees most (but not all) possessions as part of a common flow. The proper means of association together is through the giving of gifts.

The gift exchange is central to most creative communities. Scientific communities require a spirit of free exchange of ideas for the community as a whole to flourish. When one person seeks to possess things, the spirit is spoiled.

Dialogue is properly a gift relationship as well. When we speak together in a dialogue, we are speaking in a way that seeks to contribute one to the other. A conversation where the people are essentially trying to extract something from others moves away from dialogue.

In this sense, the gift dimension redefines the way power

moves in a dialogue as well. Dialogue is a discipline for developing shared meaning among disparate groups of people. But I believe that at its core, dialogue accomplishes something else: It can produce a deep shift in our understanding of the nature of power. Dialogue is a leveler, transforming repressive forms of hierarchy as it frees each individual to acknowledge what they think and feel and express it directly. But dialogue, in its fullest expression, enables the emergence of what I would refer to as genuine collective leadership, whose highest aim is ultimately to make a contribution, to give, not to take.

Warren Bennis and Patricia Biederman, in their book *Organizing Genius,* describes the world class achievements that came from groups of people that somehow achieved extraordinary levels of alignment and collaboration. The Manhattan Project, or Steve Jobs's famous Macintosh pirate gang at Apple Computer, are among the examples he cites.

People in "great groups" like the one that created the Macintosh freely give all their ideas in the service of what they believed to be their "mission from God." This team genuinely felt they were contributing something to humanity, a product and a vision of what a personal computer could be.

The principles outlined in this book attempt to articulate why and how such groups achieve what they do; in essence, they find the courage and inspiration to move out of the "breakdown" in the container state into some kind of alignment and flow. In the case of the Mac, Jobs clearly inspired people to rise out of differences they might have had and align with a larger vision. In other situations people move back and forth, but they sustain enough of the flow state to produce many great ideas and outcomes. Once this condition is reached, people discover that a great deal of power moves, power that organizes people, but more important, that reshapes and magnetizes a set of ideas, giving everyone a common focus and common purpose.

The willingness to give one's ideas freely, without the sense of having to draw close boundaries to protect or preserve them, generates a common mind and common pool of meaning out of which much can be done. Equally, when a group of people suddenly find themselves in an exchange where everyone is carefully guarding their ideas and words, to see what the other person will say, to discover how to play the situation, things break down.

The circle is a potent metaphor for the kinds of exchanges that require our minds and hearts to be open to one another in a very different way than is normally the case. The circular economy is the gift economy; the market economy is the commercial exchange economy.

~

Dialogue enables a "free flow of meaning," which has the potential of transforming the power relationships among the people concerned. As this free flow emerges, it becomes quite apparent that no one person owns this flow and that no one can legislate it. People can learn to embody it, and in a sense serve it. This is perhaps the most significant shift possible in dialogue: that power is no longer the province of a person in a role, or even of any single individual, but at the level of alignment an individual or group has with the power of Life itself. We have a familiar way of understanding power of this kind, though it comes from an unusual source. Power that respects no one but includes everyone, that calls for the best in people, and that evokes great creativity, is love. Dialogue can unleash the power of love, not in a sentimental or moralistic sense but in the genuine sense of true creativity. In this lies the secret of integration among the three languages as well. It may perhaps be the case that few "great groups" or powerful collaborations would publicly attribute their success to love, but I suspect it is often the invisible ingredient.

SPEAKING THE TRUE:
A NEW LANGUAGE OF WHOLENESS

Dialogue represents a way of working that while perhaps embedded in the genes of our ancestors is new to us. Most people lack real experience of it. We are unused to speaking together openly and consciously, particularly in high-stakes settings, without any intention of somehow possessing for ourselves something of the outcome of these exchanges. We do not know how to participate in such a way that we have not planned in advance what we are going to say, or where we are deliberately inquiring into. We come prepared, well stocked with thoughts, perhaps having sought to prepare others as well. And when the going gets tough, we fall back on argument and debate.

One implication of this is that as our experience with dialogue increases, we discover that the words we have to express ourselves are ill equipped to capture what we feel. For many of us, our language reflects the "machine age" in which we live. This is particularly reflected in the business culture. There we "force" issues, "drive change," "roll out" efforts to expand. This is true in other cases as well. Our language has become fragmented. We speak to reinforce our positions. We can see this same tendency to fragment in the fact that we have many words that seem to mean something different to everyone you ask. Words like *process* and *system* mean so many different things to different people that they might as well be in different languages. We lack a language of wholeness.

Greg is a union officer who has worked at the plant in Kansas City for over thirty years now. He is slight, a chain smoker, and talks in a tough, gravelly voice, holding the weight of experience in the lines of his face. He grew up with unions: "I've been union all my life. . . . I walked a strike line with my dad when I was six years old . . . the union's just a way of life. It's something that's very, very necessary. A poor employer makes a good union. You can't, you can't put a good union into a good employer. It just doesn't happen. There's no necessity for it."[4]

Greg was well respected among his union associates mainly because he took such a consistently hard line against management. In his view, they were *always* out to screw you; you just might not be able to tell in what way. Yet somehow he managed to maintain his credibility with management too; he spoke honestly, directly, without a cynical edge. He often would name truths management sought to hide, which they both resented and respected. He would, for instance, report the exact number of unresolved grievances submitted by the union even as management was trying to put on the best possible face about management-union relationships. And, he came, quite to his own surprise, not only to respect the value of dialogue, but also to see it as a necessary change for both management and union. Yet this realization did not come without costs.

Greg once came to me, several months after we had all been working together, clearly irritated. "I am not happy with you, Bill," he began. "Why?" I said. "You've taken away one of the best weapons I had. I can't just go to management and fight with them now. That was what I knew how to do. Now I can't. What am I supposed to do instead?"

Embracing dialogue can be perilous. It can shift your awareness in a way that causes you to be unable or unwilling to return to a more "monologic," directive, and ultimately disrespectful way of working. Yet making this transition can be challenging, because you may not immediately know what you would like to about how to navigate tough situations. Others may seem much better equipped to defeat your conciliatory proposals and attempts at greater inquiry. These are efforts to speak what is "true"—a new language of meaning. They are not always met with open arms.

Speaking what is true for us is perilous for other reasons. As with the other languages discussed earlier, the language of meaning can be similarly one-sided. It can leave out any sense of action; it can bypass or objectify people and their feelings. Our thought is often categorical and coarse, framed in either/or terms. As Alfred Korzybski, the famous theorist of semantics pointed out, a thing is always more and less than its label. No words we speak capture the full meanings we wish to convey.

But when we speak from our true nature, the words we speak have a ring to them that is unmistakable. This is the way the true becomes reintegrated into the beautiful and the good, for when we speak our voice, it has beauty, and speaks for more than ourselves, as if for everyone. The mistake is trying to put a name or a concept on this. Instead, we could simply relax and notice that something true has been spoken.

Once I was talking with a group of seventy managers and leaders in a large circle. It was the close of a five-day educational program on learning and dialogue, and people were reflecting on their experiences of the week. A British woman stood up to speak. "I have something to say," she began. "I feel as though a layer of cloudiness has been lifted from my eyes. Things are coming clearer. It seems strange to say, but it is as if it were possible to see again. And what I see is really quite beautiful. It includes all of you, and the extraordinary and yet very simple possibility of people being together in a very new and inclusive way."

The exact words she used were less important than the timbre in her voice. Her words had a ring of truth to them. They evoked a sense of connectedness and voiced the feeling in the air: spacious independence and fluid interdependence. She was conscious of what was happening as it was happening. She declared; and it was so.

Have you ever walked away from an experience and thought to yourself, *I wish I had said that* or *I should have said this*? These things indicate that you are still fragmented: You have taken in the whole of your experience but perceived only the parts; later, you put it together, one piece at a time.[5] Reflecting after the fact in this way is a valuable thing to do, and most busy people typically do not take the time for that reflection. But the most crucial dimension of awareness is to learn to reflect and be conscious *in the moment*—to realize the things you "wish you had said" in time to say them. The ability to do this regularly is a sign of dialogic competency and a mark of a new kind of wholeness of speech.

Dialogue urges us to take this capability one step further. Its aim is to engage us, jointly and severally, in a collective present-tense inquiry, present-tense truth telling, where no one person's position or thought dominates, but where larger questions and new frontiers are laid bare for exploration.

Often in these moments fears and inadequacies rise to the surface: We realize how very little we know, how little new we have to say, how wooden and predictable so many of our words and actions have been. And many things we might have been hiding are now potentially open for exploration. All this can be daunting, and I suspect that the initial discomfort people feel at this stage is one of the reasons genuine dialogue rarely happens.

Practicing dialogue well takes experience and capability. It is not an inconsequential endeavor; it requires work and personal maturation. Yet even the most experienced practitioners of dialogue come upon a further stumbling block. Paradoxically, such people are among those who are most able *not* to take an expert stance that immediately imposes an external view upon you. They can inquire openly and directly with you without evoking defensiveness and reaction. In this state we do not have all the answers worked out. We do not have a quick retort. We have to think, we may make errors, we may find questions for which we have no idea how to proceed. We discover that one of the most challenging things dialogue opens before us is the development of a new language for our experience.

BEYOND PATTERN LANGUAGES

Christopher Alexander invented what he called a "pattern language" to point the way to resolving the structural tensions he found in building problems. The pattern language gave names to categories that captured the elements of aliveness in any building project. This language was based on deep observation of the features of human activity. Alexander was able to give names to the underlying conditions that produced high-quality buildings, drawing upon his observations of common patterns of behavior in typical living and working situations, the "feel" that different places with different physical arrangements might evoke. Alexander's unique gift is an ability to perceive the order that lies beneath the surface of places that feel "alive" and give guidelines on how to reproduce this.

Take for instance pattern number 159: "Light on two sides of every room." Here Alexander points to the quality of light in rooms and the impact this has on us. He defines this pattern as follows: "When they have a choice, people will always gravitate to those rooms which have light on two sides, and leave the rooms which are lit only from one side unused and empty."[6] Alexander speculates that the glare in rooms with one side lit prevents people from understanding one another, and so they avoid going in them. Of course, if they have no choice, people will use what they must. In another pattern, "entrance room," he notes that human beings require a transition space to pass through, to go from outside to inside, for instance.

Naming the spaces in which interaction occurs requires a different way of seeing. Seeing the whole space, and not simply the objects or things that populate it, requires training. Most of us are not used to doing this with buildings or conversations. We have some names for conversational spaces: "You could cut the tension with a knife," we might say. But we can also learn to see the emerging patterns in a group and speak these languages as well.

Once in a dialogue one of the participants noticed a striking coincidence: The circle was divided by gender. All the men were sitting on one side; the women, on the other. At the time, we were speaking about creativity and the roles of men and women. We were all a little stunned to see that we had somehow enfolded into the conversation the physical seating arrangements. This conversation was somehow suddenly "all of a piece:" What people were saying was somehow reflected in the way they were saying it, which was at the same time reflected in the physical seating arrangements.

METALOGUE

An experience of this sort points to the fact that we have somehow moved out of a state of talking together and toward one where we are being together in a new way. The word *dialogue,* you will recall, comes from roots that signify "meaning flowing through." There is a spatial metaphor implicit here: One thing flows through another. But the conversation I refer to above was different from this. We were being the meaning while speaking of it. I believe this points to a state that lies beyond dialogue. The word *metalogue* captures it well. *Meta* means "beyond," or at a later stage of development, as in *meta*physics. But *meta* also means "besides." Meaning moving besides captures the essence of our experience. Metalogue describes a unified state of experience, where the meanings and structure mirror one another.[7]

The development of a language that can clothe the emerging creative spaces of conversation is, I believe, one of the more central realms of development for human beings. To the extent that we remain caught in the language of the machine age, we will always be mired, unable to soar, unable to think. Changing the way we speak will shift how we think, and so the impacts we have upon one another.

SECOND INNOCENCE

A friend of mine once described dialogue as a state out of which we are continuously falling.[8] His belief, and mine, is that a dialogic exchange is happening throughout our world all the time: the free flow of substance from one level of being to the next. For whatever reason, human beings have an ability to step out of this flow, at least in their own awareness. A significant part of each one's journey of maturation seems to entail recovering a feeling for this experience of intimate participation in the flow of one's own life. This requires a kind of innocence that has to be earned. Robert Bly once said that your first innocence is given, but that your second innocence is earned. To earn it means to let go of the impediments that lead us to believe we are in some ways flawed or incomplete, bad, and therefore we do not deserve to experience life as one continuous, coherent flow. I have found that becoming more aware of this attitude, and letting go of it, is hard work. It is often work that the process of dialogue, in the form of a conversation with and among others, greatly facilitates. It facilitates my understanding, bringing me into a quieter place in myself, one where I am again in dialogue with myself, my world, the larger ecology in which I live. I can again begin to see it as whole, coherent, even if there are many elements that are still quite incomplete or fractured. The overall context, I begin to realize, is not fractured. In that condition I have something to offer others and a safe place to stand in myself. Second innocence.

The music of dialogue within myself calls me to this state, to this living process. I am not isolated in this state; I am intimately tied to the needs and perspectives of others. This place has both depth and breadth. I am aware of a wide architecture, can see the patterns of interaction that arise around me, can act well. And the good, the true, and the beautiful live in a continuous dynamic balance within myself. I can include each of these rich voices. And so I am capable of taking action, but my actions are now revealing of a larger whole.

I enter into a dialogue with myself, and as I do so, I enter into one with you as well. In that state, as the philosopher Martin Buber once put it:

> There is brought into being a memorable common fruitfulness which is to be found nowhere else. At such times, at each such time, the word arises in a substantial way between men who have been seized in their depths and opened out by the dynamic of an elemental togetherness.[9]

Seized by an elemental togetherness, we touch the genuine power of dialogue, and magic unfolds.

Notes

Introduction

[1] *Time* magazine, July 12, 1993.

[2] Witnessing the dramatic origins of steel-making evokes an appreciation of origins. Listen to these words from Rumi, the great thirteenth-century Persian poet, speaking of this state:

> *On the night of creation I was awake*
> *Busy at work while everyone slept*
> *I was there to see the first wink and hear the first tale told . . .*
> *How can I describe this to you?*
> *You were born later*

Quoted in *The Way of Passion*, Andrew Harvey (Berkeley, Cal.: Frog, Ltd., 1994), p. 130.

[3] These ideas were first articulated by David Kantor.

[4] See Ken Wilbur's book *The Marriage of Sense and Soul* (New York: Random House, 1998) for an interesting description of these terms.

Chapter 1: A Conversation with a Center, Not Sides

[1] As Professor Blair Sheppard of Duke University's Fuqua School of Management has pointed out, however, there are important differences between the British Parliament's debates and the U.S. Congress's verbal wars. In Britain, debate in the Houses of Parliament is a ritualized battle that is carefully scripted, exuberantly honest, and disciplined. People follow a set of well-understood rules that produce a kind of safety to be honest. Despite the chaotic appearance, there are in fact bounds people stay within. In the American case, there are few such understandings. Differences take on the character of moral outrage, and people can be quite uncivil. Recognition of this very problem has led several members of the House to conduct special retreats for the full assembly on the state of their discourse.

In a sense, the ritualized process in England enables these legislators to voice controversial things quite directly, without fear of destroying the overall context within which they are working. This is an excellent example of a "container" for conversation—a setting in which there are special rules and norms for exchange that protect individuals and, more important, the overall character of the relationships among these people. It is, of course, a container that places serious constraints on the people within it. One can find parallels in a marriage, for instance, where there is at least in some cases the understanding that you can have a horrendous fight and still sustain the overall structure of the relationship—that your commitment is your container.

[2]David Bohm described this image as that of a river flowing between two banks.

[3]This line of thought was introduced to me by Emelios Bouratinos, a student of Heidegger's in the early 1950s. Bouratinos said that Heidegger had confirmed his sense that *logos* could best be understood as "relationship."

The philosopher Gemma Fiumara also confirms this line of thought in her book *The Other Side of Language* (London: Routledge & Kegan Paul, 1995). She shows that *logos* is a noun that comes from the Greek verb *legein*, which means "to gather" and "to speak." This word comes from an even earlier source, *leg*, which means "to collect." In its original sense, *logos* conveyed a sense of gathering with a deep perception of and participation in the context from which the gathering was made—of the ecology of things. This is a term that fundamentally implies belongingness, or, simply, *relationship*. Fiumara shows that conventional definitions of the term *logos* have been, since the time of the Greeks, quite one-sided and reductionist, referring strictly to the rational and orderly fashion of speech.

Principally, and amazingly, as she notes, every interpretation of *logos* since the Greeks has left out the notion of *listening*. Almost from the beginning, a word that has been absolutely central to the development of Western thought was deprived of half its meaning. By focusing on the speaking and not the listening, we have developed an understanding of logic that leaves out a perception, a hearing, or gathering—the whole which is being thought about.

[4]This is not the same as "tolerance." When we tolerate another's view, we may judge it to be wrong but grant it the right to operate. In either case, we are seeing it as somehow outside of us. In this sense, tolerance sustains separation and fragmentation.

[5]See, for instance, Mark Gerzon's book *A House Divided* (New York: G. P. Putnam's Sons, 1996) for a description of projects doing work along these lines.

[6]*The New York Times*, August 24, 1994, and September 5, 1994.

[7]Christopher Alexander, *Notes on the Synthesis of Form* (Cambridge, Mass.: Harvard University Press, 1964), p. 53. The pattern has been the same for many indigenous peoples around the world: Their rootedness in the physical earth, their artistic practices, and their language itself have been deeply violated over the last few hundred years. This

does not mean that the ways they lived were unremarkable or invalid for us today; it means that we unwittingly disturbed patterns of unselfconscious alignment.

[8]Out of this silence and the conversations that followed, this group of people planted seeds for some new ways of seeing the conflict between Russia and Chechnya. But they did not have a "breakthrough." In a way the victory was that everyone walked away with a greater sense that their interests were being heard and explored. There may well be more difficulties between these states. But they reached toward dialogue in these moments, in part because of the courageous contributions of a mother and her son. A few hours after the facilitator gave his toast, his mother died. He did not tell anyone at the time, since he felt it not helpful to a group of people who had been dealing for many months with much bloodshed. But the spirit of his contribution remained.

[9]Beneath this view is what might be called a "rights" based lonely ego theory of modern political philosophy. Starting with Immanuel Kant, and running through the utilitarian to the premises of our modern system of jurisprudence, we have come to accept the notion of individuals as Newtonian particles, separate and distinct, and have erected social superstructures on top of this. "Do not tread on me, and I will not tread on you" presumes and works from this very notion. Yet Humpty Dumpty has fallen down: The pieces are in this way of thinking all separate, and cannot be put back together again.

[10]The roots of the word *compromise, com pro mettre,* mean to "send forth or send off together." This implies sending something out in the place of something else—a substitute for what we might have sent. When we do this all together, we are "compromising." The etymology reveals why we are often unhappy with a compromise. We recognize that we are committing ourselves, promising ourselves to something that is not quite right or not quite true.

[11]David Bohm, *Unfolding Meaning,* edited by Donald Factor (London: Routledge and Kegan Paul, 1985), p. 175.

Chapter 2: Why We Think Alone and What We Can Do About It

[1]The problem with tacit ways of thinking was raised by David Bohm in a variety of different places, including the book *Thought as a System* (London: Routledge, Kegan and Paul, 1996), which can serve as a good general guide to this particular territory. See also Michael Polanyi's *The Tacit Dimension* (New York: Doubleday & Co., 1967) for a summary of the idea of tacit knowledge.

[2]I am grateful to Peter Garrett for this example.
[3]Muhammad Ahmad Faris, quoted in *The Home Planet* (Reading, Mass., Addison-Wesley, 1998).
[4]Shunryu Suzuki, *Zen Mind, Beginner's Mind* (New York. Weatherhill, 1970).
[5]See David Bohm, *Science, Order and Creativity* (New York: Bantam Books, 1987).
[6]This example, first proposed by David Bohm, reveals the flight or fight reaction in memory. It is arguable that this reaction is "instinctual," and so in a way part of a social or even biological memory pattern, one that comes preinstalled in the package, as it were.
[7]See Owen Barfield's book *Saving the Appearances* (Hanover, N.H.: University Press of New England, 1988) for a fuller description of this idea. Barfield provided the rainbow example.
[8]Juanita Brown brought this phrase to my attention.
[9]Bohm once compared our thinking to a river, and the patterns and eddies that appear in it. In this sense the larger boulders provide a relatively stable structure around which the water might flow. We see regular patterns in that water that are constantly being formed and reformed by the flow. Some of these patterns seem so stable that it appears they might never change. Call them countries: The United States has been a stable pattern flowing for some 220 years as of this writing. It seems fairly permanent to us today: But it is in fact one more pattern in the water, constantly being reformed through the processes of life and human thinking and interaction.

Chapter 3: The Timeless Way of Conversation

[1]Alexander, *The Timeless Way of Building*, p. 8
[2]Alexander, *The Timeless Way of Building*, p. 15
[3]Alexander, *The Timeless Way of Building*, p. 16

Chapter 4: Listening

[1]From Jiddu Krishnamurti, *Talks and Dialogues* (New York: Avon Books, 1968).
[2]Diane Ackerman, *A Natural History of the Senses* (New York: Vintage Books, 1990), p. 178.
[3]This was one of the reasons Plato mistrusted the "mimetic," or image based, artists; his fear was that they would distort people's sense of reality.
[4]David Bohm and Basil Hiley, *The Undivided Universe* (London: Routledge, 1993), p. 382.

[5]Henri Borftoft, *The Wholeness of Nature* (Hudson, N.Y.: Lindisfarne Press, 1996), p. 5.

[6]David Abram, *The Spell of the Sensuous* (New York: Pantheon, 1996), p. 138.

[7]David Bohm and Mark Edwards, *Changing Consciousness* (San Francisco: Harper Books, 1991).

[8]Originally told to me by Fred Kofman.

[9]The ladder is based on a theory of abstraction by A. Korzybski. See *Science and Sanity* (Lakeville, Conn.: International Non-Aristotelian Library, 1933). For more, see Samuel Bois, *The Art of Awareness* (Santa Monica, Cal.: Continuum Press & Publications, 1996).

[10]See James G. Blight, *On the Brink*, (New York: Farrar Straus and Giroux, 1990).

[11]Mark Gerzon, in his project on providing leadership and consulting help to local communities around the U.S., coined this term.

[12]This example has been disguised.

Chapter 5: Respecting

[1]Humberto Maturana connects love with this act of legitimacy. He says that love is the space in which others arise as legitimate selves: "Love is the domain of relational behavior through which another arises as a legitimate other in coexistence with oneself" (Conference Presentation, Society for Organizational Learning, June 24, 1998). I believe that respect is the quality of love that in particular allows this quality to be present.

[2]Danah Zohar, *Rewiring the Corporate Brain* (San Francisco: Berrett-Koehler, 1997), p. 12.

[3]See Leo Strauss's *The Political Philosophy of Hobbes: Its Basis and Genesis* (Chicago: University of Chicago Press, 1963) for a more detailed reading of Hobbes and his influence on Western liberal democracy. See also Danah Zohar's *The Quantum Society* (New York: William Morrow, 1994).

[4]Christopher Alexander, *The Nature of Order* (unpublished manuscript).

[5]Peter Garrett, personal correspondence, February 19, 1999.

[6]Inspired by a move by Chris Thorsen and Richard Moon, two accomplished aikido masters.

[7]See Dawna Markova and Andy Bryner, *The Unused Intelligence*, for some more physical practices (Berkeley: Conari Press, 1996). See also Richard Moon's book *Aikido in Three Easy Lessons* for a better sense of the whole art of centering.

Chapter 6: Suspending

[1]Seamus Heaney, *The Paris Review,* "The Art of Poetry" (interview), No. 144, Fall 1997, pp. 114–115.

[2]See Donald Schön's book *The Reflective Practitioner* (New York: Basic Books, 1983).

[3]Hal and Sidra Stone have pioneered something they call "voice dialogue," which is a method of externalizing the different subparts of oneself that do not always happily coexist within us. See their book *Embracing Our Selves: The Voice Dialogue Manual* (Novato, Cal.: Nataraj Publishing, 1989).

[4]Rainer Maria Rilke, *Rilke on Love and Other Difficulties* (New York: Norton, 1975).

[5]See the "Shifting the Burden" systems archetype in *The Fifth Discipline Fieldbook* (New York: Doubleday/Currency, 1990) p. 125, for a structural explanation of this pattern of behavior.

[6]This practice is derived from the family systems and Gestalt therapy.

Chapter 7: Voicing

[1]I am grateful to Marilyn Paul for providing this etymology and example.

[2]Emerson, *Essays,* "Self-Reliance" (New York: Dutton, 1978).

[3]Transcript of a talk given at the Human Unity Conference, Warwickshire, UK, 1983.

[4]The question "What is at risk?" is part of a series of questions and processes refined by Cliff Barry and Mary Ellen Blandford, founders of ShadowWork Seminars®, Inc.

[5]Michael Jones first articulated the idea that the focus of dialogue is what is in the center not the circumference.

Chapter 8: Patterns of Action

[1]See, for instance, Edward Tenner's book *Why Things Bite Back: Technology and the Revenge of Unintended Things* (New York: Knopf, 1996) for an analysis of unintended effects. Also see Dietrich Dornbusch, *The Logic of Failure* (New York: Henry Holt and Company, 1996).

[2]Thomas Davenport, "Why Reengineering Failed, the Fad That Forgot People," *Fast Company,* Premiere Issue, 1995, pp. 70–74.

[3]Davenport, "Why Reengineering Failed," p. 71.

[4]Chris Argyris, "Empowerment: The Emperor's New Clothes," *Harvard Business Review,* May–June 1988.

[5]For more on this, you might wish to learn more about the work of Diana Smith of Action Design Associates, based in Weston, Massachusetts. Diana and her colleagues Phil McArthur and Robert Putnam have developed a deep discipline in helping people learn about the art of reflection and effective action. They have influenced much of my thinking on reflection in this section.

[6]From unpublished seminar materials by David Kantor.

Chapter 9: Overcoming Structural Traps

[1]The work of people like Jay Forrester at MIT has concentrated on this dimension of systems thinking. See P. Senge *The Fifth Discipline Fieldbook* (New York: Doubleday/Currency, 1990), the chapter on "systems thinking," for an introduction to one way of thinking about this subject.

[2]The term "structure" is used in a variety of different ways by many different authors. Ideas about structure in fields like biology refer most frequently to the physical structure of an organism. In this book, by structure I mean those patterns of organizing, thinking, and acting that produce causal pressures on what human beings do in face-to-face interactions.

[3]This definition of structure is derived from D. Meadows in *Beyond the Limits* (Post Mills, Vt.: Chelsea Green Publishing Company, 1992), which comes from the tradition of system dynamics developed at MIT. It also builds on the definition of structure developed in the field of family systems therapy. It differs from those developed, for instance, in biology, where structure is seen as the physical composition of a particular form. Structure to the biologists meant external form. Structure to the family system therapists meant both the internal arrangements and their manifestations. Combining these two meanings is helpful in the social domain, because it implies that social arrangements have a kind of stability to them that "spreads" through the system, which is the original meaning of the term *structure*. In the social system, one can detect patterns of behavior over time, repeating kinds of events. These patterns of behavior are again different from the organizing "patterns" that biologists refer to when speaking of the connection of relationships that give rise to a particular kind of physical manifestation. See Fritjof Capra's *The Web of Life* (New York: Doubleday/Anchor, 1996) for a description of these terms in the physical sciences.

[4]See David Kantor and William Lehr's book *In the Family* (San Francisco: Jossey Bass, 1975) for details on this work.

[5]The material for this section was drawn in part from an article by

David Shipler, "Robert McNamara and the Ghosts of Vietnam," *The New York Times Magazine*, August 10, 1997, and by conversations with James Blight, director of the Watson Institute for International Studies, the American organizer of the event.

[6]Kantor and Lehr, *In the Family*, p. 152.

[7]From unpublished materials by David Kantor, 1998.

[8]Kantor and Lehr, *In the Family*, p. 155.

Part IV: Architecture of the Invisible

[1]Christopher Alexander's definition in his forthcoming book, *The Nature of Order*. One of the clearest thinkers about fields and their relationship to social and physical space is Christopher Alexander, a prominent architectural theorist. See his book *The Timeless Way of Building* (New York: Oxford University Press, 1979). Alexander shows how certain buildings contain a special quality of field that he calls a "center." A center is an organizing field force. A stained glass rose in a cathedral contains many centers, all aligned to produce a powerful sense of spaciousness.

[2]This notion of "fields" was once an important concept in the social sciences but lost significance as people sought to find too technical a definition for it. With the emergence of the "new sciences," particularly of quantum theory, we may now find new meanings for it.

[3]Fritjof Capra, in his book *The Web of Life*, says, "The new paradigm may be called a holistic worldview, seeing the world as an integrated whole rather than a dissociated collection of parts."

[4]For more on Lewin and his unique and seminal contributions, see Art Kleiner's book *The Age of Heretics* (New York: Doubleday/Currency, 1996).

[5]See Margaret Wheatley's book *Leadership and the New Science* (San Francisco: Berrett-Koehler, 1992) pp. 47–57 for discussion of fields.

Chapter 10: Setting the Container

[1]Alexis de Toqueville, *Democracy in America* (New York: Anchor Books, pp. 186–7), quoted in Jon Elster, *Sour Grapes* (Cambridge, England: Cambridge University Press, 1983) p. 59.

[2]See, for instance, Ronald Heifetz, *Leadership Without Easy Answers* (Cambridge, Mass.: Harvard University Press, 1994).

[3]Laurens van der Post, *A Walk with a White Bushman* (London: Penguin, 1986), p. 146.

[4]I was introduced to this notion by Cliff Barry and Mary Ellen Blandford, two magical individuals who run the best programs available on helping people integrate their "shadows," the repressed or rejected parts of ourselves that seem to leap out at inopportune times (*www.shadowwork.com*).

[5]Joseph Chilton Pierce, *Magical Child* (New York: Bantam, 1980).

[6]Five Congresses used this building until the capital was moved to Washington in 1803.

Chapter 11: Fields of Conversation

[1]A colleague of mine, Claus Otto Scharmer, has developed a theory of the evolution of conversational spaces that corresponded extremely well with the work I had done previously. His ideas, which are also outlined below, added further richness and illuminated more clearly the idea that these spaces are distinct, recognizable, and practical.

[2]See, for instance, Erving Goffman, *Interaction Ritual* (New York: Pantheon Books, 1967), and Edgar Schein, *Process Consultation*, Volume II (Reading, Mass.: Addison-Wesley, 1998).

[3]David Peat, ed., "Dialogues Between Western and Indigenous Scientists," Occasional Paper, Fetzer Institute, 1992, p. 12.

[4]Peat, "Dialogues," p. 23.

Chapter 12: Convening Dialogue

[1]I cannot do justice to all the possibilities for mapping systems here. Soft-systems modeling, which involves drawing out the causal forces in a system, is an example of the kind of effort that can help at this point. See, for example, Peter Senge, et al., *The Fifth Discipline Fieldbook* and *The Dance of Change* (New York: Doubleday/Currency, 1998). Mapping social systems can also be done using technology called "action mapping." See Action Design Associates' booklet "Mapping Guide." Pegasus Communications in Waltham, Mass. publishes guides to mapping systems using system dynamics, one of Senge's Five Disciplines.

Chapter 13: The Ecology of Thought

[1]The material in this chapter owes much to David Bohm—to the published material that Bohm made available, to the transcribed conversation published as David Bohm, *Thought as a System* (London: Routledge,

1992) and also to the unpublished work that he and I developed together as we considered how to articulate a "theory of thought."

[2] See Maturana and Varela's work in particular for a description of the "nonrepresentationalist" perspective on cognition; *The Tree of Knowledge* (Boston: Shambala, 1992).

[3] See again, Maturana and Varela, *The Tree of Knowledge.*

[4] *Steps to an Ecology of Mind,* Gregory Bateson (New York: Ballantine Books, 1972).

[5] My notion of inner ecology has grown from Bohm's though it differs from it. Bohm's notion focuses principally on the idea of thought as a system of reflexes. He does not explore the ways the system of thought informs our capacity to perceive structure or "predictive intuition," nor does he explore the ways thought produces "theories-in-use," rules one might construct to help explain why we act as we do.

[6] See for example George Lakoff's book. *Women, Fire, and Dangerous Things* (Chicago, University of Chicago Press, 1987) for an excellent articulation of the power of categories on our thinking.

[7] David Bohm, *Thought as a System,* p. 52.

[8] This idea has echoes in the notion of memes, the social equivalent of genes first proposed by evolutionary biologist Richard Dawkins in 1976. In his book *The Selfish Gene* Dawkins held that memes were culturally identifiable units that enable the transmission of culture:

> Examples of memes are tunes, ideas, catch-phrases, clothes fashions, ways of making pots, or of building arches. Just as genes propagate themselves in the gene pool by leaping from body to body via sperm or eggs, so memes propagate themselves in the meme pool by leaping from brain to brain via a process which, in a broad sense, can be called imitation. If a scientist hears, or reads about, a good idea, he passes it on to his colleagues and students. He mentions it in his articles and his lectures. If the idea catches on, it can be said to propagate itself, spreading from brain to brain.

In other words, the meme concept is one way the system of thought extends its influence—It expands the theory of evolution to propose that culture, like biology, evolves through a process of natural selection. Ideas transmit, and as they transmit, they evolve—and, like species coevolving and affecting the niches they are part of, memes affect and shape the human communities around us. See Daniel Dennet, *Darwin's Dangerous Idea* (New York: Simon & Schuster, 1995) for an exploration of memes and evolution.

[9]See Wilbur, *The Marriage of Sense and Soul* (New York: Random House, 1998), p. 56.

[10]The pursuit of the Good as it related to governance in human society was for instance part of what Plato considered the "art of politics." Today we have by and large rejected the line of thinking that says there is such a thing as an "objective" art, what the Greeks called a techne of politics.

Chapter 14: Dialogue and the New Economy

[1]The "new economy" is not, of course, all that new. In the 1960s writers heralded the age of information and the dramatic shift from the industrial age with its intensive focus on plant and equipment and the concentration of control, to what writers Jessica Lipnack and Jeffrey Stamps have more recently called the "network age." See their books *The Age of the Network* (Essex Junction, Vt.: Oliver Wright Publications, 1994; *The TeamNet Factor* (New York: John Wiley, 1993) and *Virtual Teams* (New York: John Wiley, 1997). Built upon purposeful links among people, networks are emerging everywhere to accommodate a dramatically different way of working.

[2]Lester Thurow, *The Future of Capitalism* (New York: William Morrow, 1996), p. 26.

[3]Kevin Kelly, *New Rules for the New Economy* (New York: Penguin, 1998), p. 5.

[4]I want to thank Marc Gerstein and Otto Scharmer for suggesting this line of thinking.

[5]Edgar Schein, "Dialogue and Culture," *Organizational Dynamics,* Autumn 1993.

[6]Schein, "Dialogue and Culture," p. 58.

[7]One study we did in a large technology organization showed that promoting openness in this fashion did in fact increase people's sense of appreciation for the company and sense that they could learn. But it also raised many of the undiscussable issues to the light, only to be closed down again or suppressed.

[8]Chris Argyris, "Good Communications That Block Learning," *Harvard Business Review,* July-August 1994.

[9]See, for instance, Chris Argyris, *Overcoming Organizational Defenses* (Boston: Allyn and Bacon, 1990).

[10]Václav Havel, *Living in Truth* (London, England: Faber and Faber, 1986).

[11]See Ikujiro Nonaka and Hirotaka Takeuchi, *The Knowledge Creating*

Company: How Japanese Companies Create the Dynamics of Innovation (New York: Oxford University Press, 1995), who claim that Japanese companies largely base their success on their ability to take tacit processes and translate them into shared practices, and then back again into tacit understanding.

Chapter 15: Cultivating Organizational and System Dialogue

[1] M. Beer, S. Eisenstadt, and M. Spector, "Why Change Programs Don't Produce Change," *Harvard Business Review*, November-December 1990.
[2] See Chris Argyris, "Empowerment, the Emperor's New Clothes," *Harvard Business Review*, May-June 1998, p. 98; M. Beer, S. Eisenstadt, and M. Spector, "Why Change Programs Don't Produce Change," *Harvard Business Review*, November-December 1990.
[3] Beer et al., "Why Change Programs."
[4] Argyris, "Empowerment," p. 101.
[5] This has already happened to the word *dialogue* to some degree, where its ubiquitous use spawns many different and contradictory definitions, for instance. See my chapter in *The Dance of Change*, P. Senge *et al.* (New York: Doubleday, 1999), "The Perils of Shared Ideals."
[6] A dialogic change process need not reject more rationally planned efforts. Clearly, some challenges require significant and detailed planning and coordination. But I do believe that large scale initiatives that are *not* informed by efforts to establish on an equally large scale the capabilities described here will be far less likely to succeed. "Success" in organizational change efforts is, in any event, an extremely difficult notion to assess. Depending on whom you ask, and when you ask, you can get very different answers. Some companies have worked on their change efforts for decades, and produced in that time both stunning economic performance and remarkable defeats. See, for instance, Art Kleiner, *The Age of Heretics* (New York: Doubleday, 1996) for stories about the dramatic dynamics of organizational change efforts; also Nils Brunsson, *The Organization of Hypocrisy: Talk, Decisions and Actions in Organizations* (Chichester: John Wiley, 1989), and Danny Miller, *The Icarus Paradox: How Exceptional Companies Bring About Their Own Downfall,* (New York: Harper Business, 1990).
[7] See, for instance, Meg Wheatley, *Leadership and the New Science* (San Francisco: Berrett-Koehler, 1993).
[8] Ron Heifetz and Don Laurie, "The Work of Leadership," *Harvard Business Review;* January-February 1997.
[9] "The Networked Community," Shell Oil Company Report, p. 4.3.

[10] "The Networked Community," p. 43.6
[11] Jessica Lipnack and Jeffry Stamps, personal communication, 1998.
[12] Charles Hampden Turner, "Corporate Culture for Competitive Edge," Management Guides, *The Economist* Publications, February 1990, Special Report No. 1196.
[13] Turner, "Corporate Culture," p. 112.

Chapter 16: Dialogue and Democracy

[1] *New York Times*, April 17, 1995, p. A7.
[2] Transcript of broadcast of *Prime Time Live*, ABC News, 1997.
[3] *Ibid; Prime Time Live* transcript.
[4] Their firm, Action Design Associates, evolved out of their association with Chris Argyris and Donald Schön.
[5] Several practitioners and academics have attempted such efforts, notably Herb Kelman of Harvard, who conducted workshops with Palestinians and Israelis for many years before the current era of negotiations. Many of the key players have in some way been involved in these experiences, met people on the "other side" of their conflict, and gradually formed different understandings of what motivates the other.
[6] The Oslo Accord, establishing a peace plan for the Middle East after years of failure, was finally agreed to after many months of secret meetings between Israelis and Palestinians. Nelson Mandela, then a prisoner of the South African government, and South African president de Klerk met privately in the years and months before the end of apartheid in that country. Ulster politician John Hume and Sinn Fein leader Gerry Adams met in Ireland, as I mentioned before, to talk about how to stop the violence.
[7] Transcript from The Hague I, 1995, unpublished document.
[8] "The Hague Initiative," 1998, p. 7 and personal communications with B. Allyn.
[9] *Ibid;* "The Hague Initiative."
[10] From "U.S. House of Representatives Bipartisan Retreat: A Brief History," unpublished memo, 1998.
[11] Robert Bly, *A Little Book on the Human Shadow* (San Francisco: HarperCollins, 1988), p. 17.
[12] Bly, *A Little Book,* p. 17.
[13] Alison Liebling and David Price, "An Exploration of Staff-Prisoner Relationships at HMP Whitemoor," October 1998.
[14] Peter Garrett, private correspondence, 1999.

Chapter 17: Taking Wholeness Seriously

[1]See, for instance, Kevin Kelly's *New Rules for the New Economy* (New York: Viking, 1998).

[2]From an article in *Fast Company* magazine, June 1998, pp. 118 and ff.

[3]See Lewis Hyde, *The Gift, Poetry and The Erotic Life of Property* (New York: Vintage Books, 1979), p. 4.

[4]February 1993 interview.

[5]Richard Moon and Chris Thorsen developed this analogy and have explored the implications of "state changes"—methods of bringing us rapidly back into the present through physical embodiment practices.

[6]Christopher Alexander, *A Pattern Language* (New York; Oxford University Press, 1977), p. 747.

[7]Gregory Bateson spoke about the notion of metalogue in his book *Steps to an Ecology of Mind.*

[8]I am grateful to John Gray for this observation.

[9]Martin Buber, *The Knowledge of Man* (Atlantic Highlands, N.J.; Humanitics Press International, Inc., 1988), p. 76.

APPENDIX: DIAGRAMS

DAVID KANTOR'S FOUR PLAYER SYSTEM

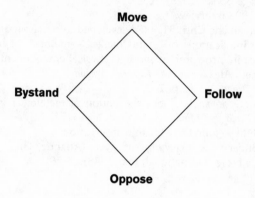

- Without movers, there is no *direction*.

- Without followers, there is no *completion*.

- Without opposers, there is no *correction*.

- Without bystanders, there is no *perspective*.

NEW CAPACITIES FOR BEHAVIOR

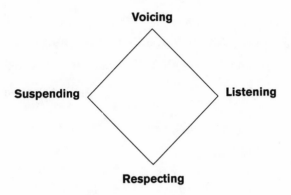

voicing

• Speaking the truth of one's own authority, what one really is and thinks.

• Asks: What needs to be said?

listening

• Without resistance or imposition.

• Asks: How does this feel?

respecting

• Awareness of the integrity of another's position and the impossibility of fully understanding it.

• Asks: How does this fit?

suspending

• Suspension of assumptions, judgment, and certainty.

• Asks: How does this work?

CORE PRINCIPLES FOR DIALOGUE

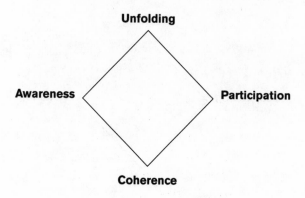

Unfolding

Awareness

Participation

Coherence

unfolding

• There is a constant implicate potential unfolding through and around us.

participation

• I am in the world, and the world is in me.

coherence

• Everything is already whole; I must look for the ways that it is.

awareness

• Self-perception; I am aware of many different voices within myself.

Index